# Girl Zines

# Girl Zines

*Making Media, Doing Feminism*

Alison Piepmeier

*Foreword by Andi Zeisler*

NEW YORK UNIVERSITY PRESS

*New York and London*

NEW YORK UNIVERSITY PRESS
New York and London
www.nyupress.org

Library of Congress Cataloging-in-Publication Data

Piepmeier, Alison.
Girl zines : making media, doing feminism / Alison Piepmeier ;
foreword by Andi Zeisler.
p. cm.
Includes bibliographical references and index.
ISBN-13: 978-0-8147-6751-1 (cl : alk. paper)
ISBN-10: 0-8147-6751-6 (cl : alk. paper)
ISBN-13: 978-0-8147-6752-8 (pb : alk. paper)
ISBN-10: 0-8147-6752-4 (pb : alk. paper)
1. Zines. 2. Women's periodicals. I. Title.
PN4836.P54      2009
305.42—dc22           2009020628

New York University Press books are printed on acid-free paper,
and their binding materials are chosen for strength and durability.
We strive to use environmentally responsible suppliers and materials
to the greatest extent possible in publishing our books.

Manufactured in the United States of America
c   10 9 8 7 6 5 4 3 2 1
p   10 9 8 7 6 5 4 3 2 1

*To Maybelle*

# Contents

# Acknowledgments

I highly recommend that other scholars delve into the world of zines. This is the only research I've ever done that has resulted in surprise packages in the mail: zines, handwritten letters, buttons, and posters—sometimes with creative doodling on the envelope itself. I've also had the great pleasure of being invited to contribute to two zines while working on this project: the Sallie Bingham Center's *My Life in Zines* and ABC No Rio's *The Art of Zines*. I was also mentioned in a third project, the tenth-anniversary issue of *The East Village Inky*.

I thank all the zinesters and zine readers I interviewed, who shared valuable hours out of their lives to talk with me about the things I was interested in, and who often called and emailed later with follow-up thoughts and to see how the book was coming along. At many points in the process I thought I should just have printed transcriptions of all the interviews because they were fascinating, and I'm grateful to have been welcomed into such a generous and creative community. Special thanks go to Neely Bat Chestnut for designing the book's cover.

I hope everyone working on archival research has a library and talented staff like the ones at the Sallie Bingham Center for Women's History and Culture in the Rare Book, Manuscript, and Special Collections Library at Duke University. On several trips to their zine collection, I never failed to find enthusiastic, supportive folk. In particular, I thank Laura Micham, Amy Hagardorn, and Kelly Wooten. I also thank Barnard College Library and the librarian of its zine collection, Jenna Freedman, and the Sallie Bingham Center for Mary Lily Grant funds that allowed me to make my first trip there.

A number of undergraduate and graduate students have been essential collaborators in this project. Thanks go to Emily Cooney, Kim Galloway, Ed Lenahan, Taylor Livingston, Shannon Madden, Rachel Reinke, and Meghann Stubel. Your insights and library sleuthing (along with your tireless transcriptions of interviews!) made this book possible. Thank you to the Undergraduate Research Office at the College of Charleston for providing grant funding that allowed Taylor, Rachel, and Meghann to work with me. The College of Charleston Faculty Research and Development Committee also provided essential support, as did the Department of English, the Women's and Gender Studies Program, and the School of Humanities and Social Sciences. Thanks, as well, to all the students who have shared their zines with me through the years, and a special thanks to Natalie Coffin for becoming a freelance photographer on my behalf.

The Super Ninja Writing Force came into being when I was at an early crisis point in this project, and the insights, accountability, and careful readings of Claire Curtis and Conseula Francis have sustained me through the rest of it. This is yet another creative community I am grateful to belong to. Catherine Bush helped with interviews, moral support, and filing.

I am grateful for the good fortune that brought this project to the attention of Ilene Kalish at New York University Press. Her enthusiasm for this project and efforts on its behalf have made it a stronger book by far than it would have been without her, and she has been a delight to work with. I also thank Aiden Amos for her support (and her zine!) and the anonymous readers who provided careful, thoughtful critiques.

Finally, thank you to Walter Biffle, who helped me understand zines as art objects, listened to my every idea, and went halves on a baby with me.

# Foreword

*Andi Zeisler*

I'll be honest. I never felt cool enough for girl zines.

I was living in Chicago when I discovered them, interning as an editor/proofreader/general office gal at a tiny literary magazine run by a thirtysomething married couple out of their apartment. I knew only a little about the medium of zines: I'd read reviews of them in *Spin* and *Sassy* magazines. My kind-of boyfriend/devoted pen pal published a one-page, double-sided newsletter about punk rock and veganism decorated with Victorian-style clip-art filigrees. And I had made the pilgrimage to Quimby's, the Wicker Park store that brimmed with alternative-publishing products ranging from poetry chapbooks to minicomics to thick, single-spaced political screeds. And I knew that—well, I thought that—okay, I hoped that—someday I would make one myself. But it wasn't until I perused the copies of *Factsheet 5* that lay around the editors' apartment that I realized just how vast the world of zines was. It was overwhelming, daunting, and occasionally scary to read this directory of zines and see, in minuscule 8-point type, just how much was out there. (And to ponder the range of humanity producing it: the editors reviewed everything sent to them and withheld most judgment, even about truly fringe zines like the one comprised mostly of graphic color photos of murder and accident victims.)

There was a zine out there for every possible quirk, interest, occupation, obsession, and kink you could imagine. *Thrift Score* was one girl's regularly published account of thrift shopping. *Guinea Pig Zero* was written by a guy who made his living as the subject of drug trials and other medical experiments. There were dozens of zines devoted to the childhood pop culture of their creators—both *The Brady Bunch* and *The Partridge Family* seemed to preoccupy many a zine maker. There were zines about sock monkeys, zines about junk food, zines like *Hate Those Jays* ("For those who can't help but disapprove of Toronto's baseball franchise"). And, of course, there were zines about being a girl: being happy to be a girl, being angry about being a girl, being anxious to be a girl. Some of them—the ones I'd heard the most about, the ones covered in *Sassy*—were Riot Grrrl zines. I wasn't a Riot Grrrl. I was shy and sheltered and about as punk rock as a dust ruffle. I wasn't going to meet the girls who did these zines at a show and bond with them over how we had to reject the patriarchal forces that made us feel bad about our bodies or our desires. But I wanted to be part of their world.

In junior high, high school, and what college I had thus far attended, it was clear that females got the shit end of the stick when it came to representation. The classics, the canon, the "universal" stories, biographies, and books were by and about men and boys. Was your name Anne Frank? If not, you weren't showing up on too many classroom syllabi. I made up the deficit on my own time, zipping through every Judy Blume, Norma Klein, Toni Morrison, Lois Duncan, and Paula Danziger book in the public library. I wrote, but I didn't think I would be a writer until someone else said I was. The girls behind these zines had probably noticed the same things I did (Hey, why are stories about boys and men universal, but stories about girls and women relegated to English-class electives?)—but, unlike me, they'd actually decided to do something about it. They weren't waiting out their awkwardness and pain so they could write about it with ironic distance in a future memoir. *I don't care if you want to hear from me, I'm saying it anyway.*

Over lunches of fish fingers and tater tots with Ed and Kim's two toddlers, I scribbled down titles and addresses for zines called *Girl Cola* and *Pasty* and *Muffin Bones* and sent off scads of envelopes, each containing $1 or $2 bills. And then came the anticipation, as I checked the mailbox every afternoon. I felt a yearning, a hopefulness, and a fear. I wouldn't have identified it this way then, but now I realize I was hoping for a kind of validation and reassurance. *You can do this, too. You don't have to wait.*

It will probably surprise no one familiar with zines to hear that I received only a handful of the ones I sent away for. The ones that did come, though, arrived like tiny presents, fancied up with glittery star stickers and hand-lettered envelopes festooned with Sharpie flourishes and, in one case, a big old lipstick kiss print. I actually remember the zines themselves far less at this point than I remember the packaging. The external trappings of zine exchanges seemed like they were the logical and only slightly more grown-up extension of the sticker trading, fortune-teller-making, bus-note-trading giddiness that had been a crucial part of my elementary school years. I may not have had everything in common with the authors of the zines that were sent to me, but the medium itself was instantly familiar.

I read and reread the zines; I bought zines reviewed in the first zines. I saw the way common threads emerged in the writing: struggles with body image, with sexuality, with anger, with feeling important in the lives of other girls, with wanting to be free in a way that wasn't tidily summed up. I didn't feel any cooler, but I didn't care. I had located the place my feminism would reside.

Not all young feminists find their ideological home in zines, of course, just as not all young feminists phone bank for NARAL Pro-Choice America, boycott sweatshop-produced clothing, take back the night, or march on Washington. But it was in zines that I and many women I came to know found a way to link the dense texts from our classes in feminist theory to the weird, should-I-say-something? moments of sexism that pockmarked our lives. *That's what I'll say next time*, I vowed, reading one girl's story of bitching out catcallers on the street. *Ugh, that's so true*, I thought as I read another's essay on how badly women can treat each other in the hopes of being one of the boys. To someone whose feminism was centered on securing reproductive rights or combating sex discrimination in the corporate realm, girl zines likely seemed too lightweight to qualify as "real" feminism. But for a lot of us, such projects reflected and underscored the way feminism was expressed in our young lives: inconsistently (the patriarchy sucks! but I really want to make out with that cute guy!), with periodic bravado (fuck corporate America! I'll never work in an office!), and as a work in progress.

Not to mention as just plain fun. *Pagan's Head*, a zine created in the late 1980s by the now-acclaimed writer Pagan Kennedy, wasn't a girl zine per se, but in remembering its genesis in her 1995 memoir *Zine*, Kennedy hits on the importance of zine-making as a process: "How had I forgotten that this—this absorbed, tongue-between-the-teeth, little-girl feeling—was the essence of art?"

Though new zines come across my desk almost every week now, it can be difficult to talk today about the impact of the medium without giving off a whiff of the Luddite—or, worse, of the wistful old-timer who would prefer to dwell in the rosy glow of the past rather than sharpen up and get with the program. In the past few years, as I've spoken to high school and college students around the country about feminism and popular culture, I've found myself explaining zines by saying things like, "Well, zines would be like, if you wrote a blog on paper, and you photocopied it and mailed it to people." I've worried that zines just wouldn't make sense to them—so sloppy and chaotic with their clip-art non sequiters and off-center layouts and crawls that revealed the use of at least three different pens of varying width and ink supply. No links. No enabled comments. *What's the point?*, I imagined them asking.

I have only my own answer to that imagined question. And it's that even in a medium as ephemeral as this one—where a creator might do one zine about her abortion and then decide that she's bored with that subject and move on to a minicomic about, I don't know, Rainbow Brite, where your $2 in well-concealed cash disappears in a wisp of anticipation never to be satisfied—the product itself remains as a marker of its time. The writing within remains as proof that those thoughts, that anger, that hope were once urgent and alive, expressed as fast as the pen would allow, stapled and mailed off to join a conversation that began long ago, that continues today. Part of what makes girl zines remain so vital as a feminist project is that they are an ongoing conversation, a way to be achingly immediate yet also provide a link to the printed matter that came before. And the book you hold in your hands is a crucial way to understand— and to appreciate–the many different ways girl zines have and continue to effect the ongoing work of feminist thought and activism. For both readers and creators, they are education and revelation, empowerment and healing, giddy secret and proud f-you, and with this book they are given a well-deserved place of prominence in the history, and the future, of feminism.

# Introduction

We have big plans for a grassroots, girl power, teenage girl movement of youth rebellion—jackets, we need jackets. The power of
style must not be downplayed in terms of political mobilization.
Can't you picture it—gangs of girls—teenage girls in gangs all
across america, breaking through boundaries of race and class
and sexual identity, girls so strong together that they don't listen
to people who tell them they are stupid or that they don't mean
anything because they don't really exist—girls so strong together
that no one dares to fuck with them when they are walking down
the street—girls so strong together that they learn to help out their
moms and help them to get away from their dads when necessary. . . . GIRL SOLDIERS . . . we need jackets. And just think
of the books that will be written, the cultures that will arise, the
bands, the movies that will be made etc.
—Tobi Vail, *Jigsaw* #4 (1991)

Fans attending Bikini Kill concerts in 1991 might have received
a small photocopied booklet with the title *Jigsaw* printed across the top in
a large typewriter font and messy handwriting across the bottom scrawl-
ing the words "true punx, real soul and the revolution girl style now." The
cover features a photograph of the band Bratmobile performing. In the
blotchy, photocopied image, the lead singer of the band stands with her
hands on her hips, mouth open, singing into a microphone. She looks defiant and also feminine, wearing retro cats-eye glasses and a dress with
a small white heart on the lapel. To the left, the guitarist chunks at her
instrument, wearing a kilt, hair pulled back with a large headband.[1] The
women, divided by a drumset, are intent on their performance: they
are serious musicians. In contrast, the top and bottom of the cover are

bordered by photocopied foil stars, like the kind that a teacher would put on an elementary school test. The cover is simultaneously—and perhaps surprisingly—friendly, playful, and fierce, like the *revolution girl style* that the scrawled handwriting invokes. Here punk girls play their own music and create their own publications, and Bikini Kill's fans could shove the booklet into their pockets and take it home to read about what it means to have a revolution not just by and for girls, but *girl style*—grounded in aesthetics, narratives, and iconography that emerge from the experiences of girls in the early 1990s.

*Jigsaw* is a zine, a frontrunner in the proliferation of zines by girls and women that began in the 1990s, catalyzed by the punk movement, Riot Grrrl—a feminist political and musical movement (sometimes identified as a subculture) that began in the early 1990s in Olympia, Washington, and Washington, D.C.—and the emergent third wave of feminism. Zines are quirky, individualized booklets filled with diatribes, reworkings of pop culture iconography, and all variety of personal and political narratives. They are self-produced and anti-corporate. Their production, philosophy, and aesthetic are anti-professional. According to Stephen Duncombe, the author of the only book-length scholarly study of zines, they are "scruffy, homemade little pamphlets. Little publications filled with rantings of high weirdness and exploding with chaotic design."[2] Like *Jigsaw*, most zines are messy, photocopied documents that may contain handwriting, collage art, and even stickers and glitter. Because zines are ephemeral underground publications, it is impossible to determine how many are in circulation, but one scholar estimated 50,000 in 1997, and overflowing stocks at zine distributor Microcosm Press and bookstores like Quimby's in Chicago and Reading Frenzy in Portland testify to their prevalence today.[3]

They cover every imaginable subject matter, from food politics to thrift shopping to motherhood. They are an example of participatory media—media created by consumers rather than by the corporate culture industries—and, as such, despite predictions of their demise in the mid-1990s due to the rise of the internet, they are part of a continuing trend in late capitalist culture.[4]

Zines created by girls and women—what this study will call "grrrl zines"—are sites where girls and women construct identities, communities, and explanatory narratives from the materials that comprise their cultural moment: discourses, media representations, ideologies, stereotypes, and even physical detritus.[5] According to girls' studies scholar Mary Celeste Kearney, zines are "the primary type of media created by

Cover of *Jigsaw* #4 (left), courtesy of Tobi Vail.

Example of zines on display at Quimby's Bookstore in Chicago (below) (photo by Natalie Coffin).

contemporary American girls," and I argue that these documents not only reveal girlhood on the ground but also are a site for the development of a late-twentieth-century feminism.[6] Though a number of scholars have investigated grrrl zines in recent years, this volume, *Girl Zines*, is the first book-length study of zines by girls and women.[7] The central questions I address in this book are the following: Why zines? What forms of expression do zines enable that may not be possible in other media? How do girls and women make use of contemporary cultural materials in creating zines, and to what ends? I ultimately contend that, considered collectively, zines are sites for the articulation of a vernacular third wave feminist theory. Grrrl zines offer idiosyncratic, surprising, yet savvy and complex responses to the late-twentieth-century incarnations of sexism, racism, and homophobia.

Before discussing the intellectual agendas and underpinnings of *Girl Zines*, I want to consider *Jigsaw* as a brief case study. Grrrl zines' informality can be deceptive: the starred and scrawled *Jigsaw* might look like girlish bedroom play—the kind of thing that scholars are quick to dismiss as trivial or unsophisticated—but, in fact, *Jigsaw* and zines like it are often offering serious reconceptualizations of gender, race, sexuality, and identity. They are tightly packed artifacts with levels of signification. This complexity is apparent in a close examination of one part of *Jigsaw*. Tobi Vail, *Jigsaw*'s editor, ends the issue with "The Jigsaw Manifesto."[8] Excerpted in the epigraph to this introduction, this manifesto reflects a number of traits that are characteristic of grrrl zines and the third wave of feminism more broadly.

"The Jigsaw Manifesto" calls for a revisioning of gender—a "girl revolution"—that links identity with the formation of female-centered community. This gender work takes place at multiple levels. Most visible is the level of content, with the image of tough girl gangs. In a culture that celebrates the catfight as the paradigmatic mode of female interaction and generally represents women as weak and physically ineffectual, Vail offers the alternative—and resistant—idea of female strength through community. She envisions girl gangs—identifiable "GIRL SOLDIERS," wearing their jackets—combating the sexist hostilities of mainstream culture. The reader can imagine these groups of girls, perhaps wearing black leather, ignoring those who tell them they are stupid, deflecting street harassment, and rescuing their mothers from abusive fathers. This image also encompasses broader identity categories than gender, as the girl gangs are "breaking through boundaries of race and class and sexual identity." She offers a vision of girls changing the world, with cultural artifacts spring-ing up to document what they have done. This is an effort both to reimag-ine girlhood and to generate feminist community, and, by calling for cul-tural productions—books, music, movies—to be part of this process, Vail makes a space for her own zine as part of this effort for cultural change.

Another level at which Vail's revisioning operates—one not, perhaps, as immediately obvious—is the level of rhetoric. Her manifesto uses ex-cessive language, as when she demands "a grassroots girl power teenage girl movement of youth rebellion." In this short phrase, she reiterates age categories four times and lists three terms related to agency: power, move-ment, and rebellion. Similarly, she repeats the phrase "girls so strong to-gether" three times in this excerpt. Throughout the manifesto, she deploys and perhaps mimics a stereotypically girlish rhetoric that suggests enthu-siasm and over-the-top affect. Her repetition of words, phrases, and ideas, however, also signals that she is struggling against constraints, struggling with saying something that is difficult to say with the vocabulary available to her. The images of girls in conflict are so overwhelming in consumer culture industries that she must reiterate "girls so strong together" as a kind of refrain to counteract the dominant message.

Her efforts to alter and control how girls are represented are also evi-dent in the visual elements of the zine. Vail was part of the Riot Grrrl movement (discussed in chapter 1), a movement that, among other things, rewrote the word "girl" to incorporate an angry growl: *grrrl*. This term be-came one of the most recognizable markers of third wave feminism and girl culture, quickly appearing not only in zines but also in mainstream media and advertising. Vail was among the cohort credited with coming up with the phrase "riot grrrl," but she later said it was a joke and didn't like to use the terminology.[9] What's interesting is that *Jigsaw* #4 is filled with the word "grrrl," but in my copy, every instance of "grrrl" has been crossed out—presumably by Vail, as a protest against the popularity of the term.

Rather than writing a new zine or a manifesto against the terminology, Vail changed the existing artifact. Her zine, then, must be understood not simply in terms of its content but in terms of its existence as a material ob-ject that can be altered to mark the passage of time and changing opinions.

It can be difficult for a reader to identify Vail's tone, and this elusive quality, rather than being a shortcoming of the writing, strikes me as in-dicative of grrrl zines more broadly. For instance, even the title "The Jig-saw Manifesto" is so earnest that it can seem sarcastic in the context of

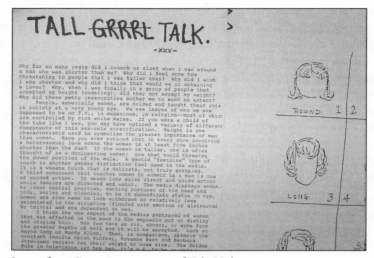

Image from *Jigsaw* #4, courtesy of Tobi Vail.

the girlish pictures and stars in the zine. A similar instability emerges in the writing itself: Vail begins the excerpted passage with what is apparently a serious call for rebellion, but she immediately follows this phrase with the insistent "jackets, we need jackets" and the emphatic statement that the "power of style must not be downplayed." Here she seems both to be mocking the media's emphasis on women's fashion and simultaneously attempting to marshal the possibility of fashion as a means of self-construction and creation of solidarity. Her unwillingness to be transparent is characteristic of zines; indeed, grrrl zines seem to offer an implicit critique of the notion of transparency, which suggests a one-dimensionality and self-awareness at odds with the identities being constructed in these zines. *Jigsaw* offers no clear distinctions between the ironic and the sincere, playing fast and loose with both and, as in the previous example, often deploying irony and sincerity simultaneously, an approach that is both cagey and strategic.

Just as the zine vacillates between irony and sincerity, so, too, does it tip between hope and cynicism. Vail's manifesto offers a utopian vision, and some of her language seems to register it as fantasy. By saying "Can't you picture it" and ending the list of ways girl gangs will be documented with a vague "etc.," Vail allows for a kind of imprecision that's more appropriate for a dream than a political précis. Indeed, the almost breathless momentum of the manifesto, propelled by dashes, suggests enthusiasm without commitment. And yet the anger that flares up in her description of "girls so strong together that no one dares fuck with them" hints at an uneasy negotiation between utopia and reality. Vail seems to want this vision to be real, but she can't really believe that it could be. This uneasy negotiation, as I discuss next, is a central element in grrrl zines' work of third wave theory production.

By calling for the creation of female community, interrupting mainstream gender norms, identifying intersectional identities, and moving seamlessly between tongue-in-cheek irony and hope, "The Jigsaw Manifesto" maps out the terrain that grrrl zines inhabit.

## Theory Production in Grrrl Zines

The themes that appear and reappear in *Jigsaw* have emerged, as well, in my conversations with grrrl zine creators. In order to make sense of *Jigsaw*, to assess the cultural work that this artifact and zines like it are performing, it is necessary to situate grrrl zines historically and theoretically. I take up their historical positioning in chapter 1. For now, I focus on the intellectual scaffolding that I used in this study to examine grrrl zines. While *Girl Zines* builds on the zine scholarship of Duncombe's *Notes from Underground*, the primary frameworks for this study are girls' studies and third wave feminism. Many scholars working in these areas are aware of zines but have either devoted limited attention to them or have approached them from a singular disciplinary vantage point (often sociological). In contrast, in this volume, I combine the existing scholarly work on zines with a much-needed broad range of interdisciplinary perspectives on book culture, activist art, and participatory media in order to map out as fully as possible the personal, political, and theoretical work that grrrl zines perform.

In taking seriously the literary, cultural, and interpersonal productions of girls and women, this volume contributes to a growing academic discussion about girls and girl culture. In particular, this study follows on such recent girls' studies scholarship as Mary Celeste Kearney's *Girls Make Media*, Anita Harris's *Future Girl*, and the work of Janice Radway.[10] These scholars position girls as producers of culture, not merely consumers, countering mainstream media depictions of girls, as well as youth culture scholarship that has by and large positioned boys as agents and girls as onlookers. Further, these scholars recognize girls' identity construction as a complex phenomenon that takes place messily at the intersections of the individual and her social context.[11] The most interesting girls' studies work undertakes interdisciplinary explorations of girls and their culture, drawing on literary, sociological, and media studies methodologies, and it is with this work that *Girl Zines* is aligned.

A related, sometimes overlapping, scholarly conversation—and one that occupies a greater portion of this study—emerges from third wave feminism. Grrrl zines are deeply and thoroughly implicated in the scholarly and cultural concept of the third wave of feminism. The "third wave" is a term that loosely defines a generational and political cohort born after the heyday of the second wave women's movement. It is not an untroubled term, to be sure; the concept of a third wave of feminism is contested, with some scholars embracing it and others arguing that it should be abandoned.[12] Those opposed to the framing of late-twentieth-century feminism in terms of a third wave contend that the "wave" terminology has lost its usefulness. They note that young feminists are still facing many of the same issues that feminists of the second wave fought, an observation that might suggest that we are still in the second wave. They point out, too, that the terminology is sometimes used to dramatize generational differences where none exist—turning feminism into a catfight—and to flatten nuanced ideological differences that aren't necessarily linked to chronological generation.

While there is merit to these arguments, I still find the third wave to be a useful concept, because it identifies and catalyzes a particular generational group—a group that encompasses a great deal of diversity of perspectives but that shares relevant similarities. It's a term I use with awareness of its problems but that I am not ready to abandon, in part because it designates certain distinctive characteristics of late-twentieth-century feminism. Girls and women who came to consciousness in an era in which second wave feminist ideals were part of the culture—taken for granted, even if not actually enacted—have a different view of gender than earlier generations. This is not to suggest their view of gender is better or somehow more enlightened; indeed, one of the characteristics of this cohort is the fact that their initial encounters with feminist ideas are often mediated through the conservative backlash against feminism, and thus they often couch their own feminist assertions in the apologetic "I'm not a feminist, but . . ."[13] In addition, this group has grown up in a late-capitalist culture that has shaped individual subjectivity, designating (in often limiting ways) what is possible and what is imaginable. These characteristics, however, are part of what makes the third wave a useful concept, because they mark ways in which this generation of feminism is distinctive. In an earlier publication, Rory Dicker and I argued that this cohort's "political activism on behalf of women's rights is shaped by—and responds to—a world of global capitalism and information technology, postmodernism and postcolonialism, and environmental degradation." Although there are certainly significant lines of connection between the second and third waves, "we no longer live in the world that feminists of the second wave faced," and it's therefore useful to examine how feminism has changed and how it manifests itself today.[14]

Explorations of the third wave as an identity group attempt to delineate who third wave feminists are, how they interact with previous feminist generations, and the ways in which they respond to and intervene in late-capitalist, backlash culture.[15] Some of the fault lines are sexuality and pleasure, race and ethnicity, engagement with popular culture, and comfort with contradiction and incoherence. Although third wave feminism, particularly in early publications about it, was often conflated with "postfeminism," the two concepts now are widely recognized as separate, with the third wave designating a distinctive incarnation of feminism and "postfeminism," a term primarily used to imply that feminism has ended.[16]

Some of the distinctive characteristics of the third wave are visible in grrrl zines. Many of the questions scholars have asked about the third wave are equally applicable to the grrrl zine phenomenon: Is it truly activist, or simply immaturely self-absorbed? Is it actually different from the second wave, or mostly a marketing scheme? Does it emerge from real postmodern theoretical foundations, or is it merely offering a fetishizing of contradiction and fragmentation for its own sake? Here I contend that zines provide a vantage point on the third wave, and considering the two in tandem will allow us to answer these questions. As vernacular third wave productions—generationally if not ideologically, but often both—zines are a rich primary source, more revealing and extensive than the television shows and music that have often been the focus of third wave studies. As I explain in chapter 1, the origin stories of the two are inextricably intertwined. Grrrl zines are coterminous with the third wave; grrrl zines and third wave feminism respond to the same world.

Beyond sharing a historical moment with the third wave, grrrl zines are often the mechanism that third wave feminists use to articulate theory and create community. The third wave is not merely a grouping of people whose ideological and generational affiliations can be articulated, nor is it simply a historical story to be told, although these are the ways in which it has most often been discussed. Indeed, since the mid-1990s, the third wave has been widely described but undertheorized.[17] I suggest that the theoretical contributions—the vocabulary, conceptual apparatus, and explanatory narratives—of the third wave have not been recognized by scholars because they're being developed in unexpected, nonacademic sites, like zines.

The idea of zines as sites of theory production may be somewhat surprising, as theory is generally associated with elitist academic practices, and zines occupy the opposite end of the spectrum, so intentionally low-brow as to be able to be mistaken for trash. Carolyn Dever usefully broadens the category of theory in her study *Skeptical Feminism*: "All feminisms, I argue—whether in the classroom, on the streets, or in the pages of *Time* magazine or academic journals—that attempt to present a systematic justification, definition, explanation, or hypothesis linked more or less concretely to a body of evidence are 'theoretical.'"[18] Dever notes that, since its inception, feminist theory has existed in a state of uneasy tension: theory requires a certain degree of abstraction, but feminist practices have rightly demanded attention to material origins and conditions that are particularized. I contend that zines up the ante on this tension because they are intensely and intentionally local, individualized, and eccentric. However, Dever explains that this tension is "powerfully useful":[19] not something to be resolved or eliminated, it produces and propels a dialectic at the heart of feminist inquiry. Grrrl zines' negotiations, then, of the specific and the generalizable—their sometimes messy careening between the local and the global, the personal and the political—are a process by which third wave theory is produced. This study draws on both aspects of third wave scholarship, viewing the third wave as a content area (particularly as set forth in chapter 1) and as a set of conceptual strategies that grrrl zines practice and enact.

One such conceptual strategy is what Radway calls "insubordinate creativity": creative construction of the self using the cultural materials that are "ready-to-hand."[20] These cultural materials—the ideas, conditions, and artifacts of late-twentieth-century America—generally do not originate with the girls and women who make zines. In fact, they don't always originate from sources that have the best interests of girls and women in mind; *Jigsaw*, like many zines, documents a culture that is actively hostile to girls and women. But grrrl zinesters are able to bring these materials together in surprising ways, leveraging them against one another to release meanings that challenge, contradict, and go beyond the cultural materials themselves. Radway identifies this creativity as insubordinate, and it often is: unruly, insurgent energy that calls into question dominant cultural norms and that, in some cases, may be so disruptive that it is invisible or unintelligible from mainstream vantage points, misread as comical, trivial, or insignificant.

Clearly, however, the identity and community construction that take place in zines are not always resistant or countercultural. Indeed, grrrl zines often reveal levels of complicity with corporate culture industries and their repetitive, omnipresent, flattening representations of girls and women. *Bust*, for instance, a feminist magazine that started as a zine, has come under fire from some feminists for its adherence to certain conventions of mainstream women's magazines, such as offering columns reviewing cosmetics and featuring fashion plates. It has also been critiqued for its approval of pornography, including its publication of explicit sex columns along with "The One-Handed Read," a pornographic story featured in each issue.[21] *Action Girl Newsletter*, too, could be seen as more complicit than resistant, as the manifesto included in each issue featured an apology for excluding boys: "This is NOT an anti-boy project. Okay, it *is* exclusionary—only projects done primarily by a female will be reviewed. But it's because this is a specialized list, not because 'boys are bad' or 'boy's zines aren't good.' . . . So don't be sad."[22] Further, *Action Girl* creator Sarah Dyer decided to appear in the quintessentially mainstream *Seventeen* magazine rather than the more alternative and feminist-friendly *Sassy* to publicize her zine.

I find, though, that I'm reluctant to read these zines and others like them as simply complicit, dupes of the patriarchy. Yet I'm also uncomfortable with the celebratory rhetorics that often accumulate in scholarly and mainstream commentary on zines and suggest that zines provide an expressive space free from cultural constraints.[23] In short, I am skeptical of the kinds of intellectual binaries that would have us divide cultural productions in terms of complicity or resistance. This binaric thinking is pervasive, particularly in conversations about girls and women. In contemporary discourse about girls, it crops up as the dichotomy of the "at-risk girl" versus the "can-do girl,"[24] categories that present girls either as victims of an oppressive culture or as resistant agents who are the success stories of late capitalism. This is another way in which grrrl zines and third wave feminism are linked, because the third wave is often categorized according to the same rubrics, with third wave feminists presented either as complicit "fuck me feminists" or as radicals who are far surpassing their second wave predecessors.[25] These categories can be seductive even for feminist scholars, particularly those influenced by some of the girl power/ power feminism rhetorics of the third wave and the marketplace. It is tempting to celebrate the resistant and to dismiss works deemed complicit with hegemonic discourses.

These sorts of binaries obscure as much as they reveal. They imply that these categories—victimization and agency, complicity and resistance— are complete, coherent, and mutually exclusive, when, in fact, they almost always coexist in the lives of individual women and in cultural discourses and practices. As legal scholar Martha Mahoney notes, "Neither concepts of agency nor of victimization fully take account of women's experiences of oppression and resistance in relationships" or in other aspects of their lives.[26] By not allowing for the coexistence of agency and victimization, these categories serve to make one or the other invisible, so that the can-do girl is seen as being unaffected by a sexist culture, and the agency of the at-risk girl—identified as a passive victim of cultural inequities and ideologies—is elided, unable to be recognized. This bifurcated thinking constructs a distorted picture of girls and women and their relationship to their culture. They are either unaffected or completely overwhelmed. In fact, our relationships with our culture are much more complex, with girls and women simultaneously affected by cultural pressures and also able to act on their own behalf and as change agents, exhibiting agency within a context of varying levels and kinds of oppression.

As much as possible, then, in this volume I avoid the binaries—either of easy celebration or snide condemnation—opting, instead, to take zines seriously as literary and cultural artifacts with weight and merit and considering what they have to tell us about the American culture within and against which girls and women are operating. With this study, I align myself with the critical theoretical perspectives of poststructuralist feminist scholars such as Lora Romero, Chela Sandoval, Susan Bordo, and Carolyn Dever, who resist these kinds of bifurcated thinking.[27] As these scholars' work would suggest, asking whether girls and women are victims or agents, or whether grrrl zines document complicity or resistance, flattens this rich resource. These are the wrong questions. Instead, in this volume, I consider what kinds of resistance are possible within this particular cultural and historical context and how girls and women leverage the available cultural materials to create personal identities and communities. How are they articulating a feminism that is grounded in the specificities of the late-twentieth century (and early-twenty-first)? Grrrl zines are operating within the contemporary culture of late modernity, a culture that Anita Harris describes as "characterized by dislocation, flux, and globalization," emphasizing "a new brand of competitive individualism" and demanding citizens who "can manage their own development and adapt to change without relying on the state."[28] In this volume, I examine what agency looks like in a social and cultural context defined by dislocation and self-creation, along with many persistent and innovative versions of the sexism, racism, and homophobia that feminists have been critiquing throughout the twentieth century.

## Blogs versus Zines

One of the important questions to address at the outset is the connection of zines to the world of the internet. When one of my undergraduate research assistants explained this book project to her friends, she found that the easiest way to describe zines was to say, "They're like blogs—just on paper." In many ways, the connection between zines and blogs is an obvious one.[29] Blogs and zines have a number of significant similarities: they're both participatory media, spaces in which individuals can become creators rather than simply consumers of culture. They allow for the public sharing of the minutiae of life. They are publications that forego the gatekeepers of the traditional publishing marketplace— editors, publishers, and others who determine who's in and who's out. Anyone who wants a blog can have one, as long as he or she has access to a computer with an internet connection. Similarly, anyone who wants to create a zine can do so, as long as he or she has access to paper and the ability to photocopy. Both forms of media allow for creations of communities beyond the boundaries of the creator's immediate physical environment.

It's clear to anyone who's paying attention, however, that digital media are becoming the twenty-first century's predominant mechanism for communication and expression. Starting as early as the 1980s, observers of the zine community began forecasting the rise of the e-zine, and in the years since then, scholars and commentators have contended that the internet, in particular the blogosphere, has superseded paper zines—or will do so soon.[30] Indeed, the rise in digital media has caused some critics to predict not only the death of the zine but the death of the book as well—the death of paper media altogether.[31] Zines, then, can be seen as a sort of nostalgic medium, harking back to a punk or grunge era that no longer exists. As I've explained this book project to colleagues, some have asked, "Does anyone even make zines these days?"[32]

The answer is emphatically—and perhaps surprisingly—yes. Zines are still being made, and in great numbers. In the course of writing this book, I've acquired approximately one hundred newly made zines, given to me by the zine creators I've interviewed or my own students, or purchased in my many forays into independent bookstores around the country or online zine distribution sites. Blogs have not replaced zines.[33] In fact, many of the zine creators I interviewed actively produce both zines and blogs. This fact alone suggests that zines and blogs, while related, aren't identical. The zine creators don't necessarily view blogs as a replacement for zines but, instead, as a supplement, a format that's doing something slightly different.[34] While I examine some of the differences at length in chapter 2, I want to take a moment here to map out why girls and women continue to make zines in a digital age.

The climate of the internet itself is part of the answer. On the one hand, girls and women play vital roles on the internet. In December 2007, the Pew Internet and American Life Project reported that girls do significantly more blogging than boys.[35] In particular, the internet has become a space where much third wave feminist activism and community-building are happening. Blogs such as Feministing, Blac(k)ademic, Feministe, Pandagon, Angry Black Bitch, and Girl with Pen, to name only a few, have become some of the main voices for the third wave.[36] In 2006, the *Guardian* (Manchester, U.K.) estimated the number of feminist blogs to be 240,000, and these sites are visited by hundreds of thousands of readers a day.[37]

On the other hand, mere presence doesn't necessarily challenge the structural conditions of the internet and cybercommunities. In an essay describing her own experiences creating and maintaining websites, zine creator Mimi Nguyen troubles the notion of the internet as a welcoming space for girls and women:

> The feminist performance theorist Peggy Phelan writes, "If representational visibility equals power, then almost-naked young white women should be running Western culture." It seems I might be able to offer a parallel observation, that if representational visibility equals power, then almost-naked young Asian women should be running a very big chunk

of cyberspace. That is, whenever I type "asian+women" into search fields I get almost nothing but them.[38]

Nguyen's observation points to a fact that many bloggers and scholars have recognized: the internet is a space that replicates many of the structural inequities of the nondigital world.[39]

The internet can be a racist, sexist space. In a 2008 issue of the zine/magazine *Bitch*, Jaclyn Friedman reports on the "violent, gendered threats" that she and other female bloggers have faced and the generally hostile climate that the internet provides for women.[40] A number of recent studies have documented the hostility of the internet for women. According to a 2006 University of Maryland School of Engineering study, "female-named chat-room users got more threatening and/or sexually explicit messages than male-named users—25 times more, in fact."[41] Similarly, a 2008 Pew Internet and American Life Project report showed that being female was a significant "risk factor" for being contacted by strangers on social networking sites, including contact described as "scary or uncomfortable."[42]

Nguyen provides an example of how this "scary or uncomfortable" vibe can play out for female bloggers and web administrators. She features many visual representations of herself in her zines, as discussed in chapter 4. However, her online publications—including her websites "Worse Than Queer" and "exoticize this!"—do not. She explains that her reasoning has to do with the climate of online communities: "The lack of photographs, of me, at least, had been a deliberate omission. . . . I have no pressing desire to cater to *that* particular urge of the anonymous voyeur, powered by a deceptively friendly neighborhood browser. (Nothing to see here, folks.)"[43] And yet she notes that the "anonymous voyeurs" found her nonetheless; she received regular hate emails because of her websites, emails that recycled old and new stereotypes about feminism, and that, she explains, "share a singular purpose, that is, to fuck with me."[44] Numerous other female bloggers have shared this experience of being "fucked with" by anonymous readers, whose tactics Friedman describes as "saturated with juvenile, racist, misogynist, and homophobic language and imagery."[45]

To be sure, zine creators like Nguyen, Lauren Jade Martin, and others don't posit the zine community as a utopian alternative to the internet; they are clear that the zine world is not necessarily a space of "true" community, where such dissent and hatred don't occur.[46] As discussed in chapter 2, however, zines do provide a kind of intimacy, and demand a kind of effort, that seems to block some of the more opportunistic aggression that is prevalent online. Writing a hostile anonymous comment on a blog is easy; taking the time to write a letter, on paper, and mail it to someone whose zine you read is a more labor-intensive endeavor. It's also a more intimate one, since only the person who created the zine will read the letter, as opposed to the ostensibly broader audience for blog comments. For these reasons, at least in part, the zine creators I spoke to reported receiving a great deal fewer hostile responses from their zines than from their blogs. For instance, Ayun Halliday, creator of the zine *The East Village Inky*, told me that she's only received one critical letter in the ten years of producing her zine, and it "was so witty that I couldn't be that mad about it." In contrast, she explains, "On my last blog tour for [her book] *Dirty Sugar Cookies*, I did swing by one parenting [blog] that was great because it got me a ton of publicity, but *whoa*, some of the *nasty* comments, you know?"[47]

It's also the case that zines as paper artifacts register the connections of bodies and the passage of time more fully than digital technologies (addressed in chapter 2). Zine creator Lauren Jade Martin wrote a post on her blog about taking one of her essays off line because she's a much different person now than when she wrote it. It was an essay she originally published in a zine, and she explained why she felt comfortable with the essay in zine format rather than digital:

> Zines are tangible, are material. The writing is contained in an object that physically ages. Ink fades. Paper yellows. Holding a zine from even just ten years ago feels like holding an historical document. It's easier to place it, the writing inside, and the person who wrote it, in a particular moment in time, to contextualize it. Words appearing on a computer screen, even if they are date-stamped, seem the opposite: decontextualized, ahistorical, atemporal.[48]

Because her zine registers age, readers can intuitively understand that they are reading something that Martin might well have moved beyond; the zine, like the human body, changes with time. Halliday makes a related observation, explaining that she appreciates the longevity of zines:

> I'm not convinced that what's written on a blog, that it's still gonna be there if you don't print it out, you know? In ten years, is it just going to be sucked into the ether? Whereas maybe a hundred years from now

somebody's going to go into an attic or a basement and find a copy of *The East Village Inky* rattling around, and that, to me, is very exciting. I like the idea of the time capsule quality of something that's on paper in multiple units.[49]

Digital media, then, strike these zine creators as both atemporal and ephemeral in ways that zines are not.[50] The materiality of zines differentiates them from blogs, not only in terms of the artifacts themselves but also in terms of the communities that accrue around them. Although zines and blogs have relevant similarities, the blog has not replaced the zine. Zines are a living medium with both historical and contemporary relevance for the lives of girls and women and for feminism's third wave. Historically they are a space where many third wave ideas and iconography developed, and as a contemporary phenomenon they allow for different kinds of community and different modes of activism than digital media.

## Organization of the Chapters

Here in *Girl Zines*, I draw on a range of disciplinary perspectives—from participatory media to print culture studies to art theory—to trace a trajectory through zines' history, form, content, and effects. Because these categories operate interdependently, each chapter builds on the preceding ones to develop an increasingly complex picture of the cultural work of these zines and the girls and women who create them. With their uneven quality, their propensity for incongruity and fragmentation, and their comfort with lack of closure, grrrl zines don't play by the rules of previous historical moments or literary cultures. Understanding zines means that we must take them on their own terms. Rather than a comprehensive history or overview of the grrrl zine phenomenon, the chapters that follow offer particular thematic explorations accompanied by close readings of zines and comments from their creators.

This study begins with origin stories. Although most often zines are identified as originating in male-dominated spaces—from the pamphlets of the American Revolution to the punk zines of the 1970s—in chapter 1, I trace a feminist trajectory for zines, from the scrapbooks of nineteenth-century women's clubs through the mimeographed manifestos of second wave feminism. Positioning grrrl zines within a feminist legacy makes women's resistance visible. This perspective also keeps grrrl zines from appearing to be an aberration when, in fact, they are part of a long-standing feminist legacy. Many grrrl zinesters have felt that they were creating an entirely new feminism, but I contend that they were revising feminism without reinventing it. Central to this origin story are the influence of Sarah Dyer's *Action Girl Newsletter* and the Riot Grrrl movement, both of which helped to spark the grrrl zine explosion that began in the 1990s. While Riot Grrrl has received scholarly and mainstream media attention, the *Action Girl Newsletter* has been less often recognized as one of the catalysts for the grrrl zine explosion and third wave feminism, and I argue for the importance of *Action Girl*.[51] The *Action Girl Newsletter* and Riot Grrrl emerged simultaneously with the terminology of "third wave feminism," so grrrl zines and the third wave help to define each other.

Third wave feminism is one theoretical lens through which to examine zines. I offer another theoretical approach, grounded in the materiality of zines, in chapter 2, where I consider the fact that zines are not merely words on a page: they are material artifacts that must be examined with attention to their visual and sculptural elements as components of their meaning. Using tools drawn from print culture and art scholarship, I offer close readings of five zines—*I'm So Fucking Beautiful, Fragments of Friendship, The East Village Inky, No Better Voice,* and *Doris*—as case studies of the different ways in which zines can deploy what print culture scholars call "the semiotics of concrete forms."[52] One phenomenon that interests me about zines is the miscellany that accumulates around them, the gifts and letters that circulate between zine creators and readers. In this chapter, I consider zines as the hub of a gift culture and argue that zines' materiality helps form a particular kind of connection between zine readers and creators, what I call an "embodied community." Pleasure plays a key role in creating embodied community. Pleasure is at the heart of the zine endeavor, motivating the creation of zines, connecting zine writers and readers, and making even bad zines worth reading. The embodied community, the attention to materiality, and the importance of pleasure are ideas that inform every subsequent chapter.

Grrrl zine creators' negotiations with the material terrain of gender—and their pleasures in doing so—are the focus of chapter 3. Most zines by girls and women address gender, taking on mainstream concepts of femininity in complex ways. As this chapter's title, "Playing Dress-Up, Playing Pin-Up, Playing Mom," suggests, zines often function as spaces not only for gender construction but also for gender play. Here I consider a broad set of grrrl zines—from one-off zines like *Grit & Glitter* to zines like *Bust* which have become full-fledged magazines—with attention to the ways in which these zines are generating complex, creative subjectivities: third wave subjectivities. These zines document the challenges of female embodiment, embrace and redefine transgressive models of womanhood, and generate communities grounded in enjoyment and pleasure. I pay particular attention to the "mama zine," a subset of zines created by women, often in their thirties, who have children. These zines offer specific reconfigurations of what it means to be an adult woman, mapping out a terrain that is far more complex than mainstream media depictions of motherhood. What the idea of third wave subjectivities suggests is that these zines aren't offering depictions of authentic, coherent selfhood—"the real girl." Instead, the zine creators make strategic use of fragmentation and incompletion, constructing tentative, multilayered, and sometimes contradictory self-representations, representations that are well suited to a late-capitalist, postmodern climate.

These third wave subjectivities are often amplified in zines by girls and women of color. Although grrrl zines are primarily created by white girls and women with access to material resources, the number of zines written by women of color suggests that the zine medium is a useful space for articulating intersectional subjectivities. In chapter 4, I consider zines that challenge the flattened, depoliticized discourses of multiculturalism and diversity in a post–civil rights era. The zines I examine in this chapter, including *Quantify, Evolution of a Race Riot, Slant*, and *With Heart in Mouth*, activate complex, shifting self-representations, with attention to the intersections of race, gender, sexuality, class, and history. They identify the personal as a site that's constrained and configured by larger institutions and power structures, as well as by the symbolic realm, and they make those constraints visible. In particular, I argue that zinesters make creative use of limiting cultural symbolism, leveraging their own self-representations against such familiar racist and sexist iconography as the sexualized "Oriental" woman and Aunt Jemima. In so doing, they give the lie to claims that we are a "colorblind" society. Notably, they challenge the rhetoric of colorblindness, not only in the culture at large but in the world of feminist politics and activism as well. Just as Sarah Dyer used the *Action Girl Newsletter* to make space for her voice within a punk community, the zine creators I consider in this chapter use their zines to make feminism more inclusive and true to its own ideals.

I culminate the book in chapter 5, in an examination of grrrl zines' political effects. While some zines are self-consciously political and others

emphasize personal reflection, all zines fit under the rubric of what communication scholar Clemencia Rodriguez calls "citizens' media," media
that "activate subtle processes of fracture in the social, cultural, and power
spheres of everyday life."[53] Zines configure resistance at the microlevel;
rather than a grand revolution, they offer resistance in small, particular,
utterly grassroots manifestations. In chapter 5, I consider three different
sets of zines that offer three different pedagogical modalities: pedagogies
of process, active critique, and imagination. While global capitalism and
media consolidation work to create homogenization for the sake of ever-
larger markets, zines embrace the unmarketable, the local, the particular,
and the quirky. They perform micropolitical interventions within hegemonic systems and within the symbolic order; indeed, their interventions
are so personalized that they are often invisible as activism to scholars
who are searching for the kinds of social change efforts that were prevalent in the social justice movements of the earlier twentieth century. By
offering an alternative to mainstream late-capitalist modes of operation,
zines enact a public pedagogy of hope.

Over the past several years, I have collected hundreds of zines by girls
and women, and I have had lengthy, in-depth conversations with a dozen
zine creators. I have also had conversations with fifteen zine readers who
are located across the country who explain what zine reading means to
them.[54] I have spoken with women whose zines went on to become successful magazines, such as Lisa Jervis and Andi Zeisler of *Bitch* and Laurie
Henzel and Debbie Stoller of *Bust*. In addition, I've interviewed women
who have created zines—sometimes many of them—with no magazine
aspirations, such as Neely Bat Chestnut and Nomy Lamm. In these conversations, zine creators answered the question of why they made paper
zines, particularly in an era of digital media, which I explore in chapter
2. Most identified zines as a site for working through ideas about gender,
ethnicity, sexuality, and other identity categories, as I discuss in chapters 3
and 4. And as I explain in chapter 5, many of the conversations revealed a
complex interplay of personal and political motives in the zines. It is worth
noting, however, that I relied less on individualized, psychological readings
and more consistently drew on tools of cultural analysis for this study.

While most of these zine creators are on the East and West Coasts, in
urban hubs where zines are familiar objects and where zine distribution
networks are often in place, I have also spoken with zine creators from
more surprising locales, including Nashville, Tennessee; Asheville, North
Carolina; and Charleston, South Carolina. As discussed in chapters 2 and

5, zines inspire other zines so that the zine phenomenon is self-sustaining, creating what Duncombe calls a "virtual bohemia." He notes that these other locales almost certainly outnumber urban hubs for zine production.[55] Often, the zines emerging from locations not known for having alternative or bohemian subcultures are the most interesting, revealing how girls and women create community and identity in the absence of a supportive in-person community.

The work that girls and women do in and through zines may seem personal, but the theoretical structures that zines build and the hope that zines offer point to the larger political project of grrrl zines. Grrrl zines provide a glimpse of the future of feminism. They document feminism's ability to transform itself to respond to a changing culture and to help girls and women construct firmer social identities and innovative political interventions.

# 1

## "If I Didn't Write These Things No One Else Would Either"

### *The Feminist Legacy of Grrrl Zines and the Origins of the Third Wave*

please listen to me you mother fuckers, i, unlike hundreds of boy fanzine writers all across america, have a legitimate need and desperate desire to be heard. i am making a fanzine not to entertain or distract or exclude or because i don't have anything better to do but because if i didn't write these things no one else would either.

—Tobi Vail, *Jigsaw* #3 (1991)

BECAUSE we must take over the means of production in order to create our own meanings.

—*Bikini Kill* #2 (1992)

In 1988, Sarah Dyer began working as producer of the successful, nationally distributed punk zine *No Idea*. She and her co-producer, who was male, started a record label and put on punk shows in addition to publishing and distributing the zine. They worked collaboratively at every level. Dyer quickly realized, however, that within the context of the punk scene, and the zine scene affiliated with it, her work was invisible. She explains, "We would get phone calls and they would ask to talk to Var because they just assumed that my name was on there just because I was the girlfriend, not because I was actually doing anything. And if people wanted to buy an ad, they would ask to talk to him. You know, we would do a show and the bands on the stage would thank him and they would be thanking the guys who helped us clean."[1] In other words, Dyer was assumed to be an accessory rather than an actual co-creator.

As a result of this lack of public recognition, she decided to produce a zine that was entirely her own, emphatically "ALL MINE!" as the masthead for the second issue of *Mad Planet* proclaimed.[2] *Mad Planet* offered Dyer's thoughts on various bands and musical genres. It was framed in terms of her own interests. Her editorial letter in the first issue of the zine explained that she designed it as a zine "that actually covers everything I like." She went on to say, "Basically, if you're a girl-type, and you work on anything with a boy-type or types, everyone assumes that you're just along for the ride."[3] Even with these explanations, however, reviewers gave credit to the men who were tangentially involved in the project—men she had labeled as "boy slaves" in her first masthead—rather than to Dyer herself. "I couldn't believe that I'm doing this zine completely by myself and people kept focusing on my friend Bill because he's doing interviews and Evan because he's doing comics," Dyer notes. She began to recognize that this was not a problem facing her alone, which led her to a radicalizing moment:

> There were so many women involved in zines, and they were all treated this way, just sort of, you know, "girls don't do that." So I decided, I'm going to find the other girls doing zines, working on zines. I started looking very carefully at the ads in *Maximum Rock and Roll*, like, "This is a girl," and trying to kind of network with them. And I went to England in 1992, found a copy of *Girlfrenzy* zine by Erica Smith, and she had reviewed girl zines, and in her review list, she had maybe three or four American zines that I had never heard of, and I was just like, I can't believe I have to come all the way to England and buy a zine in a bookstore to find out about zines in America. So when I came back I did the first *Action Girl Newsletter*.[4]

Dyer discovered that it was not enough for her to break away individually, to make her own zine so that she could receive credit. She needed to intervene in the larger zine culture, to create a community of women, and thus the *Action Girl Newsletter* was born.

Dyer describes a familiar feminist story. She was part of a punk community that positioned itself as outside of and superior to the mainstream world, a community that claimed to challenge the power dynamics and oppression that characterized dominant societal practices. And yet, like suffragist Elizabeth Cady Stanton when she was excluded from the World

Anti-Slavery Convention in 1840, feminist activists Casey Hayden, Mary King, and Robin Morgan who were accorded less status in the civil rights movement and New Left organizing in the 1960s, or radical women of color Gloria Anzaldúa and Cherríe Moraga, who experienced racism within the women's movement, Dyer discovered that the social justice movement with which she identified did not offer her full human recognition.[5] While the punk community worked to undercut mainstream American practices, Dyer experienced the sexism from the broader culture replicated in the movement, which was a space that had promised to do things differently. Dyer's invisibility as a woman creator within the punk scene made her gender visible to her. She responded as many radicalized women had before her: she took action. And in a move that she helped to make a trend among young feminists, Dyer's action took the form of a zine.

Dyer tells a particular origin story for the *Action Girl Newsletter*, a feminist origin story in which gender inequities become visible and a woman decides to make a change. Zines have a similar gendered origin story, which has mostly gone untold. Most studies of zines identify them as resistant media originating in male-dominated spaces. They are positioned as descendants of the pamphlets of the American Revolution and Dadaist and Samizdat publishing, emerging from the fanzines of the 1930s and the punk community of the 1970s.[6] According to this narrative, the zine proliferation was triggered by the convergence of punk culture and technology. Punk culture provided the "zine" terminology, along with a non-elitist, do-it-yourself (DIY) structure and aesthetic, and these ideologies were channeled into the production of zines because of technological innovations such as desktop publishing and inexpensive, widely available photocopying.

This explanation is insufficient on a number of counts when it comes to grrrl zines. Although zines are often described as though they and their predecessors have always been male-dominated media, what hasn't been discussed is the fact that these publications also have predecessors in the informal publications, documents, and artifacts produced by women during the first and second waves of feminism.[7] One reason for this omission is that zines are resistant media, and women are, even today, rarely identified with resistance. As Dyer's story shows, our encrusted gender ideology often makes women's efforts at cultural change invisible. Even if, like Dyer, women are clearly speaking out, then they may still be erased from the story altogether, identified as someone's girlfriend rather than as legitimate agents. Dyer's story makes this process of erasure visible.

Her story also shows that she longed for female predecessors, for a female community. She sought out other zines by girls and women and then created the *Action Girl Newletter* as a resource that could help solidify and expand that community of women. Her story is not unusual; many of the grrrl zinesters I interviewed explained that they began making zines either as a response to sexism or because they were inspired by another grrrl zine. Nomy Lamm didn't know much about feminism, but when she read the feminist body acceptance book *Shadow on a Tightrope*, it inspired her to create the zine *I'm So Fucking Beautiful*.[8] Similarly, Neely Bat Chestnut created the first issue of her zine *Mend My Dress* after reading *The Courage to Heal*, a book for women on recovering from sexual assault.[9] Cindy Crabb was inspired by the grrrl zine *Snarla*, while for Lauren Jade Martin it was a pamphlet from Sarah Dyer on "Doing Your Own Zine." *Bitch* and *Bust* were created as explicitly feminist interventions into pop culture, and *The East Village Inky* came about when Ayun Halliday recognized that being a mother cut her off from many of her former creative pursuits. Although some of these women were part of the punk zine community, all began creating zines because of some specifically gender-related catalyst, and that gender specificity is exactly what is missing from the general origin story that's told about zines.

Origin stories are important because they tell us where to look and what patterns to watch for. The "wrong" stories can give us a distorted or diminished understanding of the past and, by extension, the present moment. In the case of grrrl zines, if we think of them as originating from the male-dominated spaces of zines and punk culture, then grrrl zines appear as aberrations at best; as one author suggests, they seem "a side note to women's history."[10] They're not quite the same as the zines produced by men, but this difference isn't taken seriously. This commonly told origin story marks grrrl zines as a rupture and the girls and women who produce them as either trying—often unsuccessfully—to be like the boys or rebelling against the male punk community.

This story of rupture provides a limited context for understanding grrrl zines, and in that view they are aberrant, unconnected, a fun but odd blip. The story is significant because it shapes our interpretations of grrrl zines. Further, because grrrl zines are places where third wave feminism is developed, this incomplete story also has consequences for our understanding of the third wave. Third wave feminism, like grrrl zines, is often positioned as a rupture, as a kind of feminism drastically different from the first and second waves—indeed, in some cases, with no evident connection to previous generations of feminism at all. This narrative has been appealing even within a feminist context; many self-identified young feminists have relished the persona of being a rebel against feminism. In the early years of the 1990s, in particular, a number of young feminists—most famously Katie Roiphe in *The Morning After: Sex, Fear, and Feminism on Campus* and Rebecca Walker in *To Be Real*—declared their disconnect from second wave feminism. Roiphe argues, "Feminism has come more and more to represent sexual thoughts and images censored, behavior checked, fantasies regulated. In my late adolescent idiom, feminism was not about rebellion, but rules; it was not about setting loose, as it once was, it was about reining in."[11] Similarly, Walker explains, "For many of us it seems that to be a feminist in the way we have seen or understood feminism is to conform to an identity and way of living that doesn't allow for individuality, complexity, or less than perfect personal histories," and she identifies feminism as "another impossible contrivance of perfect womanhood, another scripted role to perform in the name of biology and virtue."[12] In this collection she declares the third wave to be a break from the past, denying the connections with previous generations of feminism and, like Roiphe, figuring feminism as a tool of oppression not unlike patriarchal norms for womanhood.

Third wave discourse is often complicated and contested rather than one monolithic perspective. While Walker, Roiphe, and other young feminists declared their separation from the second wave, other self-identified third wave feminists proclaimed their allegiance, arguing "to us the second and third waves of feminism are neither incompatible nor opposed" and "we see many strands of continuity between the second and third waves."[13] The sense of a debate in progress—of a contest for the definition of the third wave—is an undercurrent in many of the third wave feminist anthologies that appeared throughout the 1990s and early 2000s. "Them's fighting words," quipped one author in response to Roiphe, arguing that she had experienced feminism not as an oppressive force but as "a way for me to be an individual and break free of society's many rules about a woman's proper place" and that she, therefore, was not interested in a third wave that wanted a clean break from the second wave.[14]

While there are certainly relevant differences between third wave feminism and earlier generations, I argue that an undue emphasis on—or exaggeration of—those differences masks the far more prevalent similarities between all incarnations of feminism. This is not to suggest that feminism is a monolithic, unified movement; far from it. Feminist thought and activism have been and are multifarious, changing, unagreed upon, diverse. The dissent within feminist discourse hasn't been merely generational but has emerged from fractures of race, class, sexuality, and gender identity, and the dissent is often generative. Indeed, one of the great strengths of feminism has been its ability to alter, to expand, in order to respond to internal critiques and changing cultural experiences.[15] Focusing solely on the differences, however, perpetuates a distorted understanding of earlier feminist moments, particularly the second wave, and prevents young feminists and others from recognizing feminism as a larger historical change movement. For despite the variations—the notable differences, for instance, in the understanding of women's rights espoused by Elizabeth Cady Stanton and that espoused by Sarah Dyer—I contend that it is meaningful to keep the umbrella term "feminism." It designates movements and discourses that have at their core a belief in the full personhood of women and an agenda of eradicating all forms of oppression that keep people from achieving their full humanity.

The same sorts of distortions and misrecognitions that have influenced the third wave have occurred in the origin story of grrrl zines, as well; indeed, they seem to be interlocking distortions, perpetuating an incomplete and inaccurate version of how grrrl zines relate to feminism. A recognition of connection between incarnations of feminism is important in the name of historical accuracy; moreover, it will allow young feminists to learn from and build on the past, recognizing work that has come before so that they aren't always having to act as pioneers, trailblazers.

To that end, if we recognize the particularly feminist origins and content of grrrl zines, then the story of grrrl zines as an aberration no longer holds. Here I provide an outline of this feminist trajectory, offering an alternate origin story that recognizes a U.S. feminist continuum, starting with the informal publications of the suffragists and women's clubs of the late-nineteenth and early twentieth centuries. I also present a specific originating moment for third wave feminism: the early 1990s in which the feminist political and musical movement known as Riot Grrrl and the *Action Girl Newsletter* emerged. When framed in terms of a feminist history of participatory media, Riot Grrrl and *Action Girl* help reveal what is distinctive about third wave feminism, as well as the ways in which this feminist generation is linked to previous ones. The lines of connection between earlier feminist moments and this one become visible, and this provides not only a more accurate picture of first wave and second wave feminism but also a context for understanding grrrl zines and the third wave.

The third wave has been examined from many angles—as a movement that is sexy, rebellious, self-absorbed, and savvy—but it needs to be positioned within a larger feminist narrative. Rather than being aberrations, in my origin story grrrl zines are actually part of a significant trend in women's history. As explained in this chapter, women throughout the nineteenth and twentieth centuries have created informal publications— from scrapbooks to women's health brochures to mimeographed feminist pamphlets—and a textual and formal analysis of these publications suggests that they are the direct historical predecessors of grrrl zines. These publications were creative and resistant, and they provided a platform for women speaking from disempowered positions. The women who made scrapbooks, health guides, or mimeographed pamphlets, like zine creators, were denied access to the standard mechanisms for publication, because what they had to say didn't fit the dominant scripts.[16] Positioning grrrl zines within this feminist history makes women's continued resistance visible and enables us to begin creating a more accurate picture, not only of zines but of third wave feminism. I contend that the third wave, like the grrrl zines that helped initiate it, is part of feminist history and not a unique break from the past. An exploration of grrrl zines shows that the rhetoric and iconography of the third wave are distinct from earlier feminist generations, but many of the underlying impulses propelling this feminism are similar among all the waves of feminism.

## Feminist History of Zines: The First Wave

Dyer's story of the *Action Girl Newsletter*'s origins exhibits a number of characteristics that connect grrrl zines to their feminist predecessors. As I mentioned in the introduction, the zine is a form of what's called "participatory media," media made by individuals rather than by the consumer culture industries, and participatory media have been part of women's and feminist history since the 1850s. Participatory media represent a way of engaging with unfriendly mass culture and transforming it—if not always on a broad scale, at least at the level of the local (the nineteenth-century women's club that reads a scrapbook made by a member, the 1970s consciousness-raising meeting that distributes a mimeographed pamphlet). Historically, feminist participatory media productions have engaged with some of the themes central to grrrl zines—such as gender, identity, community, and resistance—and have offered a snapshot of their own cultural moment's take on these issues. Participatory media of the first and second waves of feminism—scrapbooks, health booklets, and mimeographed pamphlets—have significant similarities with grrrl zines, in some cases similarities of material culture and construction, in other cases ideological similarities. Like zines, they have rarely been studied—or, if they have, not in terms of their publication practices and the effects these had on their function and meaning. Rather than offering an in-depth historical examination of scrapbooks, health booklets, and mimeographed pamphlets, I identify points of connection among feminist participatory media, provocative textual similarities that are ripe for further research.

Scrapbooking was a widespread practice in the nineteenth century, a way that girls and women could document their lives and the culture in which they lived. Although some men did engage in scrapbooking, it was widely understood as an activity for women. Scrapbooks have been understood as artifacts of personal identity, "a material manifestation of memory," as a recent scholarly collection describes them.[17] The girls and women who made these books would gather together collections of personally significant memorabilia such as calling cards, newspaper clippings, photographs, and letters as a record of their lives, or they would assemble the books as reference volumes on various subjects in which they were interested.

Scrapbooks did more than offer personal commemoration, however. Like zines, scrapbooks offered a space for girls and women to comment on mainstream culture and also to construct community and solidarity. Scrapbook scholar Amy Mecklenburg-Faenger explains, "These scrapbook collections of 'rare gems' were meant to be shared with other people, and scrapbooking often, although not always, was constructed as a communal activity. That is, scrapbooks were not understood as private documents, but as artifacts meant to be shared with others."[18] Individual women used scrapbooks, according to Mecklenburg-Faenger, "to critically engage the social roles prescribed for them and to construct new possibilities for women's work, and women's identities."[19] For instance, women's organizations in the Progressive era often used scrapbooks to document their own work and challenge mainstream newspaper coverage. Scrapbooks were interventions, spaces where clubwomen and suffragists—both black and white—could construct their own legacy and public identity. Through what artifacts they chose to include, how they arranged the artifacts, the context into which they placed them, and the creators' own comments on magazine and newspaper clippings, women who made scrapbooks were offering contributions to and critiques of public life. Their hand-made publications could reframe and reprioritize mainstream media reporting by pulling particular articles out of the newspaper and giving them greater emphasis within the scrapbook. Mecklenburg-Faenger gives many examples of women including media reports of various kinds in order to comment—often critically—on them in their scrapbooks. Scrapbooks were a space for women to express themselves and communicate with other women in a culture that did not provide an abundance of public venues.

The scrapbooks created by women's clubs and individual women share a family resemblance to many zines from a century later. Mecklenburg-Faenger offers an example from a page of the scrapbook of journalist and suffragist Ida Harper:

> In her scrapbook recording media coverage of women's causes in 1912, Harper preserved one of her own articles, a response to an attack on suffrage . . . next to which she included handwritten commentary on the circumstances surrounding its publication. Harper pasted the entire newspaper page on which her article appears, including other articles that appeared on the same page. In the middle of her article, the editors of the paper had inserted a piece on "An Oklahoma Town Who Is in Need of Cats." Harper drew several wavy lines through this article, noting at the bottom of the page: "A sarcastic letter from me in regard to cutting down my important article to include one on *cats* probably led to an [unreadable] editor's dropping my department–Resumed ~~Oct~~. Sept. 1914."[20]

Harper uses her scrapbook to comment on mainstream media trivialization of her work. She crosses out the offending article in her scrapbook, a space in which she can express her own side of the story. She shares with the scrapbook's readers that when she spoke out to the newspaper editor, her column was dropped, but she faces no such censorship within the world of her own publication.[21]

Similar strategies appear throughout the world of grrrl zines. Indeed, when I saw Harper's scrapbook page for the first time, I was immediately struck by how familiar it appeared. For instance, it resembles a page from Danielle Bustian's 1993 zine, *War*. Like Harper, Bustian engages with newspaper clippings, using her zine as a space to critique media coverage of particular political figures. Both authors remove the clipping from its original context and, by placing it in their own publication, take control over it. Both write marginal notes in their own handwriting to correct what they see as misrepresentations or disrespect and, in so doing, put their voices into conversation with the mainstream media. Indeed, within their publications, their voices supplant the mainstream media. The visual difference of the handwriting of both women in contrast to the typeset newsprint pages gives a kind of authenticity to Harper and Bustian's side of the story. As I discuss in chapter 2, these women are creating embodied communities through their use of material artifacts. Although the scrapbook and the zine may seem to document two women alone with their clippings, in fact, each woman uses her artifacts to communicate and connect with a broader community of women.

Scrapbooks and zines also share methods of negotiating with a broader capitalist culture. Feminist scholars like Ellen Gruber Garvey have argued that scrapbooks and trade card books (in which girls and women would paste cards they had collected from various products purchased), while allowing space for personal expression, often served a more colonizing interest, incorporating people into a commodity marketplace rather than providing a site for resisting that marketplace. Garvey explains, "It was the work and play of amassing the cards, sorting them, and pasting them down that taught scrapbook makers how to read advertising, how to fantasize with its seeming promises within the social worlds of the home and religious life without seeing it as overwhelming or as a repeated betrayer."[22]

As advertising images entered not only the home but also the intimate space of women's own created artifacts, these images became comfortable and familiar rather than being experienced as overt marketing tools. In other words, these scrapbooks served the pedagogical purpose of fitting their creators into capitalism. While I see the sense in this reading, my work on grrrl zines suggests that this process of being trained to respond to a capitalist visual and rhetorical marketplace doesn't always mean a process of girls and women being colonized by a consumer culture. Grrrl zinesters, like their scrapbooking predecessors, often engage intimately with magazine advertisements or, as with Bustian's zine, newspaper clippings that become parts of zine collages. By so doing, they are developing marketplace literacies that they then often use to criticize the marketplace. As I discuss in chapter 5, these literacies can become not palliative but instigative. In other words, as girls and women engage with advertising images in their scrapbooks and zines, the comfort they develop with consumer capitalism can become a tool of resistance, not just a mechanism for their complicity with that system.

Another kind of informal document with a family resemblance to zines arose in the late nineteenth and early twentieth centuries: women's health

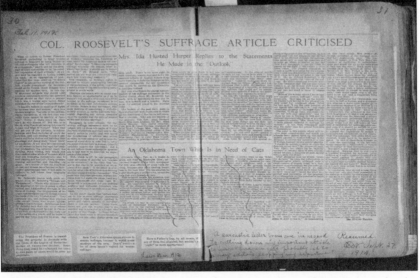

Pages from the scrapbook of Ida Harper (ABOVE), courtesy of the Library of Congress.

Page from *War* (left), courtesy of the Sallie Bingham Center for Women's History and Culture in the Rare Book, Manuscript, and Special Collections Library at Duke University.

publications. The treatment of women such as Margaret Sanger and Mary Ware Dennett illustrates how transgressive clear information about health and sexuality was considered to be, particularly when that information was created by or for women. Sanger was a pioneering activist for contraception. In 1914, after many of her columns for the socialist newspaper the *New York Call* were censored under the Comstock Law, she began publishing her own paper, the *Woman Rebel*, in which she offered information about sexuality and contraception. This publication was illegal under the Comstock Law, so Sanger spent a year in Europe avoiding prosecution. While en route to Europe, she had her supporters distribute 100,000 copies of a sixteen-page pamphlet called *Family Limitation*, a publication that explained and assessed the most common forms of contraception; it included illustrations, as well as recipes for vaginal suppositories. In this pamphlet, Sanger also advocated for women's sexual pleasure, explaining, for instance, that the condom "has another value quite apart from prevention in decreasing the tendency in the male to arrive at the climax in the sexual act before the female." She also explains of women's purported sexual coldness, "Nine times out of ten it is the fault of the man, who through ignorance and selfishness and inconsiderateness, has satisfied his own desire and promptly gone off to sleep."[23] After her husband was arrested for distributing this pamphlet, Sanger returned to the United States to face prosecution. She went on to publish a great many more things through both mainstream and informal routes, but her early publications shared many characteristics with zines. She wasn't able to find outlets in existing media for her controversial subject matter, so she created her own publications.[24]

Similarly, Dennett was a suffragist activist and writer who created a sex education pamphlet for her sons in 1915 because she found none of the available sex education literature for children acceptable. She wrote the text and included simple, hand-drawn diagrams of the sex organs that she created herself after she couldn't find any pictures in the materials of the Academy of Medicine and elsewhere. This zine-like pamphlet circulated among her friends, colleagues, and fellow activists (and their children) under the name *The Sex Side of Life: An Explanation for Young People*, until it found its way into the hands of the editor of the *Medical Review of Records*, who raised public awareness of Dennett's work. The pamphlet became popular among doctors, parents, church leaders, social workers, camp counselors, and schoolteachers, who "snatched it up by the dozens."[25] It was sold in bookstores and even used as the primary text in some childcare classes. This level of popularity led to Dennett's indictment under obscenity laws, and her case became a landmark case for censorship in the United States, ultimately responsible for changing the legal definition of obscenity.[26]

Like zines, these health pamphlets operated outside of the mainstream publishing marketplace and allowed women to convey experiences and information that otherwise couldn't be publicized. Because inexpensive technology for reproducing text was not widely available in the late-nineteenth and early-twentieth centuries, however, these pamphlets required printers and a sizeable budget for their reproduction. This medium, then, wasn't as widely available to girls and women as scrapbooking, although it did allow for a broader reach. Changes in available technology made it possible for the next generation of feminists to create informal publications, make multiple copies, and circulate them without needing the kind of budget that Sanger or Dennett had or facing legal penalties.

## *The Mimeograph Revolution of the Second Wave*

Informal publications of a different kind were integral to the second wave of the women's movement. Just as the women's clubs of the late-nineteenth and early-twentieth centuries made scrapbooks as a response to the technological innovations of inexpensive paper, photography, and mass-circulated media, women who were involved in the women's movement of the mid-twentieth century took advantage of the inexpensive technology of the mimeograph machine. Unlike scrapbooks (which were public documents with limited reach because they were unique, nonreproducible volumes) and health pamphlets (which required a budget for professional printing), mimeograph machines allowed second wave feminists to make inexpensive, multiple copies for public distribution. By typing or handwriting onto specialized mimeograph paper, called a stencil, an original copy was made. The stencil was then placed on the inked drum of a mimeograph machine, which was turned—often by hand—to press ink onto paper that was fed into the machine with each rotation of the drum. The process was imperfect; the ink was often messy (as well as purple), only one page could be reproduced at a time, and it was easy to fold and ruin stencils during the process of reproduction. Mimeograph machines were inexpensive and accessible, however, making it possible for small feminist groups to make hundreds of fliers and documents to reach a broad audience.

Although second wave feminists also created informal publications using photocopying and offset printing, mimeography has taken on a kind of iconic significance in histories of the movement, coming to stand for all informal feminist publishing. For instance, an advertisement for Feminist Expo 1996 proclaimed, "the current wave of the feminist movement began with mimeograph machines."[27] In the memoir of noted second wave feminist Susan Brownmiller, she recounts the importance of mimeographed pamphlets, leaflets, and broadsides: "In an era of technological leaps, Women's Liberation is the last major American movement to spread the word via a mimeo machine."[28] Another activist recalls that "Ti-Grace [Atkinson] said every revolution needs a mimeo machine."[29] Because there were no books or magazines that addressed the issues they were taking on, these activists had to create and distribute their own work. Indeed, many of the key second wave texts began as pamphlets or fliers not unlike zines, including Anne Koedt's "The Myth of the Vaginal Orgasm"; the Boston Women's Health Book Collective's *Our Bodies, Ourselves*; the Third World Women's Alliance's *Triple Jeopardy*; Bread and Roses's "Outreach Leaflet"; and even Mary King and Casey Hayden's "A Kind of Memo."[30]

These sorts of print media were crucial for the political work of the second wave, functioning not only to spread information but also to create what historians Rosalyn Baxandall and Linda Gordon call "a shared culture, theory, and practice."[31] Like scrapbooks, they were integral to the creation of feminist community. Baxandall and Gordon continue: "In an era before e-mail, even before xeroxing, printed publications were vital and feminists spent a significant proportion of their energy, resources, and ingenuity producing them. Mimeographed pages stapled together into pamphlets were the common currency of the early years of the movement. . . . By the mid-1970s over 500 feminist magazines and newspapers appeared throughout the country"[32]—magazines and newspapers that were often outgrowths of the popular mimeographed pamphlets. Even the feminist magazines and newspapers that took on the moniker of more-formalized publications had what I would identify as a zine-like quality: Baxandall and Gordon contend that "women's liberation publications struggled along without funds or paid staff, featuring not-quite-aligned layouts, sometimes poorly written pieces, and amateur poetry and drawings. . . . Nevertheless, it was in these homespun rags that you could find the most creative and cutting-edge theory and commentary."[33]

As with the scrapbooks, the look and feel of these second wave publications remind me of grrrl zines. For instance, the family resemblance between a *Sisters Stand* cover from 1971 and a *Riot Grrrl* cover from 1993 is immediately evident. Both feature pencil drawings of a naked woman's body that has been altered—defaced or dismembered—in some way. The *Sisters Stand* cover shows a woman with no left breast, standing in the middle of a woman symbol with her fist raised defiantly. The *Riot Grrrl* cover shows an armless, legless, headless torso. In both images, the dismemberment is making a broader point. The *Sisters Stand* image alludes to the Amazon women who removed their left breasts to enable them to be better archers; the image is clearly meant to be empowering. The dismemberment is much more dramatic on the *Riot Grrrl* cover, and the body morphs into something else: the spot where the woman's legs should be has been drawn as the cross-section of an apple, with the core as her vagina. The apple imagery is obviously a visual pun on the New York City home of this particular Riot Grrrl group, but the image is more than a joke and seems more ambiguous than the *Sisters Stand* cover. The torso makes reference to archaic/classical art images of women, but the extreme alteration and sexualization of this body gives evidence to the fact that the grrrl zinesters are in a culture saturated with a different kind of advertising imagery than the *Sisters Stand* authors faced. The lettering of the titles also registers this difference: *Riot Grrrl* is written in cursive, both girly (with extra curls on the "r" and "t") and sharp. *Sisters Stand*, in contrast, is in block print shadowed to seem as if it's emerging from the page and rising upward, along with the face of the woman on the cover. It is not at all playful or girly. Yet both covers are hand drawn, and both are reimagining women's bodies, doing something different with the naked female body than mainstream culture, claiming ownership of that iconography by printing it on the cover of the publication. Despite the differences, these covers have a family resemblance. There's no evidence that the girls who made the *Riot Grrrl* zine had seen *Sisters Stand* or were intentionally emulating second wave publications; indeed, direct lines of influence can be difficult to trace, and the propagation of social movements is often a bit haphazard. The similarities in these publications are significant, however, even if they are unintentional. Both groups of women were dealing with a culture permeated with sexist imagery and ideology, and they responded by creating their own media that resisted that sexism and envisioned womanhood differently.

Even more striking than the similar look and feel of these documents are the similarities in distribution between second wave publications and zines. Scrapbooks, of course, were one-off productions; they were individual artifacts that could be shared within a community and used to build

Cover of *Sisters Stand* (left), courtesy of the Sallie Bingham Center for Women's History and Culture in the Rare Book, Manuscript, and Special Collections Library at Duke University.
Cover of *Riot Grrrl NYC* (right), courtesy of the Sallie Bingham Center for Women's History and Culture in the Rare Book, Manuscript, and Special Collections Library at Duke University.

that community, but they could not be widely disseminated because each was unique, and inexpensive reproduction technology was not available. While health pamphlets were reproduced, the dangers of wide dissemination certainly limited their reach. Mimeograph technology allowed second wave feminists to distribute their publications widely. This was both a benefit and a challenge: activist and author Robin Morgan explains: "We were becoming bursitis-ridden, literally, from carrying around all these goddamned mimeographed papers in shopping bags when we'd go to some college for a weekend of organizing."[34] Yet this technology meant that every attendant at a consciousness-raising group could receive a copy of "The Myth of the Vaginal Orgasm." Similarly, every woman who came to a Riot

Grrrl meeting in New York City could receive one of the *Riot Grrrl* zines. They were distributed informally, person to person rather than through official publishing channels. They were often free or offered for a minimal payment (Baxandall and Gordon note that prices for Women's Liberation pamphlets ranged "from a nickel to a quarter," while grrrl zines were often $1.00).[35] As I discuss in chapter 2, this is part of how zines create community. These documents, created by hand, reproduced on a small scale, and shared in intimate settings helped to bring women together.

In addition, second wave publications and grrrl zines have ideological similarities. Although not all did, many grrrl zinesters, particularly Riot Grrrl zinesters, made conscious ideological connections with second wave publications. They may not have realized the material connections—the fact that their zines were informal, participatory media in line with previous kinds—but many zinesters clearly align themselves with a feminist legacy and see themselves as carrying on this legacy. This legacy is manifested in the many reprints of second wave documents that grrrl zinesters, particularly early grrrl zinesters, have included in their zines. For instance, Lizzard Amazon, editor of the zine *Riot Grrrlz Outer Space*, reprinted "The Bitch Manifesto" by Joreen (Jo Freeman), a publication that was included in the 1970 collection *Notes from the Second Year*. In her editor's letter, Amazon writes, "Dear Jo, Shulamith and Anne, I hope y'all are not offended that I'm reprinting this w/out permission. I just want girls today to see it!"[36] She also reprinted Valerie Solanas's *SCUM Manifesto*. Similarly, the zine *Function* #5 reprints Judy Syfer's "Why I Want a Wife" (although with no attribution or year), and many other grrrl zines include quotes from second wave publications and biographical sketches of first wave and second wave feminists.[37] Indeed, it seems clear that not only did grrrl zinesters like Amazon laud these second wave feminists whose writings they cited and reprinted, but they also created work of their own that pays tribute to or emulates second wave writings. This is evident in the many menstruation, do-it-yourself health care, and women's herbal wisdom zines that are carrying on the legacy of *Our Bodies, Ourselves* (and, although perhaps unknowingly, the health pamphlets).

These connections are also evident in Riot Grrrl manifestos. These manifestos are lists that explain Riot Grrrl; as if answering the question "Why does Riot Grrrl exist?" they begin, "Riot Grrrl is . . . BECAUSE . . .," and offer many different political explanations after the word "because." These manifestos appeared—with much consistent content—in Riot Grrrl zines throughout the early 1990s.[38] They map out a complex personal and political terrain and tie feminist social change to cultural change. They're especially strong in their eagerness to reframe the standards by which cultural productions are judged: "BECAUSE we don't wanna assimilate to someone else's (Boy) standards of what is or isn't 'good' music or punk rock or 'good' writing AND THUS need to create forums where we can recreate, destroy and define our own visions," as well as "BECAUSE we are angry at a society that tells us Girl=Dumb, Girl=Bad, Girl=Weak."[39] They are similar to a number of second wave feminist manifestos, such as the 1968 "Principles" of the New York Radical Women, the Redstockings' "Manifesto" of 1969, and the 1970 "Woman-Identified Woman" statement of the Radicalesbians.[40] These emphatic pronouncements offer clear, unambiguous claims about gender, sexism, and societal functioning, with content and tone that are surprisingly similar in the 1960s and the early 1990s. These shared characteristics demonstrate a feminist history for grrrl zines—a feminist legacy on which the early grrrl zines were building, rather than a story of rupture and rebellion. Even if they were unaware of this fact, early grrrl zinesters were sharing the rebellion that second wave feminists had articulated, rather than rebelling *against* those feminists.

However, the early grrrl zinesters didn't share ideological perspectives only with the feminists of the 1960s and 1970s. The second wave stretched over several decades, expanded, and became more complicated as U.S. third world feminists began offering critiques and reframings of feminism in the 1970s and 1980s. Grrrl zines show clear ideological links to the work of U.S. third world feminists. Third world feminist theorist Chela Sandoval identifies a new feminist paradigm, which she refers to as "differential coalitional consciousness" or "differential praxis," that "was utilized by an irreverent cadre of feminists of color within seventies and eighties United States women's movements."[41] This new paradigm is one that embraces difference and discord as sites of energy and social change, a perspective voiced, perhaps, most persuasively by poet and activist Audre Lorde:

> Advocating the mere tolerance of difference between women is the grossest reformism. It is a total denial of the creative function of difference in our lives. For difference must not be merely tolerated, but seen as a fund of necessary polarities between which our creativity can spark like a dialectic. . . . Difference is that raw and powerful connection from which our personal power is forged.[42]

Some of the central theoretical approaches characteristic of this new paradigm were articulated in the groundbreaking 1981 collection *This Bridge Called My Back: Writings by Radical Women of Color*. The editors Gloria Anzaldúa and Cherríe Moraga called for "a theory in the flesh . . . one where the physical realities of our lives—our skin color, the land or concrete we grew up on, our sexual longings—all fuse to create a politic born out of necessity. Here, we attempt to bridge the contradictions in our experience."[43]

Grrrl zines were deeply influenced by these ideas. In part, the "irreverent cadre of feminists of color" are articulating an experience that has come to be emblematic of late-capitalist culture: fragmented identities, lack of a solid moral center, and decollectivization. Further, the celebration of difference—not as a problem to be solved but as a source of energy and creativity—resonated with young women of color and white women who had come to see some kinds of second wave feminism as too restrictive. As discussed in chapters 3 and 4, grrrl zines provided a space for girls and women to explore what *This Bridge Called My Back* calls "the contradictions in our experience." The lines of transmission varied. In some cases, grrrl zinesters are, in fact, reading these scholars, hungry for the ideas they present on how to make sense of the world: many early grrrl zinesters were Women's Studies students, and bell hooks, Gayatri Spivak, Trinh Minh Ha, and other popular U.S. third world feminist scholars appear in a number of zines, including *Free to Fight, Slant, Shotgun Seamstress,* and *Doris*. In other cases, the ideas seem to have become part of the grrrl zine culture, so that zine creators could pick them up indirectly. Regardless, a comparison of these texts suggests that grrrl zines were emerging from a history of both feminist participatory media and U.S. third world feminist theory, and where they emerge from matters because of the trajectory this origin story makes visible: a trajectory of continued feminist ideology and activism that has links to the past but, as discussed in the last part of this chapter, also changes as it develops.

These informal publications—the scrapbooks, health pamphlets, and mimeographed documents—allowed girls and women to say things that weren't being said elsewhere, often because they were considered too trivial, too personal, or too controversial. In the epigraph to this chapter, Tobi Vail of *Jigsaw* identifies the silencing of women's stories as a crucial part of her inspiration for producing her zine. In emphatic capitals she announces, "i am making a fanzine not to entertain or distract or exclude or because i don't have anything better to do but because if i didn't write these things no one else would either." She frames her own zine in contrast to the "hundreds of boy fanzine writers" who presumably have the luxury of writing for entertainment, while she has "a legitimate need and a desperate desire" to publicize the stories that otherwise wouldn't be told. Vail, like her feminist predecessors, turned to participatory media because it allowed her to skirt around mainstream publishing practices, a consumer culture industry, and even a counterculture that would have denied the validity of her voice—either by seeing her words as mere entertainment or, as with Dyer, not seeing her words at all.

Of course, grrrl zines are not identical to the scrapbooks, pamphlets, and other feminist participatory media of the past. As is the case with all participatory media, grrrl zines are affected by their cultural moment; they are created in the context of available technologies, and they make use of cultural ephemera. Thus grrrl zines are aesthetically and ideologically related to previous feminist publications, but also distinct, and the distinctiveness of grrrl zines helps to create and disseminate the distinctiveness of the third wave. Grrrl zines and the third wave work within and against the terrain of femininity, promulgate an aesthetic of visual contradiction, and articulate their own over-the-top rhetorics of anger and feeling.

In the rest of this chapter, I examine these distinctions by considering the emergence of *Action Girl Newsletter* and the Riot Grrrl movement in the 1990s as a more immediate origin for the grrrl zine explosion and the third wave of feminism. As I explain, the third wave came into being and was sent out into the world in large part through the early grrrl zines. To understand the zines and the third wave, then, it's important to keep in mind grrrl zines' historical predecessors. When we bring the stories of Riot Grrrls and Action Girl together with the larger origin story of feminist participatory media, what becomes visible is a more-sustained history of women's interventions and resistance. Without knowledge of the publications that were part of previous waves of feminism, the early 1990s moment looks like nothing that's ever come before, and the artifacts of Riot Grrrl and Action Girl may be hard to contextualize. We might be baffled, as the mainstream media was, at the emergence of the third wave, this "feminism with a loud happy face dotting the 'i'" or these "she-devils out of Rush Limbaugh's worst nightmare."[44] As part of a larger origin story, though, the Riot Grrrl zines and the *Action Girl Newsletter* are revealed as the newest incarnations of long-standing feminist publishing practices.

They—and the third wave they helped initiate—exhibit ties to the past and also offer useful revisions to make feminism more relevant for young women in the late-twentieth century.

## *Riot Grrrls,* Action Girl, *and the Third Wave*

At the beginning of the 1990s, a confluence of events and trends created a perfect storm for young feminism. A brief glimpse at this cultural moment suggests the forces that combined to catalyze the third wave. In these years, the 1980s backlash against feminism, documented by Susan Faludi, was still gaining momentum, so much so that one feminist journalist could warn in 1992, "In the public world we are entering the darkest hour of the backlash."[45] High-profile rape trials such as those for William Kennedy Smith and Mike Tyson, along with the Tailhook scandal and the Clarence Thomas–Anita Hill hearings, publicized the prevalence of violence against and sexual harassment of women—and the likelihood that such crimes would remain unpunished even when acknowledged. Popular films such as *Fatal Attraction* and television shows such as *thirtysomething* demonized women with careers as miserable, mentally unstable, and desperate for a man. During this time, Teen Talk Barbie began saying things like, "I love shopping" and "Math class is tough."

And yet this same period saw the growth of *Sassy* magazine, a publication for teen girls that assumed they were smart, politically savvy, and in need of real information about their bodies, their culture, and the latest in activism. In August 1991, Girl Night in Olympia—the opening event of the International Pop Underground Festival—marked the unofficial beginning of the Riot Grrrl movement. Rebecca Walker's 1992 *Ms.* magazine essay, "Becoming the Third Wave," demanded of young feminists, "Turn that outrage to political power. Do not vote for them unless they work for us. Do not have sex with them, do not break bread with them, do not nurture them if they do not prioritize our freedom to control our bodies and our lives" and proclaimed, "I am not a postfeminism feminist. I am the Third Wave."[46] The first issues of the *Action Girl Newsletter* were published. In addition, women's studies classes and programs were becoming institutionalized at many colleges and universities. By 1993, Dyer had been featured in *Seventeen* magazine, Riot Grrrl had been profiled by media agencies from the *New York Times* to *Newsweek*, and grrrl zines were an established phenomenon. Within a few years, edited collections were published which addressed third wave feminism.

The early 1990s was a moment of hope and frustration for girls and women. It was a moment that demonstrated feminism's unfinished business, a moment in which girls and women were "caught between the hope of a world that no longer degrades women and the reality of a culture that is still, nevertheless, degrading."[47] This combination of factors—a pervasive rhetoric of equality alongside clear evidence of persistent sexism, racism, and homophobia—helped catalyze the third wave but is in part responsible for the unevenness of third wave ideology. Girls and young women in the early 1990s were likely to find feminist concepts such as equal pay for equal work commonsensical, and they were often surprised when they found that these commonsensical notions were not actually in place in the real world. And when they did encounter sexism, racism, or homophobia, the culture to which they belonged—one in which large-scale social movements and collective action were no longer seen as viable, and the emphasis was on personal success within the marketplace—was unlikely to provide them with models of how to respond.

It was in these years that the proliferation of grrrl zines began, first from major cities on the coasts but soon from towns all across the country. The grrrl zine explosion was part of the feminist tradition of informal publishing, but not all grrrl zinesters were aware of this. For one thing, the backlash had so fully defined feminism that many of the grrrl zinesters had grave misunderstandings of earlier feminist generations. For instance, young feminists Jessica Rosenberg and Gitana Garofalo, in an article about Riot Grrrl in *Signs*, claim that Riot Grrrls are "much angrier" than second wave feminists, a claim that suggests that they are unaware of the fierce anger expressed in many second wave publications and activism.[48] Also Chelsea Starr, who has done outstanding research on the Riot Grrrl movement, offers several simplistic assessments of feminism, such as, "Radical feminism and heterosexual were two categories which have not mixed since the early 1970s."[49] At several points she and some of the zinesters she interviews imply that feminism is equivalent to lesbian separatism. Nomy Lamm, Riot Grrrl and producer of the popular and influential zine *I'm So Fucking Beautiful*, said, "I'd never had feminism presented to me in any way that was interesting at all"—she thought it was only about being a corporate officer.[50] Other grrrl zinesters simply weren't aware of previous generations of feminism. In an early issue of her zine *Jigsaw*, Tobi Vail reviews Betty Friedan's *The Feminine Mystique* and presents it as a book she found in an attic and read with no sense of its historical significance. Since grrrl zinesters did not (and do not) necessarily have a more accurate view of feminism than the mainstream culture itself, they sometimes saw themselves as pioneers, re-creating feminism, rather than carrying on a particular feminist legacy.[51]

In this case, as in others, it's difficult to pinpoint exactly how or why this social movement emerged in the early 1990s. Many young feminists did know about second wave feminism, either through encountering it in women's studies classes, through their own historical studies, or through family connections (as is the case with Rebecca Walker). Others did not. Yet the grrrl zinesters *were* carrying on a feminist legacy, as one observer puts it, "rewriting feminism in a youth vernacular."[52] Their recognition of oppression, their commitment to voicing the inequities they observed in the hopes of challenging and changing them, and their attempts to document their own life experiences, experiences excluded from more-mainstream narratives, all fit within a feminist rubric. In these originating moments, two entities stand out: Riot Grrrl and the *Action Girl Newsletter.* They were instrumental in formulating a style, rhetoric, and iconography for grrrl zines, and these came to define third wave feminism, as well. The terminology of third wave feminism didn't come into the mainstream until the early 1990s, so Riot Grrrls didn't initially call themselves third wave feminists. Tobi Vail explains: "When we started there wasn't anything such as third wave, or any kind of feminism that would resemble one—it was solidly second wave. I don't know if that meant we invented it or what."[53] Her claim of invention isn't wrong: Riot Grrrl and *Action Girl* function as sites at which grrrl zines and third wave feminism emerged.

What follows is not a comprehensive history of the Riot Grrrl movement; this is a project other scholars have done ably.[54] Instead, I look closely at a few Riot Grrrl zines and the *Action Girl Newsletter* with attention to how they exhibit a distinctive style, rhetoric, and iconography. The look of these early zines, their playfulness within the terrain of femininity, their use of contradictory visual images, and their expressions of extreme rage and profanity would become characteristic of grrrl zines and the third wave. Riot Grrrl and *Action Girl* connected many of the core ideas of feminism with the trappings of their own cultural moment, and in so doing, they helped to create third wave feminism—a feminist generation with a family resemblance to previous incarnations but with its own distinctive approach. That approach was developed and deployed, at least in part, in grrrl zines. In later chapters, I explore the ideological significance of ideas explored in grrrl zines, but here I am concerned with the tools—the visual and verbal vocabularies that came to define grrrl zines and the third wave.

Image of Action Girl from *Action Girl Newsletter*, courtesy of Sarah Dyer.

Femininity was an iconographic terrain that these zines quickly began to mine. Since the second wave had destabilized some of the meaning of femininity, it was available to the next generation to start working with in a different way. It became mutable, not simply a hegemonic entity to be rejected but part of the cultural material to be considered. For late-twentieth-century feminists, femininity became a terrain of "rich and pliable symbolism."[55] The manipulation of this pliable symbolism, the celebration and reimagining of femininity, is apparent in any issue of the *Action Girl Newsletter*. *Action Girl Newsletter*, which Sarah Dyer created in 1992 as a way of bringing other grrrl zinesters together, became a popular and significant publication that helped define the iconography of the third wave. Dyer's cartoon character Action Girl, appearing in most issues of the zine, is identifiably feminine, with an outfit that resembles a drum majorette with outer space boots. She's featured smiling, with shoulder-length hair and a headband. Although she is a superhero, she has no visible musculature. She seems sweetly youthful—even cute—an image of womanhood that second wave feminists might have rejected as representing all the feminine qualities from which they were trying to divest. Indeed, she doesn't seem ironic; she is as nonthreatening as a doll.

There is more to this image, however, than a simple celebration of mainstream femininity. Dyer gives more information about Action Girl in her "Action Girl Cut and Color Activity Page,"[56] in which she does, in fact, feature the character as a paper doll. She's drawn with an array of possible outfits around her, including "Action Girl Stays Home," "Action Girl Goes to Mom's," and "Action Girl Fights Evil!" Dyer annotates each element of each outfit, interpreting her character's presentation down to the level of minutia. Several things are apparent here: although the page is lighthearted and humorous, including commentary such as "Where's a comb??" beside Action Girl's hair, the annotations also politicize the character's clothing. For instance, in describing the clothing, Dyer offers implicit recommendations: "$10 'sports bra'—comfortable, supportive, and *never* comes undone" and "Action boots! $9 from thrift shop—go with all action outfits and outlast Docs." She advocates clothing for her superhero—and by extension for her female readers—that is comfortable and functional. Indeed, although Action Girl's short skirt might seem to be pandering to mainstream fashion, the caption beside the skirt notes, "Short full skirt means freedom of movement!"

The most striking part of the page, however, is the bottom right corner—the closing space, the punch line, which features an outfit titled, "Oh No!! Action Girl Was Drawn by a Guy!!" Rather than being simply an outfit, what Dyer draws here is an entire female body missing only its head. This figure has enormous breasts and cleavage, which are visible because she is wearing a kind of skimpy bathing suit, along with a cape and fishnet stockings. All the captions for this image are observant and critical. Dyer critiques the body itself ("Like anyone has this body. Do these guys ever have dates? Have they *seen* a woman's body?"), as well as the utility of the clothing for someone actually fighting crime ("Like you can do anything in this cape"), and the image is surrounded by smaller captions reading, "Save her now!!" and "Help!" While the rest of the outfits on the page include instructions on how to cut them out and what colors each part should be, the instructions for this icon read, "Cut out, then rip up over a trash can while laughing gleefully!!"

Action Girl Cut and Color Activity Page from *Action Girl Newsletter,* courtesy of Sarah Dyer.

Indeed, the gleeful laughter of destroying sexist iconography seems to characterize this part of the page.

While it would be easy to look at the initial image of Action Girl and see her—as second wave feminists might—as complicit with mainstream images of femininity, what Dyer shows through her Activity Page is that she has constructed this image in direct contrast to the more common images of female superheroes in comics drawn by men. Action Girl has been deliberately designed as a kind of real girl; in fact, much of the commentary on this page suggests that Action Girl might have some things in common with Dyer herself. Action Girl is not thoughtlessly complicit with patriarchal views of women; instead, she represents a deployment of strategic femininity. As such, she is establishing a typical third wave move:

the creative deployment of feminine iconography comes to be a central trope of third wave feminism.

Dyer's visual vocabulary is different from that in second wave publications, in large part because she uses rather than rejects feminine ideals. Where the 1970 *Sisters Stand* cover exhibits a kind of militant refusal of the trappings of femininity, the *Action Girl Newsletter* and many other grrrl zines after it embrace femininity as a political tool. In this way the "Action Girl Cut and Color Activity Page" enacts a strategy somewhat similar to those in suffragist scrapbooks, a strategy of reinforcing the author's appropriate femininity in order to legitimize her and make her political message both stealthier and more palatable.

This page also shows Dyer embracing the iconography of girl culture. By offering a page of paper dolls and outfits in a publication meant for teen girls and adult women, Dyer is drawing on a rich reservoir of girlhood imagery and using it in unexpected ways—in this case, to mobilize critique and activism. As discussed in chapter 3 in greater detail, many aspects of girlhood and girl culture are rejected by mainstream society, but grrrl zinesters often deliberately revive those things and redefine girlhood as a space of pleasure, social change, and activism. Dyer's appropriately named "Activity Page" repeats the term "Action Girl" ten times. This rhetorical emphasis, like that seen in other grrrl zines (such as the "Jigsaw Manifesto" discussed in the introduction), combines with the visual excess of the repeated bodies and multiple outfits on the page to suggest an embrace of girlish speech and aesthetic styles, as well as an attempt to overcome a particular societal silencing of girls. Action Girl's nonthreatening cuteness merges with Dyer's political message about action and her critique of other representations of womanhood to create a different set of rhetorical and visual tools for grrrl zinesters. Indeed, Action Girl paves the way for later grrrl zinesters like Yumi Lee to write, in a 2000 essay called "Reclaiming Cute," "I think of my girliness and 'cuteness' as having been redefined. It's an enlightened, empowered cute—it's me telling the world that I may giggle a lot but that *doesn't* mean that I won't kick your ass if needs be."[57] Cute, then, does not mean apolitical. It becomes a tool for political activism, another rhetorical move that becomes characteristic of the third wave.

Another common trope in the early grrrl zines is the juxtaposition of seemingly incongruous—or even contradictory—images and rhetorics. This happens particularly often within the terrain of femininity. For instance, this trope can be seen in a cartoon that began appearing in each issue of the

Image from *Action Girl Newsletter,* courtesy of Sarah Dyer.

*Action Girl Newsletter* showing Hello Kitty wearing a Riot Grrrl dress and carrying a teddy bear with an anarchist symbol printed on its jumper.

The image accompanied the call to action that Dyer printed in each issue. The image and the call to action itself are deliberately friendly. Dyer writes, "Be an ACTION GIRL (or boy)! It's great to read/ listen to/ watch other people's creative output, but it's even cooler to do it yourself."[58] She urges her readers to "try anyway" even if they're wary, and she signs it with a heart before her name. This is an encouraging girlfriend letter alongside a Hello Kitty whose iconic rounded body hasn't been altered at all—she's still wearing her dress and a bow on her head. And yet the image is somewhat hard to read: Hello Kitty's face appears particularly expressionless when put in this context, and her Riot Grrrl clothing and anarchist bear suggest that she has a political significance far different from her mainstream market meaning.

This image captures the odd juxtapositions that came to define a particular grrrl zine and third wave aesthetic, an aesthetic that some referred to as "kinderwhore" or "kitten with a whip."[59] This aesthetic differentiates the third wave from previous feminisms; as a colleague pointed out, no self-respecting second waver would do anything with Hello Kitty imagery other than reject it, and this sort of hyperfeminine imagery does not, to my knowledge, appear in any informal second wave publications. However, third wave feminists find many cultural artifacts associated with femininity to have changeable meanings, particularly when they're combined in surprising ways. I take this up more fully in chapter 3, but the point here is that the mashing together of femininity and "fuck you" is another aesthetic element that differentiates this generation of feminists.

This aesthetic became pervasive in third wave productions. It was evident in the bodily performativity of Riot Grrrls, who often brought together apparently incongruous elements on their own skin and made their bodies into billboards. For instance, Nomy Lamm was in a band playing at a public event, and she wore a dress that she described as "this horrible silky prom-dress thing [that] was way more revealing than anything I was okay with wearing at that time."[60] In order to challenge viewers' potential condemnation of her body, she wrote "No Fat Chicks" on her chest. Other Riot Grrrls wrote "Slut," "Rape," or "Property" on their bodies. In this way, they wrested control of the language from those who would use sexist terminology to degrade women. By writing these terms on their bodies in defiant black marker scrawl, Riot Grrrls appropriated these terms and altered their meaning. Just as Hello Kitty no longer represents a silent girlhood toy, words like "slut" no longer have the same power to condemn and silence girls and women. Joanne Gottlieb and Gayle Wald discuss this bodily performativity as a means of becoming visible, and they note that "this visibility counteracts the (feelings of) erasure and invisibility produced by persistent degradation in a sexist society."[61] It was also a way of destabilizing gender standards and refusing the cultural mandate that girls' bodies be silent, viewable sex objects (and it was the single most-often-reported aspect of Riot Grrrls in the mainstream media). Riot Grrrls and grrrl zinesters often made the female body into a spectacle, but a different kind of spectacle than the one the dominant culture was comfortable with.

This willingness to take command of language and make it work differently is evident, as well, in Riot Grrrls' zines, and it becomes a familiar approach in grrrl zines and the third wave in general. For instance, many Riot Grrrl manifestos included the statement "BECAUSE i believe with my holeheartmindbody that girls constitute a revolutionary soul force that can, and will, change the world for real."[62] The neologism "holeheartmindbody" is indicative of Riot Grrrls' creative reclaiming of language. When this part of the manifesto is reprinted in other zines, the spelling is sometimes "corrected" to "wholeheartmindbody," but I think the misspelling is intentional and significant, playing on the apparently contradictory terms *hole* and *whole*, making reference to the vagina and identifying the "hole" as part of what defines a woman's wholeness as much as her heart, mind, and body. Indeed, this reclaiming of sexist terms is not only something that differentiates the second and third waves but was one of the earliest obstacles between these two populations. As young feminists in the early 1990s began using words like *girl, cunt,* and *bitch* that older feminists had struggled to undermine and eradicate, many second wave feminists took this as evidence of the third wave's apathy or lack of political understanding rather than recognizing it as a legitimate political tactic. While second wave mimeographers and first wave scrapbookers had also challenged the sexist terminology of their times, Riot Grrrls' embrace of and use of highly charged terms was different.

Even when they were making use of ideas that were common throughout the generations of feminism—such as anger at a sexist society—Riot Grrrls and *Action Girl* did so with rhetorics that were distinctive and came to define the third wave. While young feminists Garofalo and Rosenberg mistakenly identified anger solely with Riot Grrrls, they were right to note that the ways in which anger was expressed within Riot Grrrl zines was distinctive and helped to differentiate Riot Grrrls from earlier waves of feminism. For instance, a zine called *Start a Fucking Riot* was produced by D.C. Riot Grrrls and, like many Riot Grrrl zines, it overflows with expressions of frustration. One chunk of text addresses the fact that within the punk scene, a certain kind of girl the author refers to as "bimbo girl foxy girl" uses her sexuality to find acceptance. She addresses this type of girl, suggesting that she might be hurt by this sort of behavior, and the boys who take advantage of this girl, saying, "boy you have no right to use girl like that." However, the real vitriol of the essay is directed at the larger society that trains men and women to blame the victims:

no one is excluded from perpetuating this shitfuckhell we poison ourselves with. no one is justified, "well, she let me," "well, he wants it," in
their actions, their non-actions, for stopping this hellhellhellHELLhell
shitfuckhell. and i cannot/will not/refuse to apologize for being judgmen-
tal. you see, i am suffocating. my air is swiftly being sucked away by the
stifling amount of stereotypes.[63]

What characterizes this anger is its excessive, dramatic quality. The
swearing—typically a rhetoric reserved for men—represents an effort to
articulate rage at an unfair social system. Even run of the mill profanity is
not enough; she writes "hellhellhellHELLhell" and repeats "shitfuckhell"
as an attempt to amplify the language to meet up with her feelings. Overt
anger of this sort did not appear in scrapbooks or health pamphlets, in
which the authors were attempting to validate their feminine appropriate-
ness, and while profanity appeared in second wave pamphlets, it wasn't as
common there—or as emphatic—as it is in grrrl zines.[64] Kearney argues
that the Riot Grrrl movement brought together punk and second wave
feminism to create a new entity that hadn't existed before, and in the rhetorics of anger, that connection to punk is particularly clear.

The rhetorical excess and flamboyance are evident, as well, in some
of the exaggerated, over-the-top pronouncements that appeared in many
zines, such as "The Splendiferous Oath of Riot Grrrlz Outer Space":

I riotously swear to rage in glorious anger against everything that even
slightly pisses me off. I swear to be loud, vulgar, obnoxious, illogical, and
emotional whenever I damn please. As an Outer Space Riot Grrrl I will
dream of impossible utopias, make up wild political theories, laugh at
people who oppose me, and as much as I can, be full of supreme confidence and hellacious egotism.[65]

The Riot Grrrl "BECAUSE" manifestos are easier to interpret, offering
a familiar format, apparent sincerity, and transparent claims. As I discussed earlier, they are firmly aligned with the manifestos of second wave
feminist groups. The flamboyant pronouncements like the "Splendiferous
Oath" are a bit slipperier. To be sure, the talk of impossible utopias and
outer space might suggest that this is a fantasy and might cause a reader to
question the serious intent of Riot Grrrl as a political and cultural movement. Yet I contend that these tell us much about the grrrl zine as a genre
and about the emergence of the third wave. For the most part, second

wave feminists were more comfortable operating within a rhetoric of sincerity, while Riot Grrrls and third wave feminists were and are part of a cultural climate that is so relentlessly marketed to and so self-consciously savvy that they don't expect or offer straightforward points of view. Instead, these wild claims are mapping out a new terrain, challenging the terms of the conversation, using over-the-top language to counter staid, encrusted gender ideologies. To "rage in glorious anger against everything that even slightly pisses me off" and "to be loud, vulgar, obnoxious, illogical, and emotional whenever I damn please" are much more fun than being the well-behaved good girl or the "humorless feminist." These declarations are tapping into political indignation, as well as aesthetic pleasure. As a recent book about Riot Grrrl suggests, it may be more appropriate to see these statements as akin to love letters, dreams, and adventures rather than trying to understand them as rational pronouncements.[66]

Riot Grrrl zines and the *Action Girl Newsletter*, then, were crucial publications that helped establish the tools with which other grrrl zinesters and third wave feminists addressed their culture. In the remaining chapters in this book, I revisit the rhetoric and aesthetics established by Riot Grrrls and *Action Girl* again and again, as these became familiar strategies, as well as jumping-off points, for future grrrl zine developments. The excessive expressions of emotion, the embrace of denigrating terminology, and the manipulation of feminine iconography are pervasive among grrrl zines and help make these publications both distinctive and effective.

At the same time, we must remember that beneath these distinctive approaches, Riot Grrrls and *Action Girl* were carrying on a feminist legacy. Although it's appealing in some ways for young feminists to configure Riot Grrrls and *Action Girl* as an entire reinvention of feminism, this is inaccurate. The Riot Grrrl movement and the *Action Girl Newsletter* were manifesting new kinds of feminism, even as they exhibited many of the traits of earlier generations. As with scrapbookers, health pamphleteers, and mimeographers, grrrl zinesters were using the tools at hand in order to say things that no one else in the culture was saying. The origin story I offer here—one that recognizes grrrl zines as emerging from the informal publications of first wave and second wave feminists—not only corrects the male bias of previous histories by showing some of the female and feminist predecessors of grrrl zines, but it also gives much-deserved credit to those earlier generations. First wave and second wave feminists' creative, expressive, and political work is often unrecognized and is rarely acknowledged for being as clever and transgressive as the work of third wave feminists. By telling this origin story, I hope to correct some of this bias. Further, framing grrrl zines as part of this continuum of feminist participatory media means that the third wave also gets positioned as part of a continuum. Although it has its distinctive rhetorics and aesthetics—and, as discussed in upcoming chapters, ideological distinctiveness, as well—third wave feminism emerges from previous generations. Rather than being a rupture, grrrl zines and the third wave that emerged from them are framed in this volume as a development, a new stage in a feminist trajectory.

# 2

# Why Zines Matter

*Materiality and the Creation
of Embodied Community*

This is no substitute for envelopes marked with your location,
sheets of stationery with your script scratching across parallel
lines, feeling the back of the paper and an embossed pattern in
the shape of every character formed (because maybe, like me, you
press down with your pen, every letter a deliberate creation), the
smell of your house on the paper itself.
—Marissa Falco, *Red-Hooded Sweatshirt* #3 (1999)

I became aware of the significance of the materiality of zines
through my teaching. Every time I teach a class about zines, a significant
percentage of the students begin making their own. Many of them have
never heard of zines, but when I bring in a pile for them to flip through
and take home, they become inspired. This doesn't happen if I require
them to read a published anthology of zines such as *A Girl's Guide to
Taking Over the World*; getting their hands on actual zines is necessary
to ignite this creative urge. They read the long-running zine *The East Village Inky* and express surprise and delight at the informality, the quirky
portraits of zine creator Ayun Halliday and her family nestled in winding
lines of handwritten narrative. They're fascinated with the different-sized
pages (some a long, skinny 4 ¼ by 11 inches, some an almost square 4
¼ by 5 ½ inches) in *Free to Fight: The Self-Defense Project* and with the
zine's combination of collage art, comics, and scrawled stories on notebook paper.[1] They gravitate toward zines that are visibly different from
magazines and other mainstream publications, either by virtue of size or
hand-colored drawings or their sheer unprofessional appearance. Many of

them seem to feel personally invited to enter into the zine discourse, as is evidenced by the fact that they begin creating zines of their own. I have at least a dozen zines created by students who have taken my classes over three years.

In an age of electronic media, when the future of the book itself is often called into question, and when the visual and textual landscape is dominated by an increasingly voracious culture industry, zines endure.[2] Furthermore, they seem to instigate a kind of gift culture: little eddies of artifacts accrue around grrrl zines, circulating between zine readers and creators. Zines instigate intimate, affectionate connections between their creators and readers, not just communities but what I am calling *embodied* communities, made possible by the materiality of the zine medium.[3] My students have been inspired to become part of the zine community because of physical encounters with actual zines, not by reading anthologized zines. In a world where more and more of us spend all day at our computers, zines reconnect us to our bodies and to other human beings. This embodied community has implications for the zine medium more broadly but is particularly salient to the development of third wave theory and activism.

I begin this chapter with close readings of zines as visual and sculptural media. We can't understand grrrl zines or the zine medium—can't understand the communities they create, why they continue to be created, or what they allow girls and women to say and do—without examining the physical form, the materiality, of zines. This is a necessary first step. For this reason, I examine five zines—*I'm So Fucking Beautiful, Fragments of Friendship, The East Village Inky, No Better Voice*, and *Doris*—with attention to particular aspects of the medium each zine illustrates. When studying a body of material as diverse, changing, and elusive as zines, it's nearly impossible to make many claims about representativeness. In this sense, then, these five zines are case studies without being models; they are examples of rather than being representative of, and my readings of them offer hints and possibilities, showing the layers of meaning that become visible when we move beyond the written word to the artifact itself.

The community of zines doesn't demand homogeny or perceived sameness; instead, zine communities are more like what philosopher Iris Marion Young describes as "the ideal of city life," characterized by variety, social differentiation without exclusion, and a heterogeneous public.[4] These zines—created during the timeline this book follows, from the early 1990s through today—address different topics. Four—*I'm So Fucking Beautiful,*

*The East Village Inky, No Better Voice,* and *Doris*—have been widely circulated, and *The East Village Inky, No Better Voice,* and *Doris* are all long-
running. *Fragments of Friendship* is a one-off zine. Although all are easily
identifiable within the zine medium, they have different aesthetic profiles
and therefore allow for an examination of varying ways in which the
visual and sculptural elements of zines can function. The close reading of
these five zines illustrates features of materiality that produce embodied
community. By mobilizing particular human experiences that are linked
to the body, including vulnerability, affection, and pleasure, these zines
leverage their materiality into a kind of surrogate physical interaction and
offer mechanisms for creating meaningful relationships. I conclude the
chapter with a theoretical analysis of the nature of the embodied community created by zines and its implications for third wave feminism.

## Semiotics of Concrete Forms in I'm So Fucking Beautiful

Nomy Lamm's zine *I'm So Fucking Beautiful* documents her frustration
with being a large woman in a culture that derides fat and her creation
of what she later began calling "a big fat revolution."[5] Lamm produced
three issues of the zine in 1991, when she was seventeen years old. The
zine combines handwriting and drawings, collage art, and typewritten
narratives, and its existence as a visual and sculptural artifact or artwork
is a significant component of its meaning. Issue 2 ½ is filled with rants
about fat oppression. The narrative voice propels the zine, offering sarcastic commentary on Lamm's friends: "YEAH everyone knows that when
there's something sizeist, nomy's the one to tell. nomy's the one who will
do something about it. ask nomy what to do. or just sit around and wait
to see what nomy will do."[6] As the zine progresses, the voice becomes pro-
gressively angrier, until Lamm writes, "this fukin dumbass boy is in my
apartment with my roommate and he tells her that to him FAT SYMBOL-
IZES WEALTH AND AMERICAN GREED. . . . this is a boy who i would
have considered my friendly acquaintance. THIS IS IN MY OWN FUCK-
ING APARTMENT."[7] Lamm's tone is fierce and unapologetic; she emphasizes her anger and her ironic disbelief through her use of profanity and
phrases that are fully capitalized. This woman is infuriated.

It would be easy to stop at this level of analysis, considering the narrative alone as constitutive of the meaning of this zine. The zine would seem
to be a rant, a one-dimensional expression of anger and outrage, and certainly this is part of what the zine expresses. But this isn't the full meaning.

```
     scene three:                    considered a friendly acquaintance
                                     THIS IS IN MY OWN FUCKING APARTMENT.
this is the worst because it takes   i'm not there of course, but this
place in my own apartment.           asshole knows that i live here, he
   this fukin dumbass boy is in my   knows that he's talking to a close
apartment with my roommate and he    friend of mine.
tells her that to him FAT SYMBOLIZES    i know that this boy is a total
WEALTH AND AMERICAN GREED.  this is  fucking idiot and he probably just
not something new i know that        heard someone say that on mtv and
this is a common rationalization/    after my roommate argued with him for
justification for fat hating.  i know two minutes he changed his mind.  but
that fukin ian mckaye (or however you i don't care. he said something that
spell that) has said that before.    hurt me really bad and i'm not
but this is a boy who i would have   ever gonna forgive him cuz there is
```

Pages from *I'm So Fucking Beautiful,* courtesy of Nomy Lamm.

Attention to the visual elements of this zine reveals the inadequacy of a text-based approach to a visual medium. *I'm So Fucking Beautiful* is interspersed with hand-drawn images, and four of the seven address an emotion other than anger, such as the drawing of a large woman's naked torso with a heart in the center. Framed within the heart is the word "OPEN," and the heart is surrounded by lines that radiate out into the torso, each ending in an "x." The lines suggest stitches, as though the heart is sutured into the body, or perhaps they represent something emerging from the open heart. Imposed on the soft, realistic body, the x's seem harsh, and they contrast with the iconic, almost girlish heart-shape. The female body, drawn with minimalist lines hinting at folds of flesh, is vulnerable in its nudity, and the heart is vulnerable as well, with "OPEN" functioning both as a description and a command. The drawing complicates the message, adding additional layers to Lamm's expression of her responses to a fatphobic culture.

What's more, issue 2 ½ is quite small—not quite 3 by 4 inches, just slightly larger than a business card. It is a zine about fat acceptance, a zine that demands that the world make room for large bodies, and yet it is tiny, smaller not only than most mainstream publications but also than all other issues of her zine. Not only the imagery but the form—the scale of the zine—is in tension with the content, and this tension makes the zine richer, more nuanced in its expression, and harder to pin down. Clearly, the materiality of Lamm's zine contributes to its meaning; not merely the means of transmission of information, the physical imagery and interface of the zine help shape a reader's experience and understanding. As print culture scholars recognize, a document's content is not in any easy way separable from its material existence. In their seminal print culture study *Reading Books*, critics Michele Moylan and Lane Stiles explain:

Clearly, when we read books, we really read *books*—that is, we read the physicality or materiality of the book as well as and in relation to the text itself. Literacy, then, may be said to include not only textual competence but material competence, an ability to read the semiotics of the concrete forms that embody, shape, and condition the meanings of texts. Bindings, illustrations, paper, typeface, layout, advertisements, scholarly introductions, promotional blurbs—all function as parts of a semiotic system, parts of the total meaning of a text.[8]

In other words, while readers and even scholars may be content to assess the words on the page, the page itself also makes the text's meaning. This is true with small details, as well as broad marketplace structures: typographers know that the shape and style of letters affect the reading experience, and even the most casual reader can understand the promotional semiotics of books in a bookstore—distinguishing, for instance, between mystery novels and classic texts by the cover art, shape, weight, and other silent but significant factors. Although few scholars and readers

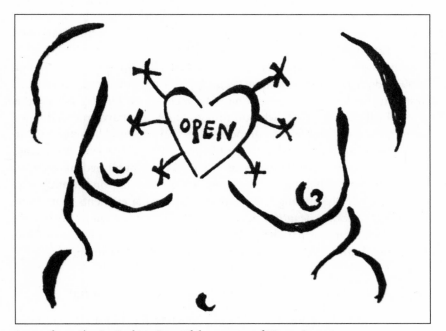

Image from *I'm So Fucking Beautiful,* courtesy of Nomy Lamm.

have identified these as relevant objects of study, zine creators like Lamm are often savvy manipulators of the semiotics of concrete forms.

Lamm deploys the visual and spatial properties of her medium in deliberate ways. Although she presents herself as powerful, a woman not to be messed with, her zine's visual components and its form do suggest vulnerability. The narrative harangues from the palm of the reader's hand, a furious message that is so delicate it could easily be crumpled and discarded. The zine's form dramatizes the difficulty of demanding fat acceptance in a society overrun with images of small, nonthreatening womanhood. Although, as Moylan and Stiles note, "often scholars, particularly literary scholars, have tended to idealize books as 'mere' texts— disembodied mental constructs transcending materiality, culture, and history," Lamm's zine is neither disembodied nor transcendent.[9] Instead, it is emphatically material, consciously designed so that the medium lets the reader see Lamm's struggle, her conflicted feelings of rage and shame. The zine is an art object as well as a literary text.

Print culture scholars and art scholars have created useful vocabularies for analyzing the sculptural and textual convergence that zines enact. However, neither set of scholars has devoted much attention to zines because they are what art theorist Gregory Sholette terms "Dark Matter," work that functions outside of and is therefore invisible to the established art world and world of academic scholarship.[10] Few scholars have sought out the self-created artifacts of a seventeen-year-old girl, even though thousands read *I'm So Fucking Beautiful*, and tens of thousands are invested in the larger zine community of which *I'm So Fucking Beautiful* is part.[11] Even among critics who do discuss zines, few have analyzed zines' materiality as a significant component of their cultural functioning. In part, this neglect may be due to the fact that some critics who study zines do so by analyzing anthologies of zines.[12] While published anthologies may be more easily attained than actual zines, relying on an anthology means completely missing the sculptural and visual elements that a zine like *I'm So Fucking Beautiful* deploys. Published anthologies also remove zines from their normal channels of distribution, and as I discuss here, these distribution methods, too, are part of the zines' meaning.[13]

## Paper versus Electronic Media and Fragments of Friendship

We can begin to see the ways that the concrete form of a zine connects creator and reader in the zine *Fragments of Friendship*.[14] Victoria Law created this zine out of a year's worth of email correspondence between herself and her friend, fellow zine creator China Martens. It adheres to a fairly standard zine format: codex, digest size, with a tan cardstock cover featuring a plain, printed title. The zine has no images, just email messages printed on paper, physically cut and glued onto other sheets of paper, and then photocopied.

This wouldn't have been a zine that particularly caught my attention except for the content: Law created no new material for the zine but simply made already existing email correspondence into this material object. She explained, "I don't remember why I actually put it together. It might've been one of the days that we were just feeling down, and I put it together and sent it to [Martens], and it brightened her day up. Being like, 'Look! You know, we got through all these things.'"[15] She was clear about the fact that this was a "one-off" zine, made primarily for Martens herself; she didn't intend to sell or widely distribute it but meant it as an artifact that would both encourage her friend and also document a year of their friendship. Somehow the emails themselves were deficient, and she wasn't inspired to archive the emails using digital means, such as a CD or website. Instead, she chose paper.

*Fragments of Friendship* makes explicit an idea that many zine creators allude and adhere to: the notion that paper is better suited for facilitating human connection than electronic media. In the epigraph to this chapter, zine creator Marissa Falco identifies a letter as a site of physical interaction. In describing "feeling the back of the paper and an embossed pattern in the shape of every character formed," she figures paper as connecting two bodies, so that the fingers of one person respond to the traces of the handwriting of the other. A piece of paper bears the marks of the body that created it as well as carrying other sensory information ("the smell of your house on the paper itself") to the reader. The paper, then, is a nexus, a technology that mediates the connections not just of "people" but of bodies.

Although blogs and zines are often conflated, zine creators know that the material matters, and they repeatedly identify zines as a paper medium. *Zine World*, one of the major zine directories, argues, "Zines are different from e-zines, which are 'zines' published on the Internet, via personal webpages or email lists. . . . There are significant differences between the two genres, and we choose to retain the distinction. When *Zine World* says 'zine,' we mean something on paper. We only review zines."[16] Indeed, this is a point that zinesters make repeatedly. Lauren Jade Martin

# 8 April 2003

Well - I am Very happy right now - if you can't tell. This is because I called my old boss and she said Hi China in a very nice voice and asked when I could come in for an interview - which we scheduled tomorrow at 10:00. I don't think there wouldn't be an opportunity for me to work there - after her asking me to come talk with her. I don't want to count my chickens before they hatch - but it looks good.

I left a year ago. I hated the florescent lights. I hated being in a cubicle 40 hours a week - plus once I moved into the city - it was nearly an hour commute to get to this suburban place where it was located! I had worked there for a year and a half and had learned everything I could from the place. They publish a lot of their shit in WordPerfect for Gods Sake - and the boss fears Word as too new and scary a program. I always had to fight to do things in Pagemaker, nevermind Quark. I made them logo's, Greeting Cards, pamphlets, formatted books. The place however was crazy! Bosses yell at you.

I really wanted to grow as a graphic designer and get a creative job in a place that would be less fishy. They threw me a big goodbye party. The boss said I could always come back (everyone loved me there, I am a perfectionist and a good worker/designer - and it was a quirky little family atmosphere going on there) - but of course I wouldn't - she had faith I would progress in my career as a graphic designer.

Well, I been out of work for a year. Made granola in a bakery for a while. It's a bad job market for designers in Baltimore.

So it was scary to ask to come back. Like I'm a loser. Plus they have lost a lot of grant money and cut back staff - I heard they are getting a new grant but ...its more insecure now. Plus I didn't want to return there - I had wanted more.

Page from *Fragments of Friendship*, courtesy of Victoria Law.

told me that "real zines are Xeroxed."[17] Lisa Jervis, too, explained: "People thought the internet was going to herald the death of print, which was a crock even in the boom days. The feeling of a printed document is never going to lose its appeal or be replaced by an electronic alternative."[18] Raina Lee notes, "Often people who have never 'zined' ask why I choose to print instead of publish online: I state that it's obvious—how will we remember websites 5 years or even 20 years from now?"[19]

As I discuss in the introduction, zines and blogs do have similarities. A too-easy comparison of the two media, however, obscures the very element that I'm interested in examining: the function of the concrete forms of zines—the function, in the case of *Fragments of Friendship*, of "something on paper." Even in an already existing relationship, such as that between Law and Martens, paper can offer a differently intimate connection than emails. Law's decision to create the zine *Fragments of Friendship* speaks to the medium's effect on the meaning: the zine had *exactly* the same content as the emails Law and Martens sent each other, but Law created a zine and saw it as something qualitatively different from the emails themselves. As a physical object, *Fragments of Friendship* was a better artifact of their friendship than their emails and a better means for Law to encourage her friend than electronic media.

In addition, zines demand a level of aesthetic decision-making that digital media like blogs sometimes don't. Sarah Dyer, creator of the *Action Girl Newsletter*, articulates this point particularly clearly:

> Your zine is visual, you have to make a choice, whether it's pasting clip art or photos or using Xeroxes of fabric or whatever behind your text, or you've made a decision to just have text on white pages, you've made that choice, but I rarely ever see blogs where people have designed them. Among the people that I know, I think I'm the only person who actually designed their blog. . . . The design element's really been removed from what you would have in the worst zine; even if its not a good look, it's an aesthetic. And most blogs, their aesthetic is, you know, one of the templates that was available with Word Press or Livejournal.[20]

Blogs are easy to create because they are a ready-made technology, but only bloggers with web design skills can play an active role in designing their pages. Certainly bloggers can and do exhibit a great deal of creativity in blog design and content, but available blog templates make it easy for bloggers to focus on the text rather than on the appearance of the blog.[21]

Zines, in contrast, are simpler technology, and because no template exists, each element requires choice and each zine is different. The look of zines, then, is individualized and significant in a way that blogs aren't always. The necessity of making aesthetic decisions with zines, of selecting paper to be the background, deciding whether to handwrite, typewrite, or word process, is a level of personal involvement that is not as often present in electronic media. This personal, physical involvement means not only intentionality but also care.

Dyer also argues that the structure of zines differentiates them from blogs:

> To make a really lame analogy, it's like singles versus albums. When you have a zine, someone collected a bunch of their ideas in some form that makes sense to them and put it together as a package, and a blog is something that, even if you decided to sit down and read a whole month's entries at once, they were not written as a grouping that would make sense. It's just coming in every day or week or whatever, and this is where I post. So the packaging of the information is completely different. And the reading experience is completely different. I'm sure that people I know who have blogs, if they sat down and did a zine, it might have the voice of their blog, but I feel like you would get something very, very different, because when you put the zine together, you're really making a whole thing out of all these little pieces and you just don't have that experience reading a blog at all.[22]

Dyer contends that a zine is conceived of as a unit, an artifact, with a beginning and an end, while blogs are a kind of running collection of ideas. While her claim doesn't ring true for every blog, she is identifying the difference that the medium makes. She sees that this "packaging" difference affects the meaning of the artifact: she notes that "the reading experience is completely different," and she goes on to emphasize that a zine and a blog are "very, very different."

This structural difference can also relate to care: Law had to decide when to start and end *Fragments of Friendship*, and that made it into something intentional and somewhat coherent. As Dyer says, Law made "a whole thing out of all these little pieces." This, then, is another reason that Law created a zine for Martens: the physical artifact represented and communicated care that the emails did not. This is true for elaborate visual texts as well as minimalist ones, such as *Fragments of*

*Friendship.* Even Law's sparse visual aesthetic announces the affectionate connection between these two women who are physically distant from one another.

## Scrappy Messiness and The East Village Inky

The visual aesthetic of zines can cover a wide spectrum, from neat to messy, from flowery to plain, but most zines do offer evidence of the creator's hand. One *East Village Inky* reader, discussing her love for the zine, explained, "I like the drawings and the scrappy messiness of the final product (I swear every issue has at least two instances of [Halliday] leaving blank spots where she obviously meant to fill in a word later but forgot)."²³ This reader didn't criticize the zine's imperfections; instead, they were among the things that delighted her about the zine. Many zine makers embrace "scrappy messiness," an aesthetic that serves to humanize the creator and the zine. Indeed, this reader spoke so warmly about her admiration for Halliday that it seems clear that the "scrappy messiness" functions, in part, to create a sense of fondness between reader and creator, to create connection. Even when the images don't visually document the zinester's fears or doubts, as is the case with *I'm So Fucking Beautiful*, the messiness of the zine conveys a sense of vulnerability and, therefore, a sense of openness and availability for human contact that creates pleasure for the readers.

*The East Village Inky* is a quarter-sized zine, black and white, photocopied, and entirely handwritten and illustrated. The zine's distinctive appearance—pages crammed with handwriting and illustrations, words snaking around pictures, footnotes making their way across the bottom margin of multiple pages—works in tandem with its narrative style. The zine medium allows Halliday a different kind of expression than her books, magazine articles, or blog. Although Halliday's narratives of her life as a mother of young children are equally raucous and humorous in her book *The Big Rumpus* or her articles in *Bust* magazine as they are in *The East Village Inky*, the zine format allows her narratives to operate with a visual energy and fluidity that the linear typescript of a standard book or magazine can't accommodate.²⁴

This chaotic visual energy is apparent on almost any page of the zine. For instance, issue 25 begins, as do most issues of the zine, with a self-portrait of Halliday greeting her readers and introducing the contents of the zine. In this issue she is carrying a bundle of mail. A large, incompletely

Page from *The East Village Inky*, courtesy of Ayun Halliday.

outlined cartoon conversation bubble takes up most of the page, but the words aren't contained within the bubble, which is appropriate as this is a wandering, digressive narrative about the challenges of mailing out this issue of the zine. Even though this commentary to the readers already contains three parenthetical statements, she adds a parenthetical footnote, as well as two illustrations of her children offering unrelated statements and an editorial comment on her own self-portrait ("crazy Patti Smith hair").[25]

A simple reprinting of Halliday's words would be inadequate to convey what's happening on this page. The reader's eyes are forced to move around in different ways than the normal linear print narrative demands. It's unclear what follows what—the chaos of the household she describes is re-created in the wandering sentence structure, as well as the visual components of the zine. Halliday shrinks her handwriting to include commentary in the space between an illustration and the margin, offering a visual representation of a crowded home and also calling attention to the materiality of the zine itself. Spatial limitations—an inescapable component of the materiality of print culture, in which the page is not an unlimited terrain—become an aesthetic element out of which Halliday creates meaning: she uses the limits of the page to create boundaries that she can fill, and she bumps up against them. Reading *The East Village Inky* offers more than a description of Halliday's full apartment and family life: it gives the reader the sense of actually being invited into this crowded, messy home and family. As with *I'm So Fucking Beautiful*, the zine offers an experience as much as a representation. Her humor, her warmly self-deprecating comments, and her minimalist, energetic sketches of her children go along with the imperfect visuals to create vulnerability, which makes space for affection.

This creation of affection is part of what characterizes the embodied community of zines. Halliday's readers concur, identifying the structure and aesthetic of *The East Village Inky* as something that appeals to them and creates connection. One reader explained: "The personal quality of the illustrations, the personal content of the narrative, the handmade ethic, even the size and shape which feel like getting a letter not a magazine, all contribute to having a specific experience of corresponding with someone."[26] Another noted, "It's almost like getting a personal letter from a friend. . . . Also, as much I as get information online, there's nothing like getting something fun in the mail and holding actual paper. The experience is different and more satisfying."[27] Another said, "I definitely feel more connected to someone like Ayun Halliday than I do reading online publications because of this aspect of her writing."[28] These readers clearly identify zines as a "personal" medium, analogous to a letter from a friend, and the materiality of the zine—the visual style, the size and shape, the fact that it comes in the mail, and that the reader can hold "actual paper"—leads to this personal connection. In fact, every *East Village Inky* reader I interviewed mentioned the personal, intimate quality of the zine—its smallness, the fact that it is messily handwritten—as being integral to their enjoyment of it.

When we spoke, Halliday observed that readers are much more willing to attack one another on blogs than they are in the zine world:

> The thing about the parenting blogs that I see is like the *nasty* comments they attract and also the nasty comments that just sort of get stirred up between the regular readers, the regular commenters. I think that the medium of the internet lends itself to that, lends itself to people speaking impolitely, off the cuff to strangers, saying things that they would never say to

the face of an acquaintance or a stranger or, not say it in those words, you know, without really realizing what the consequences are of saying it.[29]

The hostility that Halliday identifies with blogs, and that she hasn't experienced in her eight years as a zine creator, stems from the disembodied format of electronic media. She points out that people commenting on a blog will write things that "they would never say to the face of an acquaintance or stranger": the face, the body of another person—even a stranger—makes this kind of hostility untenable. The body humanizes, and zines provide a kind of bodily engagement or a bodily surrogate that encourages intimacy, connectedness.

Although not all zines are hand-lettered or as extensively illustrated as is *The East Village Inky*, most do emphasize a hand-made quality. For instance, *With Heart in Mouth* is a black-and-white photocopied zine, but the title is written on the cover with red felt-tip marker; this was clearly done on each individual zine by the author or her friends.[30]

Jenna Freedman explains that when she released the 2004 edition of her zine *Lower East Side Librarian Winter Solstice Shout-Out*, her friends Lauren Jade Martin and Eleanor Whitney—both zine creators themselves—were immediately drawn to the blue-highlighted hair on the cartoon version of Freedman on the front cover. There was something about the fact that her hand had touched every cover that made it meaningful to these readers.[31]

One zine creator notes, "The glossier and more professional my zine gets, the less mail I get from readers."[32] Imperfections and evidence of the creator's involvement invite readers into the zine community. Zines typically employ an aesthetic that sets them apart from what Duncombe refers to as the look of "seamless commercial design."[33] The handwriting of the author is often incorporated into the zine, as are the rough edges left by scissors and the lines of tape holding pieces of text and imagery to the page. The zinester's body—the actual physical acts that went into creating the zine—is thus visible, and this creates not only what Duncombe calls "a style of intimate connection" but also a kind of corporeal connection, one that brings together the body of the zine creator and the body of the reader.[34] Most zine creators reject the commercial aesthetic because they reject the ideology of commercial mass media; rather than positioning readers as consumers, as a marketplace, the zine positions them as friends, equals, members of an embodied community who are part of a conversation with the zine maker, and the zine aesthetic plays a crucial role in this positioning.[35]

Cover of *With Heart in Mouth* (left), courtesy of Anna Whitehead.
Cover of *Lower East Side Librarian Winter Solstice Shout-Out* (right), courtesy of Jenna Freedman and Davidson Mulkey.

## Sculptural Elements in No Better Voice

Some zines take this aesthetic a step further, verging into book art. Issue #25 of *No Better Voice* is a quarter-sized photocopied zine with a cover made from a cereal box spray-painted pink and gray. A picture of rabbits, presumably from a children's book, is glued to the front. Perhaps most surprisingly, the cover is tied closed with a strand of white yarn so that the reader has to untie it to read the zine.[36]

The codex format that most zines and books utilize is so familiar that most readers don't consider this structure as a sculptural element, but Jami Thompson, the creator of *No Better Voice*, uses codex components deliberately, as a way of making meaning. Unlike electronic media which are in some sense always open, *No Better Voice* can be deliberately and emphatically closed, and by forcing the reader to untie the zine before reading it, *No Better Voice* requires the reader to become physically involved. By tying the zine closed, Thompson protects the material inside, and the physical process of opening the zine evokes a sense of secrecy, of being invited to read hidden material such as a diary.

Glued inside the front cover is a photocopied note in the author's handwriting saying, "This is the zine i got the worst review ever for. i think it said something to the effect of 'pointless, vapid, self indulgent' and said the zine was about 'suicide and vomit.'" This note highlights the interiority of the zine even further; the vomit reference, in particular, offers an image of interior material inappropriately made exterior. By publicizing her bad review—a review that certainly was made in another zine rather than a literary or scholarly publication—Thompson offers evidence for why her zine has a kind of protective shell around it. Its cover acts as a literal and metaphorical layer of protection from unfriendly readers. And yet she glues the review inside the front cover of the zine, incorporating this criticism into the inner body of the zine. In this way, Thompson is claiming and perhaps even flaunting the "inappropriate" intimacy of her zine. By sharing this criticism with the reader who has already untied the zine to read it and who is holding the zine in her or his hands, she brings the reader to her side.[37]

Cover of *No Better Voice*, courtesy of Jami Thompson.

The untying helps to make the reader an ally. *No Better Voice*, then, creates allegiance through materiality. In this case, it's a materiality formed from cast-offs. The disposable quality of zines may, in part, explain the reluctance of literary and art scholars to analyze them: zines revel in informality and threaten conventional boundaries. They explicitly reject the standards, methods, and visual vocabulary of mainstream publishing and the art world. Rather than appearing as well-wrought artistic pieces, zines take the form of ephemera, notes passed in class, doodles. In the case of zines like *No Better Voice*, they may actually be constructed of waste materials, old cereal boxes, and string. They reject art economies, and they are therefore so (intentionally) low in terms of the hierarchies of printed material that they are below the radar of many academics, but even those who know of them might not consider them as legitimate objects of study.[38] And yet, simultaneously, zines have a quality of preciousness. *No Better Voice* was visibly made by Thompson's hand, tied by hand. Like a letter or gift from a friend, the status of zines as handmade physical objects means that they accrue value. They are hard to throw away. This is also what creates allegiance.

Indeed, the zine structure offers a greater sense of intimacy even than other print media. Books can pretend to be a diary or can even be the publication of a diary, but the mechanisms of publication and the formal structures of books make it apparent to most readers that they aren't actually privy to someone's confidential information. With zines, however, there are fewer layers of separation between the reader and the creator. Thompson, the zine creator, is inviting the reader into this intimate world where the reader is untying a yarn bow that Thompson herself tied before mailing the zine. As with the hand-colored covers of *With Heart in Mouth* and *Lower East Side Librarian Winter Solstice Shout-Out*, the reader knows that this publication has been touched by the zine creator; it didn't come from a machine or a factory. Zine creators like Thompson take advantage of this aspect of the zine medium: other issues of *No Better Voice* have had similar covers, made from wallpaper scraps and ribbons, for instance.

Cindy Crabb, too, worked deliberately to create an intimate physical connection with her readers in the third issue of her zine *Doris*. She explained, "I had this thing that was like, I'm going to touch every single page. I only printed 200 of that one, but I had different things glued or taped or drawn onto every page of the zine. It was really crazy. It was really time-consuming."[39] With zines like *Doris* and *No Better Voice*, then, the structure works with the content to give the reader the sense of being part of an actual human relationships. The reader feels that he or she has been brought into a privileged confidence and is assumed to be trustworthy and of the same mind as the author, and this assumption of trustworthiness helps to make the reader an ally.

## Zine Distribution

Many of these factors—a personalized human connection, informality, the evidence of the creator's hand—come together in the ways zines are transferred from the zinester to the reader. Zines are generally distributed in ways distinct from the consumer culture industry. They aren't available in most corporate venues that sell books, although independent book and music stores do carry them, particularly independent stores in the zine creator's town. Their availability online is on the rise but is still somewhat limited, with online distribution sites—also known as distros—vetting those zines they'll distribute and often featuring long-running zines.[40] The primary way that zines are distributed is either person to person (a zine creator giving or selling the zines to friends and others) or through the mail. In the 1990s when zines were in their heyday, it was often the case that zines were traded rather than sold—you could get a zine if you traded it for one that you had made—but this practice seems to be on the decline.[41] Now zines generally sell for between $1 and $5. Even so, zine distribution is still mostly personalized and geared toward creating relationships that facilitate self-expression; the few dollars that a zinester receives for her zine generally don't even cover her expenses for producing it. Zine creators widely acknowledge that zines cost money rather than making money. Zine distribution is another component of zines' meaning; it's a factor that's easy to overlook but that helps create the embodied community of zines.

This creation of community certainly happens when zines are distributed person to person. Many of the zine creators I spoke to discussed the fact that a zine is more easily shared than a web address, and giving someone a zine is preferable to offering someone a website scrawled on a piece of paper. Law explained:

> A friend who is half Latina and half white and I were talking about ethnic identity and feelings of belonging. She had said that even though she was half Chilean, she didn't feel "authentically" Latina because she wasn't raised by the Chilean parent, didn't speak Spanish, didn't grow up with

any of the culture, etc. After I read *Sisu* (a zine written by a woman who is half Asian), I passed it along to my friend, who appreciated reading someone else's take on being biracial and grappling with issues of identity. I don't feel one can really do that with a blog or other form of online media. I could have given her a url, but, not being an internet-based person, she probably never would have looked at what this other biracial woman was experiencing, thinking and writing about.[42]

For Law, giving the zine to her friend was both easier and more reliable than offering a web address in that her friend could read it immediately, whether or not she had access to (or comfort with) the internet. More importantly, giving her the zine was clearly an act of caring, a physical act that manifested Law's positive response to the zine and her thoughts about her friend.[43]

The immediacy of person-to-person distribution and its ability to create a sense of community are especially evident in a story from the zine *Doris* #4 (1994). *Doris* is a long-running zine that combines typewritten narrative with friendly, doodled titles and marginal drawings. In this early issue, Cindy Crabb describes the process of secretly slipping a copy of her zine into the backpack of a girl she sees on the train, a girl who seems outcast. She explains her motivation: "i still want the same things. to break—with this one small gesture—the crazy things we are taught; to keep distant and distrustful, alienated, lonely and safe." She explicitly frames the gesture of giving her zine as a way of connecting with another human being. By secretly offering the zine to a stranger, she wants to counter the cultural messages that keep people isolated from one another. The zine functions to create community between two young women who don't know each other and may not find community otherwise. Silently giving the girl *Doris* #1, which she describes as "full of my secrets," Crabb creates a currency of intimacy. She trades her secrets for the possibility of closeness, trust, and connection—which she implies are risky, not "lonely and safe." The exchange she alludes to here is qualitatively different than the financial exchanges that make up the capitalist distribution methods for mainstream publications, where publications are for-profit entities. The zine for Crabb is not a way to make money but a way to connect to other people.[44]

Significantly, Crabb prefaces this story with a seemingly unrelated discussion of wanting things to be small enough to fit in her pockets. She writes, "i want this thing here [the zine itself] to be smaller. may be you could fold it twice and it would fit snug in the back of your blue-jeans like doris #one did, getting dirty and ratty and torn."[45] Here Crabb identifies the physical qualities of zines that make possible the human connection she craves. Her zine is something durable as well as vulnerable. It is durable because it can be tucked into a backpack, hidden away, and found later. And yet it's vulnerable because it registers the passage of time. Its durability and its vulnerability—its simultaneous non-preciousness (something you would fold and carry in a pocket) and preciousness (an object that is cherished like a love letter, because it signifies human connection)—are linked to its ability to initiate embodied community. This is an object that communicates and conveys generosity and kindness, and that function is inextricably connected to the zine's vulnerability. It isn't an art object or a consumer item, kept at a remove from the human body; rather, it is supposed to get "dirty and ratty and torn" in someone's pocket, get warm and worn. The reader can revisit it, and although the text will stay the same, the artifact itself will change in subtle ways, like a body itself. The zine therefore brings together essential human qualities of care, fragility, pleasure, and endurance and allows Crabb and the girl on the train the possibility of a meaningful, embodied connection, even if they never meet in person again.

These qualities of embodied community can be activated in zine distribution even if the zine is sent through the mail rather than delivered in person. Victoria Law feels strongly that getting paper mail—particularly a zine—is more exciting than getting email. When I asked her why, she responded by sharing a story about receiving a zine from a friend. The friend had written Law's two-year-old daughter's name on the envelope in glitter. Law reported:

> So she's like [motions letters as if Siu Loong is spelling], "What is that?" And finally she's like, "Oh! That says Siu Loong," and it's this amazing sort of like *ding ding ding* light bulb, a baby milestone. She's recognized her name because of this wonderfully decorated envelope with glitter, and I think there was a picture on the back of it, and suddenly she could hold it in her hand and shake it around, like, what is this? Oh this is for me, you know?[46]

This anecdote conveys the significance of the material object, as well as the personal quality, of a zine as something that is "for me," both qualities that can be activated by the zine being sent through the mail. Most zines are photocopied and therefore not explicitly made for one individual, but they are still a fairly intimate medium. Although the print runs for zines differ widely, zinesters rarely print more than one thousand copies. Often the print runs are fewer than one hundred copies, and the particular aesthetic and structural qualities that characterize the zine medium make all zines feel a bit like they were made for the individual reader. In addition, the process of receiving a hand-addressed envelope in the mail—which is how many zines are delivered—enhances that creation of intimacy, an intimacy that can have meaningful results, as in the case of Siu Loong.

Zines often arrive in hand-addressed envelopes; indeed, in some years it was not uncommon for subscribers to *The East Village Inky* to receive envelopes that had been addressed by Halliday's daughter Inky herself. The envelopes are often decorated and accompanied with handwritten notes from the zine creator so that they, too, become acts of creativity, generosity, and expression.

Neely Bat Chestnut, creator of the zine *Mend My Dress*, explained to me that the envelope is a means of expression that can reach people other than the person to whom it's addressed. She said that when she's addressing an envelope, she thinks, "'What does the postal person want to see? Something that is not white and not boring.' And I picture the envelopes

Envelope in which a zine arrived, courtesy of the Sallie Bingham Center for Women's History and Culture in the Rare Book, Manuscript, and Special Collections Library at Duke University.

going through the machine: manila envelope, manila envelope, boring, boring, boring, boring, boring, white, white, white, white, *whoa*! Pink with a million things hanging off of it. Holy shit! What is this?"[47] The way that zines' distribution differentiates them from other media is particularly visible in the envelopes. If zines themselves are seen by some as disposable (so much so that some zine makers have expressed surprise that zines are being archived in library collections), envelopes are even more so—explicitly created to be discarded, only important in the transporting of what is inside, with no value of their own.[48] Therefore, when zine creators offer elaborate drawings and glittery decorations on this disposable artifact, they are making the envelopes into an additional means of self-expression, so that even the postal staff might think, "Holy shit! What is this?" The envelopes then function as part of the entire zine-reading experience, helping to evoke pleasure and affection and to create embodied community.[49]

## Gifts, Pleasure, and Embodied Community

A number of factors foster this sense of embodiment in the grrrl zine phenomenon, including the physical efforts that go into creating zines and that are often made visible in the finished product, along with the recipient's physical interactions with the zine, which then may lead to acts of reciprocal materiality. To be sure, certain aspects of zines' materiality and their activation of an embodied community aren't gender-specific—they hold true for zines made by boys and men, as well as for grrrl zines. The physical object, made by hand, typewritten or handwritten, cut and pasted together, distributed informally, and carrying sensory information (such as the smell of the house where it was made) to the recipient, engages the bodies of the creators and the recipients, regardless of the gender of the creator, and has relevance for anyone living in the late-twentieth-century moment of increasing bodily abstraction.

The embodied community of grrrl zines, however, operates in ways that have particular salience for girls and women. For one thing, grrrl zinesters often address their own bodies in the content, as well as the structure, of their zines. As shown by Lamm's *I'm So Fucking Beautiful*, female embodiment is often highly charged terrain in a sexist culture, and the late-twentieth- and early-twenty-first century moment in which grrrl zines are being produced places specific demands on the bodies of girls and women, demands that are both contradictory and dangerous. Indeed, dissatisfaction with the body is almost emblematic of growing up female, as is the fact that female bodies are vulnerable to scrutiny and abuse, and when grrrl zinesters describe and comment on their bodily experiences, they are intervening in this cultural phenomenon. For another thing, zining fosters two-way connections between readers and creators, connections that are meaningful for girls and women in a culture in which they are often figured as each others' competition rather than as allies. The embodied grrrl zine community is taking part in these gendered systems, allowing girls and women to negotiate and leverage their own bodies and the kinds of communities to which they belong and providing ways for them to create safe spaces for intimate connection.

In examining these zines, it has become clear to me that their materiality functions not simply as another component of their meaning but also as a means of linking creator and reader, creating a particular kind of community. Describing her relationship to the readers of *The East Village Inky*, Halliday explains: "I can't remember the last time I got a letter from a friend of mine, but I get these nice newsy letters from people I haven't met. And the time it takes them to mail and to stamp it, and that they have to pay to mail it—you know, it's really great."[50] Halliday's experience speaks to the creation of a zine community; her readers' letters are evidence of a connection, because they are willing to make an effort to send friendly correspondence—on paper—to someone they only know because of reading her zine. This connection is something akin to Benedict Anderson's notion of the national imagined community, of which he says, "it is *imagined* because the members of even the smallest nation will never know most of their fellow-members, meet them, or even hear of them, yet in the minds of each lives the image of their communion."[51] Halliday describes this kind of communion with people she hasn't met. Like the zine community, Anderson's imagined community is in part realized by reading; however, while Anderson's newspaper reader has the awareness "that the ceremony he performs is being replicated simultaneously by thousands (or millions) of others," zine writers and readers feel community in part because they know that *not* many others are replicating this act.[52] The embodied community of the zine world is intimate rather than extensive, and linked to the body rather than simply to an imagined other.

The materiality of zines creates community that is embodied because it activates bodily experiences such as pleasure, affection, allegiance, and vulnerability. As discussed here, these qualities emerge in various ways in the medium itself. The size of *I'm So Fucking Beautiful* and the messy drawings of *The East Village Inky* convey vulnerability. Readers feel affection when they untie the cover of *No Better Voice*, turn the paper pages of *Fragments of Friendship*, or perhaps discover a zine secretly slipped into their backpack. Pleasure permeates all the zines.

Many critics have asked zine makers why they do what they do: zines are time consuming to produce, and they don't generate any of the commodities that our culture generally values, including money, power, or prestige. One of the answers that zinesters routinely offer in response to this question is that making a zine is fun. Zine makers will explain the way their awareness of time slips away while they're creating a zine, or how putting together a zine is a "tactile rush."[53] Pleasure, then, is a key component of the zine medium. Pleasure is registered in the artifact itself in various ways. It is one of the causes and consequences of the humanized connections that zines enable and is one of the most mysterious and important elements of this embodied community.

Zine creators emphasize the pleasures of tactileness, what Victoria Law repeatedly referred to as the "physically satisfying" act of producing a paper zine.[54] One woman explains: "I found I enjoyed rubber-cementing the pieces of my zine to their backgrounds, watching the zine become a concrete product before my eyes."[55] Grrrl zine anthologists Taormino and Green note that "a big part of the thrill in making zines is the manual work it takes to put them together. Most zine makers put a lot of effort into paste-up and often zines are full of collage-art. And from the many stickered, starred and sparkle-covered letters we received, we'd say these girls enjoy the physical labor. From our experience, this labor can be cathartic as well as inspiring."[56] In a culture that celebrates ease and immediacy, zine makers are choosing to take part in a process that is deliberately messy, inefficient, and labor-intensive—they are choosing to take part in an art process. Taormino and Green offer a psychological reading of this practice: it is "cathartic as well as inspiring" to girls and women to create zines. In addition, I suggest that the physical act of creating a zine locates zine creators in their bodies or helps them connect to their bodies. Their bodies become a site of care and pleasure, and the act of reading does the same thing for the reader, and thus they are brought into an embodied community.

Zines have come into being in a moment when the body is silenced and elided by a culture in which, as zine creator Lynn Peril told an interviewer, many of us "sit all day in front of the computer." She explained, "I like *physical objects*, I like paper. I like laying out my zine; I like the fact that you can take it with you on the bus or to the gym or to the bathtub."[57] Her identification of zines as physical objects, on paper, is linked to her bodily interactions with zines. She immediately defines zines in terms of her own body—laying them out, reading them in various locations. The pleasure of creating a zine is an embodied pleasure, as Lamm demonstrated when she pantomimed thrusting her fingers hard onto typewriter keys for the satisfaction of feeling them operate: "There's something about when you feel something really intensely and you're hitting the keys and it's like, it's much more like a visceral experience."[58] Crabb describes "this very precious feeling of gluing [a zine] all together, instead of just being a product, like head, head, head, out, it's this sort of physical integration."[59] Even the technology of creating zines can become physically integrating. Mimi Nguyen, creator of a number of zines including *Slant, Slander,* and *Evolution of a Race Riot,* playfully describes her love affair with the copier: "Okay, it's true, I admit: I used to have a *thing* for Xerox copiers. For a girl obsessed with 'zine-ing, it was, after all, only natural that I develop an equally fervent love-object relationship to the machine, my big dumb prosthesis." She explicitly connects this love to an embodied experience of creating zines: "I wrote constantly, researched articles, hawked my wares to distributors and record stores across the country, spent late nights cutting and pasting. The skin between my fingers turned a nasty shade of gray."[60] Zines bring their creators and readers away from the digital world and into their own flesh. Indeed, every zine creator I interviewed spoke of the pleasures of zine making, and most linked that pleasure to their bodily engagement with zines.

The pleasures of the zine medium may, in part, explain the gift economy in which zines operate. People make zines as acts of pleasure and generosity, and they are received this way. *East Village Inky* readers refer to the zine as "a note passed in class or a letter sent to you" or "a little present in the mailbox."[61] They experience the zine as a gift, and this doesn't seem to me to be a misinterpretation of the zine exchange. Although readers often do pay for the zines they receive (usually very little), the qualities of the zine medium I've already discussed—vulnerability, care, messiness—and the means by which zines are distributed keep the acquisition of zines from feeling like a financial transaction. Instead, the zine is a kind of gift. It operates outside of economies of scarcity and hierarchy and creates, instead, "economies based on pleasure, generosity and the free dispersal of goods and services."[62] We give gifts because we care for someone and want to make a connection with them. Gift giving makes us vulnerable, because a gift can be rejected or misunderstood, unlike a financial transaction. Giving gifts is also fun because we imagine the pleasure of the person receiving them, and in imaging this receiver, we create a connection that the physical artifact—the zine as "present in the mailbox"—makes material. The zine-as-gift, then, is quintessentially an act of community-building.[63]

In fact, zine makers often up the ante on the zine's materiality, adding other artifacts and items into the zine exchange. Buttons, letters, and stickers often accompany zines; for example, one issue of the zine *No Better Voice* arrived at my house with a tiny button that said "No Better Voice," and the zine *Brother Dana* came with a pink "Erica Rules, boys suck" sticker stapled inside each copy. An issue of the zine *Design 816* included two homemade Huggy Bear patches made of cloth and glitter.[64] The zine *First Person: True Stories by Real People* regularly contained a "free toy surprise" such as a moist towelette or Elvis Presley trading card stapled in a tiny envelope on the back page.[65] *Gogglebox* #3 contained a bottle rocket, and *Two Cents* #2 contained a "fortune teller" or "cootie catcher" toy.[66] It is almost as if the zine itself is not enough, since the zine makers are inspired to add additional objects. Some of the add-ons are random and somewhat inexplicable, such as the "free toy surprise" of a moist towelette; others are explicitly tied to a girlhood gift culture, such as the "cootie catcher," a paper game that girls often make in elementary school. In all these cases, the zine makers are activating an affectionate relationship by offering material gifts.

The zine exchange seems to inspire reciprocal materiality, with zine readers sending gifts and artifacts to zine makers, as well. Halliday explains, "I get fan mail, I get love letters, people send me all sorts of interesting little toys for the kids. Like, one time I wrote about making mojitos when we were here in Cape Cod, and this *East Village Inky* reader sent me a big package of mint so that I can make mojitos in New York."[67] This perhaps more than any other example shows the importance of the materiality and how that materiality facilitates the creation of community. Only a sense of connectedness, of individualized relationship, would inspire someone—ostensibly a stranger—to send mint or children's toys to Halliday. Materiality enables a special kind of community, even among those who aren't strangers. The tangible object transforms an imagined relationship into an embodied one.

The function of physical objects to invoke bodies is evident in an anecdote from media scholar Henry Jenkins. Describing his son's romance with a girl he knew only online, Jenkins observed that the teens sent each other objects: "These objects were cherished because they had achieved the physical intimacy still denied the geographically isolated teens. . . . Even in an age of instant communication, they still sent handwritten notes. These two teens longed for the concrete, for being together in the same space, for things materially passed from person to person."[68] Zines pass materially from person to person, as do the gifts sent by readers. When a reader holds *The East Village Inky* and reads about mojitos, perhaps the longing to be "together in the same space" with Halliday inspires her to send mint and thereby to share an object that her hands have held, that has been in the same space with her, and that will concretely engage with Halliday's body. It is this sense of embodied community that zines create; it isn't created by other print media. As one colleague pointed out, no one is sending mint to *Cosmo*.

Zines make visible the connections among pleasure, gift economies, materiality, and the human body. We can see some of these connections in the book medium, as well: William H. Glass, in an essay in *Harper's Magazine*, discusses the pleasure of shaking an old book to see what detritus of human life falls out, from gum wrappers to old telegraphs. In the same essay, he refers to how he can "enjoy the memory of my dismay when, perhaps after years, I return to my treasured copy of *Treasure Island* to find the jam I inadvertently smeared there still spotting a page."[69]

To be sure, books have a special relationship with the human body. Our bodies alter them, and they collect material that characterizes human life. We find jam, a ticket stub, we smell our old house, and these things are pleasurable. This pleasure, however, has more in common with Anderson's *imagined* community: imagined because there is not necessarily a physical other with whom the book reader is connected. Books are generally vetted by a publisher, mass-produced, and sold for profit. The ticket stub that falls from the pages of the book wasn't placed there by the book's creator as a surprise for Glass.

In other words, unlike books, zines register the *care* that is a crucial part of embodied community, care that is invested in the material. Although Glass recognized his personal relationship with his copy of *Treasure Island*, he was under no illusion that *Treasure Island* was created— written, bound, and transported—for him in particular. But zines do feel like something "for me." They offer a more intimate, personal, human connection than books, a connection that is mediated through the body and that connects the bodies of the zine creator and reader. Zines manifest and materialize human care. Siu Loong recognized her name in glitter on the envelope in part because of the care that had gone into making this physical object.

This care has implications for grrrl zines' functioning in terms of third wave feminism, as well. Zines have provided and continue to provide a space for third wave ideas to emerge and be tried out, and this can be explained, in part, by the care that undergirds the embodied grrrl zine community. For instance, grrrl zines have been a site for affectionate connections between girls and women, and this quality of the zine medium helped propel the Riot Grrrl ideology of "girl love," an ideology that deliberately countered the patriarchal notion of female relationships being troubled "cat fights," as well as challenging the heteronormative idea that girls should (or naturally do) compete with each other for the affection of boys. What's more, the embodied community of zines also created a safe enough space that girls and women could come forward to criticize the white privilege inherent in many iterations of "girl love," as discussed here in chapter 4. Zines became sites for productive, thoughtful expression and dissent.

The interactions of zines with bodies are also important for girls and women because of the particularities of female embodiment, which I address in the next two chapters. Within patriarchal cultures, female embodiment is complicated—indeed, often painful, vulnerable, and troubled—because of the ways that girlhood and womanhood are defined and situated. Scholars and participants often look to media, print as well as digital, for a sort of "freedom" from the body, particularly where women are concerned, but this freedom often proves to be apocryphal.[70] Rather than offering freedom from embodiment—a formulation that figures the female body as entrapping—zines offer girls and women a way of leveraging their embodiment, experiencing it differently, or utilizing it in particular expressive or activist ways. Indeed, as discussed in this chapter, zines can allow girls and women a space to amplify their bodies and the constraints they experience, as with Lamm's *I'm So Fucking Beautiful*, or they may provide for mediated bodily intimacies, as is evident in *Fragments of Friendship*. The zine medium doesn't demand that girls and women abandon their bodies in order to experience empowerment but provides them with tools for resistance within an embodied space.

In addition, the aesthetic demands of the zine medium mean that grrrl zine creators gather examples of the cultural ephemera that surrounds them and use that cultural material to construct their artifacts

and their communities. Zines require an engagement with material culture that's not necessarily present in other media. Grrrl zines, therefore,
help document their cultural moment, down to its most trivial and easily forgotten components—and often the components of culture with
which girls and women engage are the ones defined as trivial and thus
most readily dismissed and forgotten. Zines also demonstrate how girls
and women are able to negotiate within that culture. As artifacts, zines
reveal the lives of girls and women on the ground, with layers that other
artifacts might not offer.

The embodied zine community, then, allows for kinds of self-expression that are different from those of other media, and the formal and
physical elements are an essential part of the meaning-making. Further,
this community allows for different political possibilities, ones that are
keenly suited to the experiences of girls and women in this late-capitalist
cultural moment. I began this chapter with the story of my students feeling invited to take part in the zine community, and although I don't claim
that this invitation is unique to the zine medium, I do think it speaks to
zines' cultural functioning and political implications. Zines bring people
into conversation, provide them with a space to be creative and imperfect,
and remove some of the stakes—the dangers of online media, the gatekeepers of mainstream publishing, the slickness of corporate media—that
make other forms of expression less (or differently) available. In this way,
they do make different kinds of political interventions possible.

In the one-year anniversary issue of her zine *Fern*, Kim Fern wrote,
"finally, after all this time of trying to claim a voice of my own, i have
one. and it's sometimes strong and it's sometimes weak. and sometimes
it's confusing. but i have found it. i have the guts to say things now that
i never thought i could said two years ago. and it's so amazing. i can't
even say that enough."[71] Fern was enabled to speak out in part because
the zine medium allows for expression that is "sometimes strong," "sometimes weak," and "sometimes . . . confusing." The messiness and imperfections of zines help make them appealing and humanize both the creator
and the reader. The proliferation of voices within the zine world counters
the hegemony of corporate culture industries, and the evident pleasures
of coming to voice—what Fern describes as something "so amazing"—
encourage others to try, as well.

It seems to me that zines counter the cultural imperative that Crabb
voices in *Doris* #4, the imperative "to keep distant and distrustful, alienated, lonely and safe," and they make visible the desire for community

and human connection. They also provide a set of tools to allow girls and women to say things that aren't being said elsewhere and to create embodied communities of support to allow them to do so. When studied as multilayered artifacts, with visual, material, and distributional semiotics, grrrl zines offer an unsurpassed resource for understanding girls and women and the strategies and mechanisms of third wave feminism.

# 3

## Playing Dress-Up, Playing Pin-Up, Playing Mom
### Zines and Gender

Because i live in a world that hates women and i am one . . . who is struggling desparately not to hate myself and my best girlfriends, my whole life is constantly felt, by me, as a contradiction. In order for me to exist, i must believe that two contradictory things can exist in the same space.
—Kathleen Hanna, "Jigsaw Youth," *Jigsaw* #4 (1991)

I fight like a girl. I fight like a girl who refuses to be a victim. I fight like a girl who's tired of being ignored + humoured + beaten + raped. I fight like a girl who's sick of not being taken seriously. I fight like a girl who's been pushed too far. I fight like a girl who offers + demands respect. I fight like a girl who has a lifetime of anger + strength + pride pent up in her girly body. . . . I fight like a girl who *fights back*. So, next time you think you can distract yourself from your insecurities by victimizing a girl think again. She may be me, and I fight like a girl.
—Stefanie Moore, *World without Lard* (no date)

Disrespect and violence form a constant background noise for girls and women, defining features of a culture where "fighting like a girl"—or doing anything "like a girl"—is an insult. Stefanie Moore describes life in a body that is liable to be "ignored + humoured + beaten + raped," as well as "not . . . taken seriously." In order to survive, in order, as Kathleen Hanna says, "not to hate myself and my best girlfriends," girls and women must develop resistant consciousness. Both epigraphs to this chapter articulate what this resistance might look like. Hanna, Moore, and grrrl zinesters like them are often inspired to create zines as reactions to the misogyny around them. Their zines, however, shouldn't be misinterpreted as mere oppositional documents. Misogyny may be their starting point, but they don't end there. Their resistance is creative, and they expand the available subject positions for girls and women, by, for instance, broadening what it means to fight like a girl.

Following on the discussion of the material construction of zines in chapter 2, I now consider how zine makers negotiate the material terrain of gender itself, and how they use the zine medium to generate gendered subjectivities. Although zines do have explicitly political effects, which I take up in chapter 5, here I examine grrrl zines' interventions into the common tropes, representational modes, and stereotypes surrounding girlhood and womanhood. These interventions have far-reaching implications; as Patricia Hill Collins reminds us, "the authority to define . . . symbols is a major instrument of power."[1] Moreover, these interventions are informed by third wave sensibilities that embrace contradiction and emphasize both aggressive and playful engagement with the semiotics of femininity.

Play is a key concept in this chapter. Grrrl zines' gender interventions are often irreverent, mischievous. For instance, when Neely Bat Chestnut fills her *Mend My Dress* zines with images from Disney films such as *Cinderella* and *Sleeping Beauty*, or when *Bust* offers instructions on how to crochet a bikini, they are playfully using familiar—often disparaged—icons of femininity as sites of enjoyment and components of feminist critique. Many grrrl zines creatively recombine cultural categories associated with girlhood and womanhood in ways that destabilize their meaning: What does it mean when China Martens's zine *The Future Generation* presents the welfare mother as a pin-up girl? Further, zines allow for unconventional or transgressive models of womanhood.

Sometimes zines become a way to document changing gender roles, as is the case with the burgeoning phenomenon of the "mama zine"—zines by women, often in their thirties, who have children. These zine writers are "playing mom," using the zine as a site for negotiating what it means to be a different kind of mother than the one represented in mainstream media depictions. Hundreds of zines by girls and women are intervening in gendered representations in various ways. In this chapter, I consider four particular modalities—body image, girlhood vulnerability, pleasure, and motherhood—by closely examining several zines. The zines I examine here offer rich case studies to show what kinds of gendered interventions are possible within the zine medium. These interventions are facilitated by the embodied community, which helps zine creators create a space in which to experiment and play.

## Grrrl Zines and Identity

Some commentators have sought a coherent, solid identity in girls' and women's cultural productions, identifying zine creators as "at-risk" girls who are documenting their experiences with victimization (since many grrrl zines discuss rape, incest, anorexia, and other vulnerabilities associated with female identity) or as "can-do" girls who are manifesting individual success through their self-expression. However, these sorts of interpretive frames obscure what we're more likely to see in grrrl zines: identities that are deliberately fragmented, often with no effort being made to resolve the fragmentation, and in which the mechanisms of construction are clearly visible. Certainly, the construction of fragmented identities appears throughout the zine medium, but it seems to operate differently for grrrl zines. Stephen Duncombe argues that "zine writers use their zines as a means to assemble the different bits and pieces of their lives and interests into a formula that they believe represents *who they really are.*"[2] He sees zines as the space for zine creators to draw together all the disparate parts of themselves. However, he interviews two zine creators who, rather than drawing together the parts of themselves, used their zines as a space to fragment their identities, by creating multiple characters who conducted interviews and wrote for the zine. He explains, "I don't think it was any accident that Kali and Franetta—the two people I discovered 'passing' as others in their zines—are women of color. As both women and members of ethnic minorities they are acutely aware of the constraints of identity as defined by others."[3]

I'd like to expand beyond Duncombe's point and argue that Kali and Franetta do not represent an interesting aberration; their zines, instead, map out one of the predominant characteristics of grrrl zines. While grrrl zinesters are assembling the "bits and pieces of their lives" in their zines, in many cases they are not pulling together an authentic self, something that represents *"who they really are."* Instead, this idea of "who they really are" is the thing that's being destabilized, called into question, or even rejected in many grrrl zines. Kathleen Hanna voices this concept in her essay "Jigsaw Youth," excerpted as an epigraph to this chapter. She rejects the notion of coherence—of what she calls "some forever identity"—as impossible, given her social location as someone who "lives in a world that hates women and i am one."[4] She defiantly claims contradiction as her standpoint and articulates a perspective that is key to the kinds of identities circulating in grrrl zines.

Nomy Lamm, too, critiques an understanding of the zine as an expression of the "authentic girl." She demands that zines be seen as tools, conscious constructions:

> I really hated when people would be like, "Oh, it's all just girls in their bedrooms, sprawled out writing in their diaries, and then they'll send them to each other." I'm like, that's an aesthetic choice. You're still constructing something when it looks like a diary entry. I wasn't photocopying my diary, or if I was, it was for a specific reason. . . . Girls grow up to be like someone's looking at you all the time, so when I was creating zines, I was like, okay, so what would I say to people who are like me? And instead of asking for validation from whoever controls the media, I'm creating this kind of media that's literally from my most sacred place to somebody else's most sacred place.[5]

Even as Lamm identifies her zine as something "from my most sacred place to somebody else's most sacred place," she also recognizes zines as interventions, mediations, carefully constructed interpretive frameworks. Because of her social location as a girl, she recognized that she was often being watched, and she used the zine as a way to interrupt the more familiar narratives of girlhood objectification. Similarly, zine creator Mimi Nguyen notes in her zine *Slant*, "I'm tired of being asked to expose myself to prying eyes. Everything in here is completely strategic: I agonized long and hard, debated endlessly, over every word."[6] For the most part, zines are not fictional texts, but, like all autobiographical texts, they must be understood as complex literary artifacts that are "completely strategic" rather than as simplistic records of what happened or "who I am."

Those seeking coherence in zines will be disappointed—and will miss the point. As Janice Radway suggests:

> I think we need to pay more attention to zines as complex and contradictory forms, as fractured productions that respond to and thereby mobilize multiple technologies of subject construction. Zines are interesting

precisely because they are chaotic jumbles of material culled from mass culture, everyday life, and affective experience. They ought to be read, it seems to me, less for the way they are expressions of emerging, idiosyncratic selves or earnest, searching explorations of singular identities. Rather, I think zines should be read more for their radical generativity, for the way they combine and recombine rich repertoires of contradictory cultural fragments. They are experimental, multifarious performances, it seems to me, instantiations of multiple subject-positions.[7]

Kearney, too, explains that in her analysis of grrrl zines she is "less concerned with examining those forms of discourse that work to construct the girl zinester as an intelligible self than I am with discerning how female youth use zines to 'try out' various forms of identity."[8]

The zine, then, is a medium that captures flux, contradiction, and fragmentation and uses these things not as problems to be resolved but as sources of creative energy. It is a space for experimentation and play. Rather than looking to zines for a representation of "the real girl," Kearney's "intelligible self," or Hanna's "forever identity," it is more revealing to see zines as sites of fluctuating gender interventions, where girls and women chop up, compile, and recycle mainstream cultural images, ideologies, and materials related to femininity. Gender becomes an important site of this fragmentation because it is such a highly charged category.

Indeed, what Radway refers to as zines' "radical generativity" arises in part from the fact that girlhood and womanhood are "densely mythogenic, the object[s] of layered fictions produced by others."[9] Certain identity configurations—the fat chick, the sexy girl, the welfare mother—are particularly loaded with cultural meanings, many of which are unfriendly at best and dangerous at worst. Zines function as a space where girls and women can intervene in this set of myths, not to create a monolithic counterimage such as a "positive role model" to counteract the proliferating negative imagery but to destabilize the familiar cultural narratives and imagery, to borrow some of their power and use it to open up space for different kinds of female subject positions. For instance, see Moore's reversal of the insult "you fight like a girl." Rather than simply refuting this insult for its sexism, or rejecting the label "girl," Moore does what has been referred to as "linguistic jujitsu,"[10] absorbing the insult's power and throwing it back against those who would try to silence her or frighten her with it.[11] Indeed, this linguistic jujitsu is at the heart of the grrrl zine phenomenon, a technique by which grrrl zinesters can go beyond accepting or rejecting the images and ideologies of femininity and can, instead, tinker with them and deploy them with altered meanings. Here I examine the ways in which zine creators like Moore make use of the mythogenic properties of girlhood and womanhood.

Fragmented identities—the contradictions that Hanna refers to—are part of the gender intervention in grrrl zines for two reasons. First, these zines are responding to the larger culture, a culture in which girlhood and womanhood are composed of sometimes radically contradictory ideas, unresolvable double binds, double standards, and mixed messages. Although this has always been the case in a patriarchal culture, these messages have become amplified at the end of the twentieth century and beginning of the twenty-first. As Courtney Martin notes in *Perfect Girls, Starving Daughters*, girls today "carry the old world of guilt—center of families, keeper of relationships, caretaker of friends—with the new world of control/ambition—rich, independent, powerful."[12] Similarly, Merri Lisa Johnson explains in *Jane Sexes It Up* that these same contradictions affect adult women: "The twenty- and thirty-something women of today inhabit a transitional period in United States history, with deferential femininity from the not-so-distant past layered beneath (not simply replaced by) hard won career-related advancements toward equality."[13] Both Martin and Johnson note that girls and women are affected by ambition and sexism, by previous models of appropriate womanhood along with new expectations for egalitarian gender roles. Grrrl zines often display these competing identity categories, making the double standards and double binds visible. Indeed, they seem to be an ideal medium for the expression of these contradictions.

Grrrl zines are not simply responding to a series of impossible cultural messages about girlhood and womanhood. They are also offering subject positioning that is congruent with third wave feminism.[14] Kearney makes connections between grrrl zines and feminism throughout *Girls Make Media*; in particular, she notes that grrrl zines are responding to broad feminist discourses, such as cultural feminism. However, she does not discuss the ways in which zines are enacting third wave theory. Some of the earliest (and still strongest) theorization of the third wave comes from Leslie Heywood and Jennifer Drake, who base their definition of the third wave on paradox and contradiction: "Because our lives have been shaped by struggles between various feminisms as well as by cultural backlash against feminism, we argue that contradiction—or what looks like contradiction, if one doesn't shift one's point of view—marks the desires and strategies of third wave feminists." They go on to say, "we are products of all the contradictory definitions of and differences within feminism, beasts of such a hybrid kind that perhaps we need a different name altogether."[15] The fragmented, incoherent identities girls and women struggle with are therefore not simply a result of the cultural moment but are related to how feminism interfaces with this cultural moment.

Currently, high expectations created by feminism battle with resistant sexist ideologies, ideologies that have been shaped by and incorporated into late-capitalist structures so that they are often obscured or invisible. The lip service given to equality and the cultural emphasis on individualism and meritocracy can make it difficult to identify sexism's structural and symbolic effects. This is the milieu that demands third wave sensibilities. Those sensibilities move in multiple directions, containing, for instance, "elements of second wave critique of beauty and culture, sexual abuse, and power structures while . . . also acknowledg[ing] and mak[ing] use of the pleasure, danger, and defining power of those structures."[16] This is an understanding of third wave feminism that is widely shared. According to Johnson, for third wavers, feminism is always contradictory and capacious: "Feminism exists in us in *both* forms: resistance to authority, and the authority we resist; permission to explore our sexuality, and the sexual limits we transgress."[17]

Grrrl zines offer a legitimate, timely model of third wave subjectivities that are well poised to negotiate within what Chela Sandoval calls "the co-opting nature of so-called postmodern cultural conditions."[18] It is worth noting here—as other third wave authors have done—that what I am identifying as third wave subjectivities are heavily indebted to the theoretical work of U.S. third world feminists, who demand, according to Sandoval, "a new subjectivity, a political revision that denie[s] any one ideology as the final answer, while instead positing a *tactical subjectivity* with the capacity to de- and recenter, given the forms of power to be moved."[19] Although not all grrrl zines do this, the modes of thinking evident in many grrrl zines demonstrate this sort of tactical subjectivity, not permanently grounded in particular identity configurations but mobile, flexible, and responsive to a culture of late capitalism and late modernity.

As Johnson puts it, "There is no clear moral to this story."[20] There is, however, a direction. Just because grrrl zines offer perspectives that are fragmented and ambiguous does not mean that they are apolitical or empty. Instead, their interventions in the symbolic realm challenge—however messily—the ideals of femininity circulated in the consumer culture industries and offer politically salient alternatives.

## Beauty and Body Image

Many grrrl zines document the dangers of life in the body of a girl or woman. Indeed, when the mainstream media first became aware of grrrl zines, they often voiced shock at the fact that so many of these zines discussed incest, sexual assault, and eating disorders. In 1992, a *USA Today* article warned, "Hundreds of small, photocopied pamphlets now circulate, offering gut-wrenching confessional poetry and angry honest prose on topics such as rape, feeling ugly, boys, sex, masturbation, cures for yeast infections and the latest girl groups."[21] Similarly, an article in *Time* magazine identified zines as sites "through which teenagers who had been molested could communicate with one another."[22] Girls and women discuss these sorts of highly charged issues in zines in part because zines are a more accessible medium that provide a space for bridging the intimate and the public.

The ability of zines to bridge these realms is directly related to the embodied community that zines generate. As philosopher Linda Martín-Alcoff explains, identities are publicly constituted: "To say that we have an identity is just to say that we have a location in social space, a hermeneutic horizon that is both grounded in a location and an opening or site from which we attempt to know the world." Identity consists of two interconnected components—public identity, an identity which is "external, visible, and under only limited individual control," and subjectivity, by which she means "my own sense of myself, my lived experience of my self, or my interior life." Martín-Alcoff contends that we cannot have one without the other: "Without a social space, such as a civil society or neighborhood or perhaps a family, in which the individual can operate as a free, moral, decision-making agent, the individual cannot become a moral agent, indeed, is not a moral agent."[23] In other words, identities are not merely internal but are locational, shaped by context, and as such, they depend on the public world and some kind of community in order to be formed. The embodied community, then, plays a crucial role, functioning as a social structure into which girls and women send the "ping" of their zines so that they can develop ambitious or experimental gendered roles and subjectivities.

Furthermore, because zines mobilize a bodily experience, they are useful sites to divulge and reimagine certain gendered forms of embodiment—from the bodily traumas of sexual assault to the challenges of living in a body that doesn't adhere to mainstream norms. Even as they often contain deeply personal autobiographical information, zines facilitate the construction of a particular kind of mediated public identity, reliant, in part, on the embodied community that is built as an affectionate, supportive social space. Nomy Lamm's experience provides a revealing example. She used her fat-positive zine, *I'm So Fucking Beautiful,* as a tool for her own public self-construction by using it to shape her community. She explained, "I wrote the zine specifically so I would have something to hand out at this event that I was performing at. It's a kind of security blanket, pretty much, being like, I would feel naked, here, here's me exploiting myself." She would give the zine to people she met before she spoke with them. When I suggested that her zine itself—which discloses a great deal of personal information—seems to expose her more than physical exposure, she responded, "Saying things doesn't bother me. . . . Growing up I didn't feel I was losing anything by saying anything; it was just more of how people looked at me or like physically interacted with me. So exposing my body was a bigger deal than exposing my actual self."[24] In a way, her zine became a kind of preemptive strike, a way for her to present an interpretive lens so that people she encountered, who "looked at me or . . . physically interacted with me," would not have to rely on their own stereotypes of large women—the densely mythogenic figure of the "fat chick"—to understand Lamm. In addition, writing is a form of agency. She had control over the representations put forth in her zine, and those representations could affect the way her body was viewed. Her zine, then, helped her construct an in-person embodied community, as well as a broader community of readers she wouldn't meet except via her zine.

Lamm is not the only zine creator using her zine to help her negotiate the way her culture views her body. Many grrrl zines are concerned with the unrealistic beauty standards that pervade mainstream media, particularly advertising aimed at girls and women.[25] Beauty and body image are some of the central issues of young feminists because they disproportionately affect girls and young women in the late twentieth and early twenty-first centuries.[26] Lamm's *I'm So Fucking Beautiful* was one of the first fat-positive zines, but it was soon followed by others, including Marilyn Wann's *Fat!So?,* Krissy Durden's *Figure 8,* Jenny San Diego's *Not Sorry,* and Pat Wilkinson's *Shameless.*[27] These zines attack the pathologically thin image of female beauty and attempt, though humor as well as anger, to reclaim the fat body as an acceptable, beautiful, female form.

*Not Sorry* addresses many aspects of Jenny San Diego's life, not only her body, and it is illustrative of the interplay of subjectivity and embodied community. *Not Sorry* #3 is a quarter-sized zine consisting primarily of text (typed, word-processed, and handwritten) pasted onto a variety of background images such as maps and cartoons. In the zine, San Diego describes the personal harm she experienced as a result of growing up in a social context that demanded a particular version of female beauty. Reflecting on her younger self, she explains, "i did nothing else in that time, but hate myself. i was so smart and worthy and i could've done so much with all of that extra energy and i get so fucking angry about all of that precious time LOST. not to mention the extra money i would've had from not buying diet aids and clothes that were too small for me so that they would 'motivate' me to lose weight. no, i squandered it all in maniacal self-hate."[28] San Diego uses the space of the zine to document her suffering and her vulnerability as a large girl in a culture that valorizes thinness.

However, the intense self-reflection in this zine functions beyond the personal. Like Lamm, San Diego uses the zine to create a sympathetic community, in her case actually attempting to call into being certain elements of that community. For instance, *Not Sorry* features a handwritten letter to a potential lover in which she explains, "i'm fat. ok, i know yr not blind, but with that comes stretch marks and cellulite and other so-called undesirable physical features. are you ready to be faced with these things and not only find them *not* ugly, but find them beautiful because they are mine? are you ready to touch, kiss and appreciate these very things?" In a tactic suggestive of Lamm's preemptive strike, San Diego discloses her culturally unacceptable features so that they can't be used against her, so that she has control over them, and then offers the challenge to her future partner (and other readers of the zine) to perceive those features differently. She goes on to present her own reframing of her body, a reframing that functions as a pedagogical strategy for developing an alternative way of seeing and experiencing fatness: "my body is big, full and soft. my curves will leave you speechless. my stretch marks are like paths to a treasure."[29] In a culture saturated with media images of the beautiful female body as pathologically thin, San Diego celebrates her large female body and imagines stretch marks not as defects but as paths that redefine her body as a treasure. In so doing, she invokes and educates an embodied community that will provide a space for her physical size to become something different than it could be via the interpretive frames of corporate cultural productions.

Beauty and body image can become a differently contested terrain in zines by transgender girls and women who may be struggling to be defined as women while not conceding to the pathological beauty standards that may signal "woman" to a mainstream public. For instance, in the collaboratively produced zine *We Will Determine Our Own Bodies*, nine transgender zinesters describe the challenges they face in trying to understand and accept their bodies. In the introduction, Suzie Cyanide writes, "how is my body to be understood in terms of trans-identity? how am I to share that? . . . I want to rewrite my body. I want to rename my body. to reinvent my body."[30] Essays, poems, charts, and drawings in the zine explore what it might mean for transgender people to reinvent their bodies—what kinds of reinvention are possible within a gender binaric system, and what it might mean to love a body that is multiply nonconforming to that system.

The zine's centerfold features a twelve-panel cartoon, drawn by Suzie Cyanide and Kylin, that encompasses many of the issues featured in the zine as a whole and makes visible one way of challenging stereotypic bodily norms. In this cartoon, an ambiguously gendered person—bald-headed, round-stomached, with two protruding teeth and a naval but no sexualized characteristics—considers his/her reflection in a mirror. The sequence begins with a scream that seems to be one of bodily shame. With a caption reading, "i want to be beautiful," the figure looks into a mirror showing a stereotypical image of female beauty: a woman with large, naked breasts, long flowing hair, an hourglass figure, and several conspicuous eyelashes. The next frame reads, "Uhm, not really!" followed by, "or really but me." In this frame, the figure sees him/herself in the mirror, with hands protruding from the mirror, and this seems to mark a turning point in the image. The cartoon celebrates bodily diversity: one of the center panels reads, "i like difference," and this frame features six vaguely humanoid bodies that are connected, happy—an abandoning of stereotypes of appropriate embodiment and gender norms altogether. The sequence ends with another scream, this one clearly of happiness, as the final panel shows the figure hugging him or herself, hearts floating in the air around, and a caption reading, "How could it be so good."

What's striking about this cartoon is that the images are friendly, inviting, like images from a children's book. Although the cartoon protagonist does reject the image of standard female beauty, this isn't a cartoon propelled by oppositionality. Like San Diego's essay in *Not Sorry*, this cartoon serves a pedagogical purpose, validating unconventional bodies and training readers to accept these bodies. Because the images are so friendly,

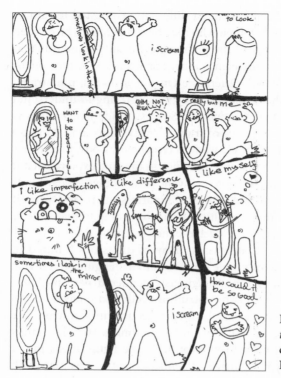

Image from *We Will Determine Our Own Bodies*, drawn by Suzie Cyanide and Kylin.

they function to normalize bodies that aren't operating within a standard beauty system or gender system. Through dramatizing the protagonist's pain, the authors show the dangers of bodily hatred that can accompany any gendered experience but may be particularly challenging for transgender people. Many of those writing for this zine still find themselves, as River-A-Genda writes, "feel[ing] bad about our bodies unless we're straight white men,"[31] and this cartoon—at the center of the zine—serves to destabilize hurtful bodily norms and propagate an appreciation of difference that's akin to what Audre Lorde calls for, difference "as a fund of necessary polarities between which our creativity can spark like a dialectic."[32]

## Girlhood Vulnerability

While beauty and body image are one potential site of vulnerability and harm addressed in grrrl zines, the theme of the dangers of girlhood and womanhood is pervasive in these zines. When I asked her about her use of girlhood imagery—hearts, stars, and other friendly doodles—in her zine *Doris*, Cindy Crabb responded by talking about growing up female: "I feel like a lot of us were really damaged at that time in life, do you know what I mean? A lot of us suffered abuse in adolescence or before, and so I feel like with hearts and stuff I'm making it allowable for this hurt part to be not hurt, and be incorporated into our full lives."[33] Like *Doris*, Neely Bat Chestnut's *Mend My Dress* offers a complex, nuanced, and skillfully constructed picture of multifarious girlhood vulnerability. Although Chestnut writes in a diary-like, stream of consciousness style, her work should not be misinterpreted as simple autobiography; instead, it offers artistic and literary mediation.

Each issue of *Mend My Dress* has a different thematic focus. In *Mend My Dress* #3, subtitled "The Little Match Girl or, my dead grandmother," Chestnut offers reflections about her grandmother as a way into thinking about mental illness, family relationships, and gender. She includes the text of the Hans Christian Andersen story of "The Little Match Girl" as part of her description of her relationship with her grandmother. She introduces it with, "almost every year for christmas she would give me a copy of this story. i think she was trying to tell me that if she could help me she would have. but she just could not. so hear it is."[34] The story, which describes a dying little girl's vision of her grandmother as something that eases her into death, suggests that the relationship between Chestnut and her grandmother is fraught with difficulty. The first issue of *Mend My Dress* is all about incest, about Chestnut's victimization by her father and stepfathers. Every subsequent zine touches on this issue, and it is one of the subtexts of Chestnut's meditations on her relationship with her grandmother, the mentally ill woman who was the mother of Chestnut's abusive father.

The zine's visual and textual elements work together. This is the smallest of the issues of *Mend My Dress*, quarter-sized rather than digest-sized, and as with many other small zines, its size enhances the sense of vulnerability expressed in the text. The last page of the zine offers a visual/textual artwork that uses fragmentation to great effect, combining a snippet from a description of 1950s mental hospitals with repeated images of the fairy godmother from Disney's *Cinderella* (one of the thematic elements that ties together all issues of *Mend My Dress*) and a line from "The Little Match Girl," cut from strips of paper.

This page generates a number of meanings. First, it calls into question the known and the unknown: in some ways, the zine suggests that Chestnut has more access to the fairy godmother figure than to her own grandmother. She experiences her grandmother—and her memory of her grandmother—through literary and fairy tale lenses, assembling this intergenerational female relationship through fragments of memory and pop culture imagery. The repeated image of the fairy godmother—the happily ever after older woman who can rescue Cinderella—is juxtaposed with a horrific description of the tortures enacted in mental hospitals like the one in which her grandmother was incarcerated. At the bottom of the page, in a position that implies closure, is a quote from "The Little Match Girl"; however, the quote is not from the end of this story and does not offer resolution. Instead, the quote—"This time it was her grandmother who appeared in the circle of flame"[35]—comes from the moment when the little girl is dying. It's painfully sad to read this page. Through these compiled images, Chestnut offers a complete evisceration of the myth of the fairy godmother, one of the iconic myths of girlhood: that if you're a good little girl and suffer stoically, you will be rescued.

ecently as the early 1950s sights
sounds in even the best mental
pital could be harrowing—the vio-
patients kept under restraint by
ps or bed sheets; seriously dis-
ped psychotics yelling in mental
nent; others huddled in frozen si-
ce.
This
time it was her grandmother who appeared in the
circle of flame.

Image from *Mend My Dress*, courtesy of Neely Bat Chestnut.

The zine highlights Chestnut's own victimization, along with her growing awareness of the systems of oppression that entrapped her grandmother as well. She explains that as a girl, "i wanted her to see that bad things that where happening to me, not just inside her mind."[36] And yet the grandmother wasn't able to help Chestnut, and at some level she recognized that she couldn't. The repeated gift of "The Little Match Girl" seems to show this. This zine, like the others in the series, is to a certain extent about the failures of these gifts—the failures of the cultural trappings of femininity to follow through on the promises they make. Chestnut uses images from the 1972 Disney children's book version of *Cinderella* to illustrate each issue of *Mend My Dress*, and the title comes from this book: after the stepsisters have torn Cinderella's clothing from her body and left for the ball, Cinderella says, "Oh, dear, how will I ever mend my dress?" By juxtaposing the fairy godmother with her own grandmother, Chestnut exposes the lie.

Girlhood as a space of danger and damage appears in all the *Mend My Dress* zines. In *Mend My Dress* #2, the centerfold is an excerpt from *The Wizard of Oz*, in which Dorothy encounters the China Doll Princess, who warns Dorothy that if she falls she might break. Dorothy asks, "But couldn't you be mended?" "'Oh, yes; but one is never so pretty after being mended, you know,' replied the princess."[37] Here again is the notion of being broken and needing to be mended. I asked Chestnut if this was about her, and she said, "I think so. I think that my childhood and my young adulthood were so fucked up that if I would have continued living that way, I would probably be dead by now, and there were things that I needed to fix or mend as you might say in order to be a human being."[38]

Clearly, there is a personal level to this recurring theme in the zines, but this theme is interesting not just because of what it reveals about one zine creator's personal life but because of what it reveals about the social identity of girlhood and womanhood. The zines suggest that to be a girl is to be vulnerable, breakable, a constructed thing that will need to be repaired. And although the quote itself suggests that this is problematic—"one is never so pretty after being mended"—*Mend My Dress* by its very existence makes the opposite argument. It is the broken, pieced together thing. It is made of chopped-up and reconstituted fragments of mainstream culture. It rejects the valorization of prettiness and offers a mended version of female identity, not one that pretends at wholeness and unity but boldly exhibits its seams and scissor marks. "Bricolage" is a term often used to discuss zines: they are constructed of whatever materials are

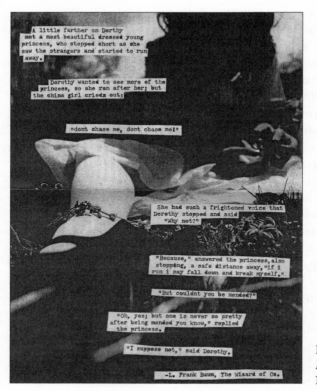

A little farther on Dorthy met a most beautiful dressed young princess, who stopped short as she saw the strangers and started to run away.

Dorothy wanted to see more of the princess, so she ran after her; but the china girl criedx out:

"dont chase me, dont chase me!"

She had such a frightened voice that Dorothy stopped and said "Why not?"

"Because," answered the princess, also stopping, a safe distance away, "if i run i may fall down and break myself."

"But couldnt you be mended?"

"Oh, yes; but one is never so pretty after being mended you know," replied the princess.

"I suppose not," said Dorothy.

-L. Frank Baum, The Wizard of Oz.

Image from *Mend My Dress*, courtesy of Neely Bat Chestnut.

"ready-to hand."[39] I argue that what Chestnut and other zinesters are doing through these zines is acting as the bricoleurs of their own subjectivities.

These zines are enacting a version of third wave theory through their emphatic reversals and revelations, their mobile and shifting engagements with pop culture imagery, and their slippery intentions. Although some of the messages in *Mend My Dress* seem clear—Chestnut's expressions of love for her grandmother, for instance, and the pain she voices about the victimization she's suffered—other aspects of the zine are more opaque. Just as with the zine *Jigsaw*, discussed in the introduction to this book, it can be difficult to identify what's ironic and what's sincere in *Mend My Dress*. Certainly, there is a level of irony in Chestnut's inclusion of iconic images from Disney's *Cinderella*, as this is a fairy tale that has been widely rejected by feminists, and she herself notes that this is a story that promotes a "false idea of love." And yet she also admits, "I kind of have an obsession with, well, like, I really identify with Cinderella as a character."⁴⁰ Chestnut's zine isn't offering a straightforward rejection of this cultural imagery but, rather, uses it in partly deconstructing and partly celebratory ways.

Her zine, then, generates and circulates modes of subjectivity that draw from social justice movements of the twentieth century, as well as post-structuralist epistemologies. She and other grrrl zinesters use the valida-tion and experiential authority of identity politics while also, in Heywood and Drake's words, "emphasizing ways that desires and pleasures subject to critique can be used to rethink and enliven activist work."⁴¹ Chestnut claims Cinderella and girlhood, but in creative rather than merely con-sumptive ways. Her inclusion of Disney imagery in her zines doesn't repli-cate oppressive tropes, nor does she reject those tropes. She is untroubled by contradictions, the "impurity" that Maria C. Lugones identifies with complex identities,⁴² and yet her zines do not posit a radically poststruc-turalist view of identity as entirely performative and limitless. Rather, she (and other grrrl zinesters like her) operates within a field of subjectiv-ity with boundaries: just as the boundaries of the page provide structure within and against which Chestnut constructs narratives, so, too, does her social location and the embodied community of the zine world provide functional limits.

## *Bad Girl, Good Girl: The Pleasures of Femininity*

Grrrl zines don't simply expose the dangers of being a girl or woman in a patriarchal culture. They also often engage with familiar configurations of girlishness and femininity—playfully reclaiming and reworking them. To a certain extent, this has become an identifiable grrrl zine visual style: the kinderwhore or "kitten with a whip" aesthetic, in which girlish im-ages are given a twist or are recontextualized in ways that change their meaning, making them tough or resistant.⁴³ For example, as discussed in chapter 1, Sarah Dyer's famous anarchist Hello Kitty became an almost ubiquitous image in grrrl zines in the 1990s. There are countless examples of this phenomenon, from the celebration of children's book protagonist Pippi Longstocking in numerous grrrl zines to Cindy Crabb's use of girl-ish doodles, such as hearts, stars, and flowers, in conjunction with discus-sions of weighty subjects such as sexual assault.

The incongruous connections happen rhetorically, as well, as in the re-working of the insult "you fight like a girl" in the epigraph to this chap-ter. These reframings of femininity are examples of zines' "insubordinate

Image from *Doris*, courtesy of Cindy Crabb.

creativity," and they function as challenges to corporate culture industries that position girlhood in terms of passivity and consumption.

To be sure, many grrrl zines are fronting these challenges in ways that embrace certain aspects of femininity. Rather than simply rejecting sexist culture, many zines are engaged in the project of identifying the pleasures of femininity. This work is sometimes seen as "not feminist enough" because it can be understood as complicit with patriarchal gender roles and, indeed, corporate culture; during the early 1990s heyday of the Riot Grrrl movement, "girl power" quickly became a marketing strategy, even while it was being developed as a tool of resistance. Although I understand this sort of skepticism about reclaiming femininity, I contend that this skepticism can quickly lead to a flattening of feminist resistance. According to this approach, the only appropriate feminist response to patriarchal tropes of femininity is outright rejection. bell hooks asks, "How do we create an oppositional worldview, a consciousness, an identity, a standpoint that exists not only as that struggle which also opposes dehumanization but as that movement which enables creative, expansive self-actualization?" She warns that, in these efforts, "Opposition is not enough."[44] Like hooks, these zines and their creators suggest that a dichotomous framing of feminism's gender interventions, in which feminists are supposed to voice monolithic opposition to corporate culture, is inadequate. These zines are playing in the spaces between resistance and complicity and as such are creating third wave tactics.

One publication committed to the pleasures of femininity is *Bust*, which began as a zine but is now a full-fledged professional magazine. Debbie Stoller, Laurie Henzel, and Marcelle Karp started the zine in 1993 because, as Stoller explained to me, they wanted a publication that was like *Sassy* for adult women. In particular, Stoller admired *Sassy*'s framing of girlhood as a positive space: "Whereas other teen girl magazines were saying things like, you're gonna get breasts and boys are gonna want to touch them and make sure they don't. You know, *Sassy* was kind of like, you're gonna get breasts and if someone touches them it's gonna feel really good, so pick a cute guy to do it, you know, just sort of embracing, trying to really show the positive things about being a teen girl and all the great new things you could do as a teen girl . . . rather than pretending it was always in such a negative light." She was well aware of the dangers and vulnerabilities that zines such as *Mend My Dress* (and magazines such as *Ms.*) documented, but she was searching for something different. She wanted *Bust* to create "an embraceable feminist culture that's positive, that gives us stuff that we can relate to, to talk about how difficult it is to be a woman and about how much culture is misogynist, but I wanna just try to present an alternative, just try to create an alternative that you can read and be happy and feel good about."[45]

The pleasures of girlhood and womanhood have been a theme in *Bust* since its inception. The publication has featured articles that celebrate such stereotypically feminine acts as flirting, shopping, developing your own sense of style, and lipstick. However, *Bust* also tries to broaden the terrain of fun for women, emphasizing the pleasures of more stereotypically male activities such as nonmonogamous sex, physical aggression, and swearing. As *Bust* demands pleasure for women, it also documents the cultural tension between appropriately performed womanhood and female pleasure. For instance, the second issue focused on fun, and the editors' letter offered the question, "As women, is it even acceptable for us to want to have fun? . . . we are expected to undergo a kind of pleasure-ectomy so that we may become the selfless keepers of compassion, moderation, serenity, and responsibility that is the definition of 'womanhood.'"[46] A few years later, the editors upped the ante in the "Bad Girl" issue of *Bust*, an issue that came to set the thematic course for the publication. This issue discussed the pursuit of pleasure, and the editors argued that what really makes a bad girl bad is "simply doing the one thing that is truly un-feminine: *acting on your desires*."[47] *Bust* leverages two available cultural categories—the bad girl and the good girl—against each other, and the good girl, the one who has experienced the "pleasure-ectomy," gets pushed off the page. The bad girl becomes the primary iconographic terrain for the publication.

The bad girl is an agent rather than simply an object of desire, and *Bust*'s covers often highlight this social identity. In so doing, however, they often illustrate the tension between competing notions of femininity, the fact that, as they noted in the "Bad Girl" issue, "female badness seems to only be acceptable as long as it remains *attractive*—as long as it benefits someone else."[48] The cover of the zine's second issue challenges this emphasis on the bad girl as attractive. This cover features a cartoon of a giant female dog (note: bitch) with bared breasts, carrying a stereo, a beer, sex toys, movies, comics, and junk food. She is stomping through a theme park called "Fun City," her booming feet crushing some of the tiny cartoon creatures below her who run for cover. She is not particularly attractive— she is, in fact, google-eyed, drooling, and dangerous—and this is at least partly the point. She is not the typical woman's magazine cover model, and therefore she doesn't function as an easily assimilable image for women to aspire to become. The discomfort this cover might produce in a reader is part of how zines work, keeping the reader from the passive consumption mindset produced by mainstream capitalist media.[49] It functions more specifically in this case to interrupt assumptions about femininity and force the reader to consider how femininity and pleasure interface.

Many other *Bust* covers enhance this tension, as well, such as the cover of the first "Sex" issue, which features a woman's enormous pregnant stomach with the word "SEX" scrawled across it, in Riot Grrrl fashion.[50] This is the pregnant woman not as beatific, sanitized symbol of maternal instinct but as sexy, bikini-wearing, defiant girl, insurgent and owning up to the act that led to the pregnancy in the first place. Again, *Bust* celebrates the bad girl as a figure who is so colorful and dramatic—even uncomfortably so—that she completely overshadows and upstages the more familiar, palatable models of appropriate femininity.

The *Bust* editors see celebrating femininity and the pleasures of femininity as a tactical political move. Stoller explained:

> When men's magazines were starting to come out, like *Details* (there was no *Maxim* yet), there was always emphasis in those magazines about men's pleasure and how fun it is to be a guy and all the great things you can do as a guy, and so that was very consciously an important part of what shaped our ideas for how to do *Bust*, that we wanted it to keep emphasizing the pleasures of being female and feminist and making it feel like it was a great, cool club to be a part of.[51]

Pleasure is an energy, a generative force and a connective one. As discussed in chapter 2, pleasure helps create the embodied community of

Covers of *Bust,* courtesy of Laura Henzel.

grrrl zines, and *Bust* is using it intentionally, as a way to mobilize their community of readers. Certainly, there are benefits for the publication: *Bust* grew from a zine to a magazine, in part, because the zine was fun to read and it promoted consumer culture as part of the enjoyment of being a woman. By the second year, the publication was running with glossy color covers, and by the time I spoke with Stoller and Henzel in 2006, they were selling nearly 100,000 copies per issue, with around 22,000 going to subscribers and the rest being sold in bookstores (the magazine is for sale in major retailers such as Barnes and Noble and Borders) and on newsstands. Even as it moved from zine to magazine status, *Bust* maintained much of its thematic focus—its celebration of the bad girl and of female pleasures in general.

Its magazine format is necessarily less intimate and inviting than the scruffy, informal publications that readers identify as "a present in the mail," and this has had consequences for the way the publication is perceived. One complication from *Bust*'s success came in 1999, when the publication was bought out by an internet company that planned to grow the magazine but, as it turned out, "they weren't really that interested in running a magazine so the magazine was losing money with them even though it was looking great." When the stock market began to fall, the magazine's owners decided to find other investors to help grow *Bust*, but their big push for investment began with an article in the *New York Times*, which came out on September 10, 2001, the day before the terrorist attacks in New York City, Washington, D.C., and Pennsylvania. Stoller explained, "And then that was really kind of the end of it. Within a month, they closed the entire company down basically."[52]

Stoller, Henzel, and Karp were able to buy *Bust* back from its owners, a move they decided to make because they started receiving so many letters from readers expressing their love for the publication and asking what they could do to help. Stoller and Henzel explained what a frightening time that was: "We had nothing except for [the rights to publish a magazine called *Bust*]. We had no money in the bank, no money to publish the next magazine with," but their understanding of the publication and of their readership was so solid that, Stoller explained, "within six months we were able to start paying ourselves and our staff. Not very much at first, but it grew and grew."[53] It's worth noting here that, although *Bust* struggled financially due to their magazine status, they benefited from an embodied community of readers who felt such attachment to the publication that they helped bring it back from ruin.

Another complication the publication has faced is that, as a successful, visible publication, *Bust* has been a lightning rod for both praise and criticism from feminists and others in a way that seems less likely within the smaller zine community. This, however, is part of what Stoller was striving for with *Bust*. She explained to me, "I never wanted it to be some well-kept secret, some little underground thing, cause that wasn't the function, the function was to reach as many people as possible and to have, to try to have an actual cultural influence."[54] The pleasures of womanhood became a successful marketing strategy for *Bust* as the pleasures of "being a guy" were for men's magazines like *Maxim*.

More than this, though, *Bust*'s deployment of pleasure also helps alter the terrain of femininity, not to mention feminism. Stoller explicitly identifies this intervention in the terrain of femininity as a form of feminist activism: "I really believe that the thing that is incredibly influential to the way we live our lives and what restricts us and what we think about ourselves is our culture and our values, and that if you can change, those are the things that really need to change."[55] It may be worth noting here that one of the ways in which self-identified third wave feminists have sought to distinguish themselves from the second wave is via this emphasis on pleasure. Several grrrl zine creators said, on conditions of anonymity, that reading more mainstream feminist publications identified with the second wave, notably *Ms.* magazine, was akin to "eating your green vegetables" or "doing your homework"—in other words, not fun.[56] *Bust* has made tactical interventions into mainstream notions of girlhood and womanhood, using pleasure—the idea that it should be fun to be a girl or a woman—as their barometer for accepting or rejecting the parts of the culture with which they come into contact.

*Grit & Glitter*, a zine cowritten by Neely Bat Chestnut and Hazel Pine, uses a slightly different approach to rehabilitate femininity. The zine explores "femme" as a space that is personally recuperative. The inside cover of the zine offers this statement, written by Chestnut:

> As i wrote this, it became very clear to me that being femme is a big fuck you to my father, to my brother. By being femme, i am getting back [my] girlhood, my womanhood that they stole. I am saying fuck you for making me feel weak and like I was bad. Fuck you, I'm going to drink tea and cook meals, i'm going to wear skirts every fucking day and i'm going to love it. Fuck you world, I am femme.[57]

Rather than claiming the bad girl identity as *Bust* does, *Grit & Glitter* draws on the iconography of the good girl while using the rhetorics of the bad girl, the "fuck you"s that are familiar in grrrl zines. The authors of *Grit & Glitter* are claiming the pleasures and the trappings of girlhood as a personalized act of healing and redemption.

Chestnut and Pine recognize the fact that girlhood and womanhood are defined as dangerous identities, sites of attack and victimization, and locations of inherent weakness. Both relate incidents, growing up, when they learned that female bodies were vulnerable, as when Pine recounts, "By the time I was 11, I had realized I had tits and this made people want something from me," and Chestnut explains, "To be female was to be a victim, to be a sex plaything for my father."[58] Both retreated from girlhood and from identifiable gendered markers (clothing, hair) as an attempt to find safety. In this zine, they reject their own androgyny as a defense mechanism they no longer need. They are not denying the vulnerability described in zines like *Mend My Dress* but are reclaiming their girlhood and their femme subjectivities as acts of agency.

Throughout the zine, they're recuperating visual images of femininity. The zine is filled with pictures of flowers, and the spine of the zine has been stitched with a sewing machine, so even its structure draws on a skill set affiliated with women. However, through their juxtapositioning of

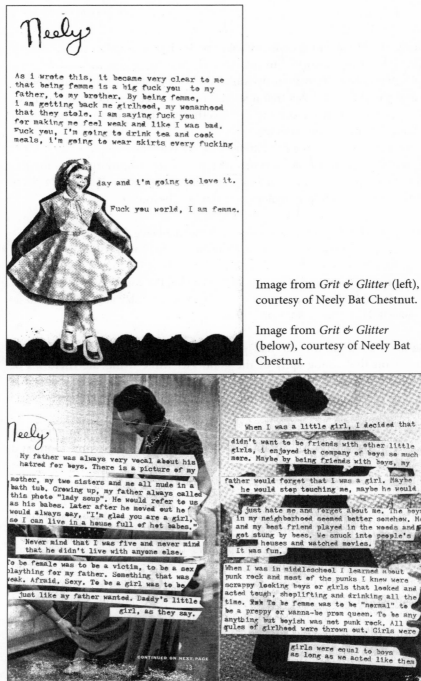

*Neely*

As i wrote this, it became very clear to me
that being femme is a big fuck you to my
father, to my brother. By being femme,
i am getting back me girlhood, my womanhood
that they stole. I am saying fuck you
for making me feel weak and like I was bad.
Fuck you, I'm going to drink tea and cook
meals, i'm going to wear skirts every fucking

day and i'm going to love it.

Fuck you world, I am femme.

Image from *Grit & Glitter* (left),
courtesy of Neely Bat Chestnut.

Image from *Grit & Glitter*
(below), courtesy of Neely Bat
Chestnut.

*Neely*

My father was always very vocal about his
hatred for boys. There is a picture of my

mother, my two sisters and me all nude in a
bath tub. Growing up, my father always called
this photo "lady soup". He would refer to us
as his babes. Later after he moved out he
would always say, "I'm glad you are a girl,
so I can live in a house full of hot babes."

Never mind that I was five and never mind
that he didn't live with anyone else.

To be female was to be a victim, to be a sex
plaything for my father. Something that was
weak. Afraid. Sexy. To be a girl was to be

just like my father wanted. Daddy's little

girl, as they say.

When I was a little girl, I decided that
didn't want to be friends with other little
girls, i enjoyed the company of boys so much
more. Maybe by being friends with boys, my

father would forget that I was a girl. Maybe
he would stop touching me, maybe he would

just hate me and forget about me. The boys
in my neighborhood seemed better somehow. Me
and my best friend played in the woods and
got stung by bees. We snuck into people's
houses and watched movies.
It was fun.

When I was in middleschool I learned about
punk rock and most of the punks I knew were
scrappy looking boys or girls that looked and
acted tough, shoplifting and drinking all the
time. Fuk To be femme was to be "normal" to
be a preppy or wanna-be prom queen. To be any
anything but boyish was not punk rock. All
rules of girlhood were thrown out. Girls were

girls were equal to boys
as long as we acted like them

CONTINUED ON NEXT PAGE

13

images and text, their compilations of contradictory material, they change the meanings of these icons. The little girl curtsying in her dress and Mary Janes is positioned next to Chestnut's statement, "Fuck you world, I am femme," while pearl-wearing 1950s women in gowns form the background for Chestnut's story of her father's abuse.

These images do not communicate the familiar sense of femininity; indeed, the little girl curtsying comes to seem almost maniacal in the context of Chestnut's text, her smile not cloying but devious, dangerous. The images become infused with resistance, and Pine and Chestnut also locate resistance in particular performances of girlishness, as when Pine explains, "femme is the little girl in the corner glaring, the girl who always wear skirts, but never learned to cross her legs," and Chestnut relates a childhood incident of cutting up a jumper that her mother was attempting to force her to wear.[59]

As the resistant girliness suggests, in the zine, femme becomes not only a personal healing performance but also a kind of tactical subjectivity. Chestnut's "Fuck you world, I am femme" gives evidence that claiming femininity can be an act of aggression against both individuals and the culture that have made girlhood so vulnerable. The zine presents drinking tea, cooking meals, and wearing skirts as an attack on patriarchal norms rather than a concession to those norms. Rather than retreating from these sorts of gendered behavior as both zinesters once did in an effort to maintain bodily safety, Chestnut and Pine now see their defiant performance of these behaviors and their pleasure in these performances as resistant. Further, by using the term "femme," a term affiliated with the performance of feminine roles within queer relationships, Chestnut and Pine additionally complicate their subject positions. Both authors identify as queer, and by claiming "femme" rather than "feminine" identities, they disentangle both categories from compulsory heterosexuality and "[make] . . . femininity unreliable as a marker of heterosexuality."[60] Pine writes: "Then there is of course, the implied queerness of femme. The subversive nature of femme—the double whammy to heteronorms by not only being queer, but a hidden queer." Their use of "femme" also points to the performative quality of femininity. Their identities are clearly positioned as chosen rather than default states: "Femininity," Pine writes, "we know is something taught, not ingrained."[61]

Zines that reclaim femininity are sometimes identified as enacting a version of cultural feminism, but I don't think it's useful to frame them in these terms.[62] Cultural feminism, usually defined as a feminism that celebrates women's unique perspective, is a somewhat outmoded category that doesn't capture the complexity of these zines' gender interventions. What these zines are doing is offering a contradictory stance: yes, girlhood and womanhood are dangerous, and, yes, they are culturally constructed for particular political ends, but I can do something different with them and enjoy them. On the one hand, this approach can be seen as politically suspect; indeed, in earlier writing I myself have labeled it "the feminist free-for-all" and have suggested that these sorts of actions represent the bankrupting of feminist politics.[63] But I question that stance now. Just because these zines don't offer a coherent political standpoint, just because they don't fully undermine mainstream gender performances, doesn't mean that they are complicit with cultures of domination. Again, I stress that the binary of resistant/complicit is inadequate to the task of assessing these zines (or texts more generally). In fact, I think the incompleteness I see in these zines, their "yes, but" approach to feminism and femininity, represents a valid theoretical stance, a tactical subjectivity that's keyed to this cultural moment and is characteristically third wave.

This "yes, but" approach encodes resistance and attempts to move the feminist discussion of female subjectivities beyond opposition. Johnson suggests that many young feminist scholars—and I would extend her insight to many grrrl zinesters as well—are so familiar with the discourses critical of racism, sexism, and homophobia that they do not mention them. She argues: "Our redirection does not constitute a turning away from . . . skepticism and critique . . . but a thoroughgoing acceptance of skepticism and critique as the givens of our approach, joined with a desire to go beyond them."[64] This is obviously not to say that young feminists or grrrl zinesters see racism, sexism, homophobia, or other oppressive systems as being gone; in fact, just the opposite. The cultural critique of these systems is the foundation on which they are building, but they don't necessarily stay in that space of critique, choosing, rather, to generate alternative subject positions and to tap into the pleasures of creation and cultural intervention.

There are potential problems with this approach, of course. One of the concerns regularly raised about third wave feminists is that, having come to consciousness in a hyperindividualistic backlash culture, they often don't recognize pervasive problems or know how to address them. A related concern, which I address in chapter 4, is that white zinesters, who make up the majority of those producing zines, often give only lip service to racism, ultimately replicating societal hierarchies around race and ethnicity. Ultimately, though, I think it would be reductive (and condescending) to understand the celebration of femininity and pleasure as merely a form of false consciousness or denial. Better to take seriously the desire to create what Stoller calls "an embraceable feminist culture that's positive," a desire that helps animate a community.

Even as these zines reclaim femininity, a tension between girlhood and womanhood often emerges. In many zines, girlhood is identified as the space of play and pleasure, while womanhood is seen as a space of sacrifice, self-abnegation, and labor. The editors of *Bust* contend, "It's clear that fun seems to be what separates the girls from the women," and later they ask, "what's a thirty-year old gal supposed to do for fun? Can we still behave the way we did as girls, or is it just too embarrassing? Do we even still want to?"[65] Many grrrl zinesters have used the iconography of girlhood to redefine adult womanhood, but the *Bust* editors suggest that this might be "embarrassing," and the mainstream media have done the same, as when an *Entertainment Weekly* reporter queried, "who outside the alterna-culture is likely to take a female over the age of 8 wearing pink barrettes and a plastic Barbie watch all that seriously?"[66] Mama zines are a subset of grrrl zines that have addressed this tension. These zines construct a symbolic terrain for adult womanhood that includes pleasure and that does not simply rely on the iconography of girlhood.

## Mama Zines

The production of mama zines started at the same time as the grrrl zine explosion of which they are a part, in the early 1990s. China Martens's *The Future Generation* may have been the first, in 1990, and she explains that she felt a bit like a pioneer because motherhood essentially did not appear in zines at that time. According to Martens, "When I started, there weren't any [mama zines], literally not any, and I was pretty cued into the radical zine scene."[67] As of this date, mama zines are a sizeable and identifiable subgenre of grrrl zines, with hundreds of mama zines in fairly regular production at the time of this printing. A collective of mama zinesters, including Martens, have produced three *Mamaphiles* zine anthologies, which together have published the work of fifty-eight mama zinesters (and one dad), and many of the longer-running and more recognizable grrrl zines these days are mama zines.[68]

These zines are stylistically diverse, from Ayun Halliday's frenetic line drawings in *The East Village Inky* to Martens's full pages of typed text, from Victoria Law's collaborative photo albums made with her daughter to Kristin McPherson's poetry and photo montages in *Yoga Mama*. They're also diverse in terms of the race and ethnicity of the zine creators; while the burgeoning publishing niche of motherhood memoirs is almost exclusively white, approximately 20 percent of the contributors to the *Mamaphiles* zines are women of color.[69] In some ways they're atypical of the grrrl zine genre: generally older women produce them (women in their late twenties, thirties, and even forties) rather than the teens and twenty-somethings who are more often zine creators.[70] However, like grrrl zines more broadly, they are reclaiming language and the symbolic realm, using the word "mama" rather than "mother" as way of reframing motherhood in terms of informality and warmth—and, by extension, reframing adult womanhood.[71]

Many mama zines originate in the same sense of alienation and exclusion that triggered the larger grrrl zine explosion. Just as Sarah Dyer started the *Action Girl Newsletter* because she felt excluded from the punk community and the zine community by virtue of her gender, many mama zinesters start producing a zine because of feeling alienated from their home communities when they have children. For instance, *The East Village Inky* began when Halliday wasn't able to take part in an acting workshop with her husband because of their childcare needs. She reports that the actors in the workshop

> all saw me as the mother of [Greg's] baby. You know? And like, "oh, Greg's wife is so nice!" And none of them knew my name. And then I think out of that cloud of *desponse* came the realization that I gotta find something that I can do that will be a creative outlet that will put me in some kind of community, even if it's not one that I'm actually seeing and having over for dinner and coffee. But to feel like I'm part of something.[72]

Similarly, Law, creator of a number of zines, including *Fragments of Friendship* and *Tenacious: Writings from Women in Prison*, found when she had her child that "the activist scene was not really set up for dealing with parents and children and children's needs." She continued:

> I ended up dropping out of a lot of things, and the things that I still did go to, people would say things like, "Oh, it's great to see you here! Most women, when they become mothers, they drop out, I guess they just don't care anymore." And I was just like no, but maybe I really wouldn't

be able to table at this loud smoky event with a newborn. You know? It was really kind of frustrating to see that so many people had this opinion that motherhood equals complacency, or motherhood equals political indifference.[73]

Halliday and Law both encountered themselves as the objects of others' projected stereotypes when they became mothers. Halliday became the auxiliary to her husband, and Law became someone who was complacent or indifferent, as if she were no longer an activist. They began creating mama zines as a way to express a more complex subjectivity than the one projected onto them, and to construct an embodied community that would give shape to their redefined subjectivity. Mama zinester Ariel Gore has called *The Future Generation* (and, by extension, mama zines in general) "a little Xeroxed island home in a sea of alienation."[74]

Zines are a good fit for parenthood because the zine is an informal, immediate medium. Halliday explains the process of creating her zine:

> Every day I could count on about maybe two hours of naptime. I didn't know when they would happen, but it seemed like, okay, if I make the zine handwritten I'm not going to be wasting time trying to figure out how to use the computer, how to do desktop publishing. And then I can also put it in my purse and then if she falls asleep when we're nine blocks from home, I'll just go sit on a bench somewhere and, you know, pull out a pen and work on the zine there. And that's what I did, and not only did it work out from a practical standpoint, but I think a lot of other mothers of young children or mothers who had gone through that experience of having young children related to that aspect of it as well. And then you know, that's why the run on sentences and the drawings that are incomplete where I forgot—I like white-out a hand and forget to go back and redraw it.[75]

Other mother zinesters agree. China Martens writes in an issue of *The Future Generation*, "This writing style is called spontaneous. . . . Their is no time to edit. This is the poor womens style of writing, get it out and share it with you, a slice of life. I don't have the luxury to have a respectable article, but I do have the guts to print this anyway. I'm all for real communication. When was the last time your corporate communication or newspaper, gave you as much?"[76] The zine medium does not demand perfection; indeed, the messiness of zines—the incomplete

drawings that Halliday refers to, or the misspellings in Martens's zine—
are part of what defines the zine medium and helps create connections
between readers and writers. Halliday suspects that her readers relate
to this aspect of her zines, and they report that this is the case. One
*East Village Inky* reader explained, "Often I'll read it when I'm grabbing
a meal, or while standing at the counter waiting for the pasta to boil.
Occasionally I'll even sit down on the couch to read it."[77] Another said,
"I read it when I am nursing the baby (nice handy size!) and I read it
in the late hours after my kids are asleep and I am winding down." She
continued, "it's incredibly portable—if I'm going to pick my kids up at
school I can flip through a few pages while waiting for the bell to ring.
I find my reading time is very broken up, so a zine can be read in small
chunks without having to keep the running thread of a novel."[78] The
zine medium, then, fits with the demands of motherhood whether one
is a zine creator or reader.

One reason that mama zines "can be read in small chunks" is that, like
other grrrl zines, they are constructing subjectivities and perspectives that
are fragmented and multifarious. They provide a space for inconsistent,
complex representations of motherhood. For instance, *The East Village
Inky* features the recurring character Bitchmother, who emerges periodi-
cally to do things such as "complain about the state of the apartment and
how people should feel lucky to live in proximity to so many amazing
museums and why one shouldn't launch an unending campaign for a
light saber the day after one has received a brand new fluorescent green
samurai sword and that she's not a waitress *or* a short order cook . . . well,
you get the picture."[79] Bitchmother is a separate character who enters the
zine, offering another example of fragmented subjectivities in grrrl zines.
Halliday uses this character to make gentle fun of herself, as well as to
normalize the anger that is part of motherhood. Although Bitchmother
is generally drawn in ways that make her fairly ferocious, such as with
fangs, she is not an unsympathetic character. Rather, like the household's
vicious cat Jambo, Bitchmother is presented affectionately, as a difficult
but loved family member.

More pointedly, China Martens' welfare mother pin-up girl is the cover
image of issue #9 of *The Future Generation*. This image features Martens
herself wearing fishnet stockings and high-heeled platform shoes, with
dark hair falling seductively over one eye and glossy lipstick. The caption
on which she appears to be sitting is outlined in red and pink and reads
"Welfare Mothers make better LOVERS."

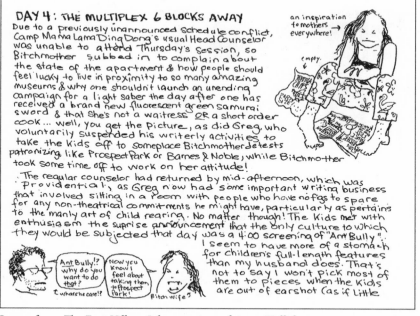

Image from *The East Village Inky*, courtesy of Ayun Halliday.

Inside the front cover, she explains: "Welfare moms have been so slandered in the press—so I'm just saying, I'm not ashamed that I am an economically-disadvantaged-single-parent-head-of-the-house-holder-as-a-group-using-One-Percent-of-the-tax-budget. (the lover on the cover is a picture of me—china doll)."[80] Here Martens contextualizes state support of welfare mothers within the larger picture of national spending. Throughout the rest of the zine she addresses national spending issues, with harsh critiques of the amount of money spent to subsidize corporations and national defense as compared with the money spent on quality of life for women and children. These issues are now somewhat familiar within the mothers' movement, but in 1998, when Martens produced this issue of the zine, they were not as widely discussed, so Martens is on the cutting edge of a particular politics of mothering.[81]

In the process of making her political point, Martens leverages a number of symbolic variables in surprising ways. First, she reframes the welfare mother as an attractive white woman, countering the prevalent images, particularly in the 1990s, of the "welfare queen" who was black.

Cover of *The Future Generation,* courtesy of China Martens.

Moreover, the welfare mother is a pin-up girl, a sex object, and a "better lover." She claims welfare mother status as something acceptable—even desirable—rather than shameful. She also doesn't shy away from sexuality, as she herself is posing as "the lover on the cover" in a tactical subjectivity she calls "china doll," one of many versions of herself that appears in issues of *The Future Generation.* Later in this same issue, Martens describes her struggles as a working mother suffering from depression and someone who romanticizes home and family. She offers no coherent identity; instead, the zine churns out multiple personas, many, as with the welfare mother/lover/pin-up girl, layered on top of one another in the collage fashion typical of grrrl zines' aesthetics.

As Martens's zines demonstrate, mama zines offer alternative narratives to those told in mainstream parenting publications. They publicize varied emotions, not only happiness but also many emotional responses to parenting that are essentially prohibited in mainstream publications, such as deep ambivalence—even intense sadness—about motherhood and children. For instance, Lauren Eichelberger of *Are We There Yet?* describes early motherhood as "the hardest time in my life. I don't remember a lot of happiness. I remember a lot of struggle. I was tired, I was depressed. It was all very confusing. None of the books seemed to talk about me. I did not want to be a mom but it was too late."[82] Sometimes the ambivalence or sadness are contextualized in terms of the personal experiences of exhaustion or depression; other times they are linked to specific socioeconomic or cultural challenges. For instance, Jackie Regales of *Esperanza* writes a letter to her daughter in which she explains, "I've been depressed for months. I've felt trapped, anxious, lonely, isolated. I've been drowning slowly day by day. Your dad and I are barely living from paycheck to paycheck. I've spent a year ministering to your every need and sacrificing my own ambitions."[83] Similarly, Noemi Martinez of *Hermana, Resist* writes a poem to her newborn son listing aspects of Martinez's Mexican upbringing that her son will never experience, from "Duranzo trees under the sun" to "the paletero/ Friday mornings/ at el mercado." She ends the poem by mentioning a fruit her son won't taste, "that fruit with the/ milky flesh./ I forget the name./ I forget."[84] The poem is filled with rich detail and language that clearly convey an experience of Mexico. This contrasts with the ending, where her description of a particular fruit dissolves into the single phrase "I forget," with no punctuation at the end, suggesting the dissolution of her connection to her Mexican heritage, or her fear of that dissolution. Having a child brings back to Martinez a culture that she fears she has lost or is in the process of forgetting. Rather than a celebration of motherhood, these authors express the grief and pain that motherhood can evoke.

The media construction of motherhood is bifurcated, featuring celebrity mothers who radiate an effortless, blissful maternity, or pathological women who kill their children: what Susan J. Douglas and Meredith Michaels refer to as "celebrity moms" and "maternal delinquents" (further versions of the "can-do" and "at-risk" designations).[85] Zines provide a space for the articulation of different models of motherhood, including the expression of depression, fear, and regret. Just as Martens attempts to destigmatize the welfare mother, so, too, do these mama zines publicize and thereby demystify the suffering that can be part of the experience of motherhood. By bringing these experiences out of a space of secrecy and presenting them publicly, these zines provide more viable subject positions for mothers.

Mama zines are not, however, all about the difficulties of motherhood. They also offer descriptions of the joys of being a mother. The pleasures they unleash are not the of the pink plastic barrette and Barbie watch variety; rather, they are constructing a semiotics of adult female pleasure. For instance, *The East Village Inky* is emphatically playful, funny, and charming. Each issue discusses not only the humorous events of the household but also Halliday's explorations of New York City—often with children in tow—to ethnic markets, museums, and, in one issue, a specialty bra store. *The East Village Inky* and zines like it show motherhood not as a space of self-abnegation and denial but as something fun for the mother and the children.

As we have seen, zines themselves are sites of pleasure—fun to create and to read—and this is sometimes a shared pleasure in mama zines when the children help create the zines. When Martens's daughter Clover was a child, *The Future Generation* often featured small drawings and captions that Clover contributed. Taking it to the next level, Victoria Law began creating a series of zines in collaboration with her daughter Siu Loong, age 5. These zines, called *Nefarious Doings in Revisionist Tourist Attractions*, document their travels and showcase photographs taken by Law and Siu Loong. Law offers narrative for the photographs, explaining some of Siu Loong's aesthetic choices, as well as the fact that creating the zines was Siu Loong's idea.[86] These zines not only *describe* the pleasures of mothering but actually *demonstrate* them, becoming a documentation of the collaboration between parent and child. If the social location of womanhood remains, as *Bust* contends, to be "the selfless keepers of compassion, moderation, serenity, and responsibility," then motherhood is an amplified version of that.[87] Motherhood may be challenging for third wavers who have grown up with a notion of the "revolution grrrl style"—with the valorization of girlhood implied in "grrrl style"—which may be why they create zines, as a way of asserting agency over the cultural meaning of motherhood.

## First-Person Singular Feminism

There has been a great deal of talk recently about the emphasis on the personal within contemporary feminism. Linda Hirshman has famously—and, to my mind, rightly—critiqued what she calls "choice feminism," an informal ideology which suggests that women's choices, "everyone's choices, the incredibly constrained 'choices' they made, are good choices."[88] This entirely individualized feminism (which is arguably more a consumer ethos than a political one) is indeed problematic, and yet it is indicative of the current late-capitalist cultural moment in which the possibilities for collective action seem so remote as to be ancient history.

As Astrid Henry explains in her excellent study of second wave and third wave feminism, *Not My Mother's Sister,* "Women entering feminism today are much less idealistic—and hopeful—about the possibility of revolutionary social change than were early second-wave feminists. Paradoxically, then, younger women may have a strong sense of their own personal power while feeling ambivalent about their power to effect real change."[89] She also shares a more personal reaction: "In looking back on this period in feminism's history [the second wave], I have often found myself feeling envious of the enthusiasm and confidence with which feminists of the early second wave were able to write about their own historical moment. One can't help but notice a great sense of exuberance in these early second-wave texts, a feeling of being part of something larger than oneself, of being an agent in history."[90] Unlike the second wavers, Henry and her cohort have a sense of individual, personal power that is unconnected to a belief in political power. As Hirshman argues, the ability to make an individual choice is more relevant to shopping than to social justice. Henry and Hirshman are identifying an important set of characteristics of this cultural moment, which has led to a feeling in many quarters that something is missing from the third wave, a sense of political commitment, theoretical rigor, and/or agency.

I take up the issue of the activist potential of grrrl zines and the third wave more fully in chapter 5, but I want to spend a moment here reflecting on the significance of the personal emphasis in these zines. Henry has referred to third wave writings as "first-person singular feminism," a feminism that is obsessed with itself to such an extent that it might not even fit the label "feminist."[91] I suggest that this "first-person singular" quality need not be seen as the third wave's bankruptcy. These grrrl zines *are* deeply invested in personal reflection, but this is not mere naval gazing. There are other, and perhaps more optimistic, ways to read what's happening in grrrl zines. To a certain extent, the focus on the personal operates like second wave consciousness-raising, allowing individual girls and women to recognize inequities in their own lives and then begin to articulate them to others so that outrage—and then activism—can emerge. For example, Jenny San Diego recognizes inequalities based on body image so that she can begin to agitate for change. Zines, then, can be seen as laying the foundation for activism.

In addition, some of these zines do operate within a more familiar political framework. Mama zines, for instance, are an integral part of the mothers' movement, a broad-based activist effort at social change promoting "the well-being and empowerment of mothers and their fami-lies."[92] Martens's *The Future Generation* has a clear political impetus, from critique of welfare reform to making the activist community more sup-portive of parents and children. Similarly, when Law felt shut out from the activist community because of her responsibilities as a mother, she began creating zines as activist spaces for herself and other mothers. Her collaborative zine *Mama Sez No War*, for instance, allowed her and other mothers to voice their resistance to the invasion of Iraq, even if the au-thors' parenting responsibilities kept them from participating in protests.

In many mama zines, however, this political impetus may not be straightforward. These zines enact what Patrice DiQuinzio calls a "par-adoxical politics of mothering," one that "does not require for its foun-dation a univocal, coherent, and exhaustive position on mothering."[93] Indeed, Heather Hewett critiques those observers who demand unity from the mothers' movement, suggesting that "'disunity' might instead represent an expanding number of organizations and agendas."[94] In other words, unity may no longer be the most productive or functional political mode; instead, the shifting subjectivities and affiliations of the mama zine community are broadening the terrain of how we see motherhood and adult womanhood. Their interventions not only demand policy changes relevant to women and children but also construct a symbolic realm in which mothers can be angry and loving, can have fun and be imperfect, and can experience motherhood as a complex social location.

But even those grrrl zines that aren't activist, which are describing a relationship with a grandmother or the pleasures of lipstick, are perform-ing meaningful symbolic work. Indeed, that's one point I want to stress: challenges to the realm of the symbolic matter, even if they don't imme-diately result in changed material conditions. The personal emphasis of many grrrl zines and their emphasis on subjectivities that are fragmented, multiply constructed, and coalitional can be seen as meaningful creative processes and tactical moves. As discussed in chapter 5, the emphasis on the local, quirky, and uncategorizable in zines offers a counterforce to the homogenizing impulses of late capitalism. The challenge to the symbolic realm is not enough, but in a world in which power is more closely af-filiated than ever with public discourses, the ability to shape the symbolic realm has real effects. As Moore suggests in the epigraph to this chapter, if we change what it means to "fight like a girl"—and, by extension, the meaning of girlhood—then those who "think [they] can distract [them-selves] from [their] insecurities by victimizing a girl" might think again.

# 4

# "We Are Not All One"

## Intersectional Identities in Grrrl Zines

I don't have conclusions, only questions and frustrations. I'm a mess of contradictions myself—a bi-queer Asian girl madly in love with a straight white boy. I don't deconstruct, I just bask in the glow.

—Mimi Nguyen, *Slander* (1999)

These beings were not either/or, Clark Kent *was* Superman, Autobots were both robots *and* automobiles at the same time. In that vein, in real life I, too, could be more than meets the eye. Not "just" Lauren, but many Laurens, different versions of who I am, not competing with one another, but all of them calmly resting inside. Chinese *and* Jewish, and that's not a contradiction (although even I can recognize it as one hella pomo racial identity), neither is having queer gender/s and sexuality/ies necessarily a cause for conflict.

—Lauren Jade Martin, *Quantify* #5 (2003)

Grrrl zines are a space for girls and women to articulate complex identities, with attention to the intersections of race and ethnicity, gender, sexuality, class, and history. As a number of scholars have noted, "multiculturalism" and "diversity" are now popular, pervasive ideas that have, in the post–civil rights, post–black power era, been drained of radical political power, becoming individualized, apolitical tropes linked to brand identities and market demographics.[1] Asian iconography appears on merchandise from tattoos to t-shirts, Mexican music and language have become affiliated with food sales ("Yo quiero Taco Bell"), and hip-hop music is used to market every kind of product to white Americans.[2]

The visibility of such pop culture characters as Dora the Explorer, not to mention President Barack Obama, have been taken by many in the corporate culture industries and the political realm as evidence that we are in a post–race era, an era in which we've transcended race—or at least we're getting close.[3] As Mimi Nguyen observes in her zine *Slant*, "in the day and age of transnational cultural commodification, the market value—both material and cultural—of 'difference' is amazing."[4]

The incorporation of images of "diversity" into consumer culture has meant the erasure of an understanding of structural problems, a phenomenon that Patricia Hill Collins refers to as "the new colorblind racism."[5] In other words, a common assumption is that, because white Americans eat at Taco Bell and feel comfortable with Oprah Winfrey, the United States no longer has a race problem. This despite the continuing prevalence of systemic inequalities based on race and ethnicity. As feminist media scholar Sarah Banet-Weiser explains:

> Empowerment is thus discursively figured in at least two ways in this historical moment: as media visibility and market demographic. It is true, however, that there is a particular lack of substance that supports these representations for the number of people of color living below the poverty line in the United States continues to increase, women continue to make only 78 cents to the dollar of their male counterparts, and sexism and racism seem to be as institutionalized as ever.
>
> There is, however, no lack of the *image* of diversity and gender within media culture.[6]

The image of diversity that's prevalent in mainstream media is both apoliticized and flattened. It is the newest guise of a backlash culture, the image of success—empowerment as media visibility—masking widespread failures.[7]

The zines I examine in this chapter are closely attuned to the paradoxes of this cultural moment, and they offer sophisticated responses. They respond to the flattening of race, ethnicity, and gender in mainstream discourses by presenting identities that are not merely complex but intersectional, with attention to how various identity categories interlock and affect one another. They respond to the de-politicizing, market-driven discourses by making race, ethnicity, and other aspects of their social locations vibrantly political, attending to the larger institutions, power structures, and histories that shape their subjectivity.

Zines discussed in this chapter describe identities that don't fit into familiar cultural narratives or stereotypes—identities that are, as the epigraphs suggest, "a mess of contradictions" and "more than meets the eye." This chapter builds on many of the ideas from chapter 3, in particular the notion of grrrl zines as spaces for girls and women to articulate fragmented identities that they aren't trying to reconcile. These zines go further, describing and mobilizing identities that demand an intersectional approach, and in so doing they illustrate feminist theory on the ground. There is not an expectation of universally shared opinions or experiences within these zines, nor is there an expectation of individual consistency. In the excerpt from *Slander* cited in the epigraph, Mimi Nguyen isn't coming to conclusions about her complex identity, "just bask[ing] in the glow." Similarly, Lauren Jade Martin rejects the notion that the various parts of her identity are competing for prominence, instead seeing them as "calmly resting inside." Both zinesters allow their identities to be multifarious and ambiguous. Their zines provide a space for them to spin out multiple possibilities rather than pin down any sort of essential or "true" identity (Martin resists the notion of being "'just' Lauren") or transcend the specifics ("Chinese *and* Jewish, and that's not a contradiction").[8]

As discussed in other chapters, these zinesters use cultural tools that are ready-to-hand to create these images of complexity, as when Martin describes her identity in terms of the children's toys and narratives of Superman comics and Transformers. She takes cultural materials that were not created with her in mind—a girl like Martin arguably wasn't even considered as a potential consumer of these products and narratives—and creatively reappropriates them for her own purposes. In Transformers and Superman, she finds models of identities that aren't *either/or* but *both/and*: transient, cumulative, and intersectional. Just as Transformers aren't expected to pick sides—are you more car than robot?—so, too, does Martin proclaim her inability to reduce and simplify herself. She is all the things she is, and she can deploy the various aspects of her identity tactically; indeed, the combination of factors benefits her rather than functioning as a negative aberration.[9] She's aided in her creative use of cultural materials by the fact that zines like *Quantify* aren't as constrained by a capitalist marketplace as magazines like *Jane*. Readers are advised not to look to these zines for the real girl but to look to them for complex, theoretically rich constructions that are grappling with individual subjectivities meeting the politics and history of social locations.

Grrrl zines that examine intersectional identities often offer a kind of vibrant feminist theorizing, an articulation of intersectional theory that is methodologically and visually different from that emerging from many mainstream third wave feminist publications. Girls and women of color are forced on a continual basis to confront and grapple with intersectionality. Though every chapter in this book features zines by girls and women of color, the zines here are doing a specific kind of work: they are illustrating theories and tactics of intersectionality and putting these theories into practice in particular ways, using the characteristics—such as materiality, visual aesthetics, embodied community, comfort with process—that make the zine medium distinctive.[10]

## Intersectionality

Intersectionality has been one of the key theoretical ideas of contemporary feminism. The idea is important enough that it's been incorporated into mainstream feminist discourse (virtually every major feminist organization in the United States acknowledges intersectionality in its mission statement) as well as scholarly discourse, and it has been a foundational concept for the third wave.[11] Although the term was coined by critical legal scholar Kimberlé Crenshaw in 1989, the concept has been part of the women's rights activism of women of color in the United States since at least the nineteenth century.[12]

The notion of interlocking or simultaneous oppressions gained currency in the 1980s through the writings of U.S. third world feminists, such as the Combahee River Collective. In 1983, the collective argued, "we are actively committed to struggling against racial, sexual, heterosexual, and class oppression and see as our particular task the development of integrated analysis and practice based upon the fact that the major systems of oppression are interlocking. The synthesis of these oppressions creates the conditions of our lives."[13] Crenshaw developed the idea further; the notion of intersectionality explicitly rejects the idea of categories of identity as being separable and additive. Instead, this concept proposes that any individual's identity exists at the intersection of multiple identity categories, and that when identity categories meet or intersect they change qualitatively, so that, for instance, an African American woman experiences racism differently than an African American man, and sexism differently than a white woman. Crenshaw argues the need for intersectional analysis: "Contemporary feminist and antiracist discourses have failed to consider the intersections of racism and patriarchy. . . . The experiences of women of color are frequently the product of intersecting patterns of racism and sexism, and . . . these experiences tend not to be represented within the discourse of either feminism or antiracism."[14] Intersectional analysis allows for more complex accountings of individual life experiences and for tracking the political valences that shape individual experiences. Not limited to race and gender, the concept of intersectionality allows for analysis of multiple identity categories and the ways in which they influence each other.

As I discuss throughout this volume, many of the originating texts of third wave feminism address intersectionality as a foundational concept. Rebecca Walker's "Becoming the Third Wave," for instance, begins with the Anita Hill–Clarence Thomas hearings as a case study in the necessity for feminist and antiracist politics that encompass race and gender. In addition, all third wave anthologies—which have functioned as the canonical publications of third wave feminism—offer a diversity of voices, not allowing white feminists to be the de facto spokespersons.[15] Black feminist scholar Patricia Hill Collins explains that "intersectional paradigms view race, class, gender, sexuality, ethnicity, and age, among others, as mutually constructing systems of power. Whereas all of these systems are always present, grappling with their theoretical contours is far more difficult than merely mentioning them."[16]

Collins's point can be applied to the problems with many third wave texts that address intersectionality: they mention it without "grappling with [its] theoretical contours."[17] Many of the autobiographical writings of third wave feminists, such as those published in anthologies like *To Be Real*, *Listen Up*, and *Colonize This!*[18] offer more description than analysis. The description is a useful starting point; for instance, in my teaching I often return to Sonja D. Curry-Johnson's essay in *Listen Up*, in which she explains, "As an educated, married, monogamous, feminist, Christian, African American mother, I suffer from an acute case of multiplicity." She expresses the need for a place in her life where she can "bring my whole self to the table." This is meaningful and useful, but it doesn't go far enough, relying on the notion of "multiplicity"—which suggests an additive understanding of identity—rather than the notion of intersectionality, which demands a tracking of symbolic and institutional power structures and their influence on individual lives. The theoretical grappling that Collins calls for is taking place in the writings of U.S. third world feminist scholars and in these grrrl zines.

In some cases, zines are a site where this theoretical work happens because they aren't bound by the formal or editorial constraints of mainstream publications and media. A zine creator like Lauren Jade Martin, for instance, is able to produce dozens of zines over the course of many years, giving her more space and time to explore ideas than what is allowed to a contributor to an anthology like *Listen Up*. Indeed, it's interesting to trace Martin's life in zines, because she begins creating them while she is in high school, in zines that offer analysis based almost exclusively on her gender; in some of her high school and college zines, such as *Boredom Sucks* and *You Might as Well Live*, she doesn't even mention her ethnicity or her sexuality. Her writing becomes more complex as she moves through college, work in the nonprofit sector, and graduate school, until she's producing the *Quantify* zines which, I would argue, are as theoretically rich and sophisticated as many academic feminist publications, grappling in nuanced ways with the power structures that shape her social location and the ways in which she can manipulate those structures and work within them. Unlike contributors to an autobiographical third wave anthology, Martin has room to develop ideas and experiment; indeed, her age becomes an identity category that's at play in visible ways as her ideas change over the years—something that's not always the case in discrete essays, with their limited space and an expectation of coherence. The proliferation of zines and their accessibility and mutability as a medium make them a site for different sorts of illustrations of intersectional analysis.

Furthermore, the materiality of zines also facilitates theoretical engagement: being able to work with visual, textual, and sculptural media allows zine creators a variety of ways to address the issue of complex, politicized identity. In this chapter, as in the last, zine creators are shown to be dealing with a terrain of "densely mythogenic" images. These zines engage with images—visual and rhetorical—such as the mammy, the compliant Asian woman, the ungrateful immigrant, and the gang member, images that are "layered fictions produced by others."[19] Because the zine is not merely a text-based medium, zine creators can reproduce and alter these images, mobilizing the imagery for political ends, and the visual images can mark intersections in ways that text alone might not. Indeed, many zinesters use visual imagery in their zines to work out and explore the ways their bodies are visually available to others—a useful tactic in a culture in which race and ethnicity are often visually defined and identified.

Zines also provide a functional space for working through theoretical ideas because of the embodied community they create. Saying things that might be inflammatory to readers, trying out theories that are not fully formed, and experimenting with modes of identity that are unfamiliar—are all facilitated by the affectionate, care-driven space of the embodied community. The embodied community of grrrl zines is not automatically intersectional, but it is a diverse community in which some zinesters are able to articulate intersectional analyses. As I discuss in chapter 2, this community fits with Iris Marion Young's notion of "the ideal of city life." She problematizes the desire for sameness and homogeneity that characterizes many framings of "community." Instead of sameness, she offers the trope of the city as a space that allows for the heterogeneity not only of groups but also of the subject: "any individual subject is a play of difference that cannot be completely comprehended."[20] These grrrl zines—taken individually as well as collectively—mirror the ideal of city life. The embodied community of grrrl zines experiences dissent and critique, as when Nguyen castigates Erika of *Fantastic Fanzine* for claiming to be African American because she discovered a black ancestor, explaining, in a lengthy essay in *Slant*, "As part of her racial privilege, Erika can 'choose' to be black without having to deal with either its realities or damaging consequences in a white supremacist society."[21] These authors are calling each other on their blind spots and working to develop more inclusive, empowered approaches. In these ways, they mirror the scholarship of U.S. third world feminists and work, through their own zine methodologies, to construct communities that more fully embody third wave ideals.

The zines discussed in this chapter are related materially, ideologically, and historically to the zines discussed in other chapters in this book. The feminist publications that preceded zines and the early grrrl zines (discussed in chapter 1) made a space for women's voices that otherwise weren't heard in public; similarly, Martin characterizes the purpose of zines like *Quantify* as "knocking on the door, like, 'hello, I exist, and people like me exist so look out, cause we're here, we're not silent.'"[22] Like the other grrrl zines, these zines address the terrain of pop culture images that make certain identity configurations and social locations seem inherent and obvious rather than politically constructed and perpetuated.[23] These zines reveal the social construction of images and customs, and they denaturalize them in part by describing identities that aren't mythogenic but, rather, are complex, living, transient, and unfixed. They also denaturalize through play, through making fun, through anger—tactics and rhetorics we've seen before in grrrl zines.

And yet there are key differences between the zines in this chapter and others in the book. For one thing, the zines I examine here are often indicting feminism and the grrrl zine community for white privilege. *Quantify* isn't simply saying "hello, I exist" to the larger world but to a white feminist community. While *Action Girl* was reacting to sexism within the punk community, zines like *Quantify* are calling for *feminism* to be a different kind of space. Further, these zines describe and mobilize identities that are so unspoken in popular discourses that they're often invisible (biracial identities, queer identities, identities that are ambiguous and fluid, "hella pomo").[24] In using the zine medium to make these identities visible, zinesters articulate and illustrate intersectional theory. As Anna Whitehead explains in *With Heart in Mouth*, "oppression comes in waves and values and it builds a matrix, and we are not all one. I am not the same as a transgender Chicana dyke living in South East below the poverty line, and I never will be, and I can't claim to know what it is like to be her."[25] Indeed, as we will see, these zines interrogate easy tropes of togetherness and unity like sisterhood, attending to the overt and subtle differences between women and grounding their cultural commentary in an awareness of these differences.

In identifying and theorizing intersectional subjectivities, the grrrl zines creators I discuss in this chapter must negotiate with a complex cultural terrain. As I explain in chapter 3, grrrl zines present and construct identities not as stable and self-created but as locational, tactical, and contextual. Therefore, the zines address key components of their cultural moment—in particular, the whiteness of mainstream feminism, the purported "colorblindness" of a postracial culture, and the interplay of media representations and self-representations. In so doing, they illustrate intersectional theory on the ground, joining the abstract with the intensely personal and bringing that analytical perspective into third wave discourse in ways different from those in more traditional publications.

## Challenges to *"The White-Girl Ideal of Feminism"*

Many zines by girls and women of color offer what I consider "generative" critiques of mainstream, implicitly white, feminism: generative because in large part these kinds of critiques are where the third wave came from, from U.S. third world women. Although many white feminists over the years have made the mistake of framing these critiques as originating "outside" of feminism, these are clearly feminist critiques, aligned with feminist ideologies of inclusion and eradicating oppression.

One of the main generative contributions of these writers is that they make visible the unexamined whiteness that shapes many feminist arguments and identities. This is one way in which the intersectionality of zines is connected to third wave theorizing. *Evolution of a Race Riot* (1994) is a zine that takes a leading role in this discourse.[26] This ninety-four-page compilation zine with contributions by forty-four zinesters of color was edited by Mimi Nguyen in order to "subvert the dominant punk rock order & yes, whiteboy/girl hegemony."[27] The digest-sized zine features the standard aesthetics of typewritten and handwritten text, along with comics, photographs, and clip art. In her contribution to the zine, Chandra Ray writes:

> Many white girls talk about sisterhood. They really mean: you're my sister as long as you don't confront me on my bigotry. You're my sister as long as you know your place. (Which usually means underneath or behind you, hidden from view or maybe as a token to show how diverse your movement is.) I don't give a shit about how many meetings you've been to or how many unlearning racism workshops you've undergone. . . . Until you stop expecting women of color to conform to the white-girl ideal of feminism, I don't want anything to do with you.[28]

Ray's piece is the first in the zine, after the editor's letter, setting the tone for the zine as one of righteous anger. This two-page word-processed essay—which discusses both "white-girl" feminism and her own experiences of overt racism in and out of feminist settings—is framed by torn notebook paper with handwritten versions of key phrases from her essay. She points out the hollowness of the sisterhood that many white girls talk about: it's a sisterhood that flattens differences or, more insidiously, functions to mask racial hierarchies. As an African American woman within white feminist settings, Ray is expected to be silent about the bigotry she observes and experiences, because her speaking is seen as disruptive of the "sisterhood." Instead of being silent, however, she's verbalizing the whiteness. This is a move that appears in many zines by women of color, taking the Riot Grrrl rhetoric of challenging the "whiteboyworld" of punk and pointing out that the same kind of work needs to be done around race—both in the punk community and in feminist groups.

Ray is addressing white girls and women who are in a feminist context in which they're attempting to challenge racism and to be aware of white privilege: the women to whom she's writing, probably women she encounters at Riot Grrrl and other social justice gatherings, obviously offer up to her the fact that they've been to diversity meetings and "unlearning racism workshops." What Ray and other zinesters note is that this alone isn't enough.[29] Riot Grrrl and zines by white girls and women often frame racism as a problem that takes place in interpersonal interactions, but Ray and others demand that they recognize racism as structural. As Nguyen explains in an academic essay recounting her experiences as a zine creator, "in speaking of race and racism only in terms of personal and individual relevance, questions of history and social and structural inequality were reduced to manageable psychological scripts that too often cast girls of color into two-dimensional roles and 'social change' a matter of behavioral and attitudinal adjustments."[30] The white girls who attended "unlearning racism workshops," she argues, were reducing racism to an interpersonal dynamic, seeming to believe that if their individual views changed, then the problem was solved.

What zinesters like Ray are positing is that individualized efforts to address white privilege don't automatically result in a paradigmatic shift in feminism, and it's such a shift that Ray demands. She refuses to be "a token to show how diverse your movement is," and she observes that lip service to diversity has not undone the "white-girl ideal of feminism." Indeed, in some ways, this lip service to diversity buttresses white supremacy by both masking it and keeping it central. What Ray offers here is a critique of white feminism very similar to that made in books such as *This Bridge Called My Back*, translated into the zine medium and directed at the grrrl zine community.[31]

Many of the other zinesters who indict white feminists directly do so carefully, mitigating or moderating their anger—another deployment of tactical subjectivity. For instance, Liz McAdams writes a letter for *Evolution of a Race Riot* in which she criticizes white men and women in the punk scene for their privilege and their willingness to ignore the prevalence of racism. The left and bottom margins of the first page are framed with ten hand-drawn stars, and on the second page, she draws a large heart shape over her typed text, a heart centered over the words "there are alot of people who are actively working on this, who support us/me and listen. and i am not dismissing them. they are invaluable to me as allys and they are the reason that I'm brave enough to talk about my race in the first place." Within the heart, in a spot left blank in the typography, are the handwritten words, "this is my heart."[32]

The heart and stars are familiar iconography within grrrl zines, and by including them in her text, McAdams signals her status as an insider to

you disguise yourself as conspirators in revolution but
you need to examine who's revolution this is gonna be.
who's owning and who's not?

    i want to ask you if you ever think about
these things on yer own, becos you know they are on my
mind all the time. I can't stop thinking about them, I
can't shut my race identity/credibility on and off.
            do you realize that?
    or are you just nodding yer head again like you
    want this girl to shut the hell up?

    there are alot of people who are actively working on
.his, who support us/me and listen. AND I AM NO DISMISSING
THEM. they are *my heart* invaluable to me
as allys and they are the reason that I'm brave enough to
talk about my race in the first place.
    This letter is for the rest of you, the rest of
the punkrock community who wuld rather buy a new record by
some white boy band than read a zine that questions yer
motivations and YER ROLE in drawing the lines between
white and right and the rest of us/me.

    So I'm thinking there won't be anymore next times. YOU
need to get this now because some are fucken sick of living
in these cycles and playing these games by the rules yer
    silence and apathy creates. And oh yeah, fuck you
    for never listening.
        all my love,

        *liz*

    write me-po box 1535 mentor ohio 44061-1535

        this dialogue is
        way the fuck important.
        ask questions.

P.S.—   you had better respond. there are no
        excuses this time, ok?

pps-thanks to mimi

Page from *Evolution of a Race Riot,* courtesy of Mimi Nguyen.

the grrrl zine community. They are playful, girlish images that make her letter feel like a combination of a manifesto and an actual letter from a friend. Indeed, the drawings provide a sense of McAdams's vulnerability. She constructs a literally multilayered narrative, in which the typed text expresses her anger and the handwriting and drawings establish and re-inforce her friendly, connective intent. She ends her letter with "P.S.—you had better respond. there are no excuses this time, ok?," clearly indicating to the reader that she doesn't want to cut off conversation but to begin it.[33]

The visual construction of her letter allows her to challenge one-dimensional understandings of her message. She refuses to be reduced to a stereotype of the angry woman of color; she is angry *and* frightened, needing support to be "brave enough to talk about my race in the first place." She is frustrated *and* eager for this community—"the punkrock scene"—to be more than "yer white boy/girl world."[34] By writing her essay as a letter, she also taps into the embodied community of zines, inviting the reader, addressed in large handwritten script as "dear You," to feel personally spoken to. This is a complex approach. McAdams works around the presumed defenses of her audience, humanizing herself without diluting her message. In part, this approach is necessary because of the larger context of feminist dissent: women of color have often observed that white female groups interpret conflict as damaging and nonfunctional rather than seeing it as a deeply feminist intervention.[35] By framing herself—visually and rhetorically—as an insider, an ally, and a critic, McAdams negotiates this context.

This combination of critique and connection is reflected in other zines, as well; when Nguyen and Martin critique Riot Grrrl, both are careful not to allow their critiques to be read as outright dismissals of the movement. For instance, Martin discusses her high school experiences with Riot Grrrl, initially finding Riot Grrrl zines, music, and online discussions to be a place where she belonged and felt part of a community. She explains that this sense of belonging was facilitated by the fact that it was not a face-to-face community. When she attended her first Riot Grrrl convention in 1996, it "turned out to be a real wake-up call for me, when I could see with my own eyes just how white the composition of riot grrrl was, and could hear with my own ears the racist and classist words that came out of some riot grrrls' mouths."[36] Her experience points to one of the limitations of the embodied community of zines: Martin actually didn't realize the ways in which her own social location, as a woman of color, differed from that of many of the other participants in Riot Grrrl, until she met these participants in person.

Her experience, of course, also points to a significant limitation of white-identified feminism. When she and I spoke, Martin explained, "In the Riot Grrrl era, talking about intersections of gender and sexual orientation was a very easy intersection to make, you know it was just fine and dandy, but when you threw in race and class it got very messy and people did not really care to take it."[37] Certain identity configurations were more comfortable than others for the Riot Grrrl community; it was a space where Martin could be a queer woman, but being a queer woman of color was not as "fine and dandy." She notes in her zine that "I declared riot grrrl to be dead" and yet acknowledges, "But I had also been invigorated by the summer's conventions, by chalking feminist slogans on playgrounds on the Lower East Side . . . by meeting so many punk rock girls who rocked my world, by finally feeling a real sense of—dare I say it—community."[38] Martin articulates a complicated point of view: wanting to value those parts of Riot Grrrl that were of use to her—the sense of belonging, the power she felt as a woman—while also critiquing those parts that were alienating and painful. Like Ray and McAdams, she recognizes what's at stake in making this critique: "people [do] not really care to take it." White people, that is. And yet she's not trying to dismiss Riot Grrrl altogether.

Nguyen, too, addresses the difficulty of generative critiques of white feminism. She begins an essay called "Revolution don't come easy, honey" with the note, "I want to make it crystal clear that I totally support riot grrrl as a feminist project, period. I care, therefore I critique. If I don't push, the car doesn't go, right?"[39] Later in the same zine, she writes, "in the past, critiques i've written of riot grrrl's weak investment in social justice issues and 'leaky' antiracist analyses have been selectively mis-read as an all-out attack on riot grrrl's total political project. . . . sure, for all my criticism of riot grrrl, i still think it's one of the best things that ever happened to punk and to mostly-white young women in the past twenty years."[40] Like McAdams, Nguyen resists reductive interpretations of her critique. She can be an insider—someone who's been part of Riot Grrrl and rec- ognizes its value—*and* a critic. Indeed, her status as an insider qualifies her to make the critique, a critique that she frames as necessary and func- tional. Clearly the ideal—for Ray, McAdams, Martin, and others—is that feminism change, live up to its own ideals, that white girls and women begin doing the serious work of undermining white privilege, not just giving lip service to it. Their critiques, while biting, are well grounded, constantly pushing young feminist communities to achieve their own standard, to be more than a re-creation of "white feminist myopia."[41]

One point I want to stress is that these critiques are part of the ongoing process of third wave theory and praxis. Some of the zinesters don't use the rhetoric of feminism; Noemi Martinez, for instance, who publishes *Hermana, Resist*, explained in an interview, "I consider myself a mu- jerista and am of the thinking that feminism is planted on the backs of women of color."[42] Many, however, do explicitly claim feminism, although it's often an intersectional feminism, a "feminism *and*" kind of perspec- tive. Martin identifies herself as a feminist—"what I write, it's exclusively feminist, I don't know how someone could read it and not think it was feminist"—although she is reluctant to give that feminism a specific la- bel (third wave, liberal, postmodern): "Honestly, I'm in opposition more to particular types."[43] In *Matapang*, Michelle Peñaloza describes herself as both a womanist and a third wave feminist. Nguyen describes herself in *Slant* as "a feminist, leftist, social justice activist, cultural worker, etc."[44] The point is not that they do or don't identify as particularly third wave; the point is that because the zines are self-published, the writers are able to wrestle with feminism—develop their own frameworks and contexts for feminism—in a way that authors in an anthology framed as feminist, such as *Listen Up*, may not be able to.

These zines are fracturing the feminist façade of sisterhood and unity—the "we are all one" trope—and thereby making space for individual subjectivities and public identities that are more complex: third wave subjectivities. They destabilize whiteness and the hierarchies that hidden whiteness buttresses, thus enabling a feminist community more like the ideal of city life. All these zine creators identify with an intersectional political goal of eradicating multiple oppressions, with emphasis on race and gender, and often sexuality as well. Whether or not they call this feminist, it is a feminist mission, and one that is essential to a healthy third wave. They stand outside "the white-girl ideal of feminism." This is why the metaphor of intersectionality is useful: some aspects of their identities are shared, such as commitment to feminist politics, while others are not, such as unexamined white privilege that can lead to a response of "colorblindness."

## Colorblindness: Where Are You From?

The critiques of white feminism are related to the larger indictment these zines level at the racial and ethnic politics of this "postracial" cultural moment. Because we all know to give lip service to racial equality (this relates to the rhetoric of "sisterhood" that Ray criticizes), the workings of racism are coded, masked. The assumption underlying the notion of a postracial culture—like the idea of a "postfeminist" or backlash culture—is that the goals of civil rights and antiracist activism have been met and all is well, so we don't need to talk about those things anymore. This is a phenomenon that Collins refers to as "the new colorblind racism," and she explains: "Despite protestations to the contrary, this new colorblind racism claim[s] not to see race yet manage[s] to replicate racial hierarchy as effectively as the racial segregation of old."[45] The rhetoric has changed, as have the societal institutions themselves, but the racist power structures are intact. Zinester Madhu comments on this phenomenon of colorblindness in *Evolution of a Race Riot*:

> it is soooo easy for people to say that race is no big deal when they are
> in the majority, it is not that easy otherwise, when someone is so hyper-
> conscious about race, to the point of blatantly ignoring it, then of course
> they notice it, and by pretending they don't they are being hypocritical or
> just fooling themselves. people use things like saying they are color blind

to alleviate their own guilt. you feel bad cuz you're white and someone else is not and they get shit for it, so what do you do to make yourself feel better? you ignore their race, pretend like it's something else that is causing the problem, then you don't have to feel guilty for having the blessed white skin. (80)

What Madhu observes is that ignoring race is another version of being "hyperconscious" of it. The pretense that it doesn't exist or doesn't *matter* masks the actual workings of racism—allowing them to continue unimpeded—and perpetuates white privilege. Madhu notes that it's a lie: "of course they notice it." The pretended invisibility, then, is actually a cover for the hypervisibility of race and ethnicity. This paradoxical invisibility/ hypervisibility is one way that the new colorblind racism functions: people of color continue to be "othered" but in ways that obscure the workings of racism, pretending that "it's something else that is causing the problem." Individualizing racism, a phenomenon that zinesters as well as antiracist, feminist scholars are noting, fits in well with a market-driven system.

A number of zines address this paradoxical status. One form it takes is the "where are you from?" phenomenon, which both Nguyen and Peñaloza describe and politicize in their zines. In her one-off zine *Matapang*, a digest-sized, individually distributed zine, Michelle Peñaloza, who identifies herself as "a Filipina American: feminist-writer-teacher-daughter-activist-⊠," discusses her experiences of being asked "Where are you from?" She explains that this is "a question I've been asked my entire life," and she maps out the form these conversations usually take in a brief, word-processed dialogue:

Person #963: No, I mean, *where are you from?*
Me: Nashville.
Person #964: Okay . . . well where are your parents from?
Me: Oh. They met in Detroit (*smirk—Hmmmm. What are you really trying to ask me?*)
Person #965: (*Awkward silence/uncomfortable shifting/averted eyes/defiant annoyance*)
Me: (*Just go ahead and say it! Why are you not white or black and in MY country?*)

The numbers designating the person asking the question increase throughout the dialogue, suggesting the excessive number of times

Peñaloza has had to rehearse this same conversation. The emotional response of the questioner is a variable, but the basic structure is unchanging. By offering this conversation as a template, Peñaloza takes this personal encounter and exposes its political workings. Part of why it's so insidious—its politics so masked—is that, as Peñaloza writes, "it seems like an innocuous question to whoever asks me." Each questioner believes that he or she is simply curious. But the fact that it is "a daily question" means that each questioner is actually reproducing a common script, not responding to individual curiosity. In fact, Peñaloza reveals individual curiosity to be a culturally constructed phenomenon with political origins and consequences. She explains that the constant questioning is productive of a "state and status as *foreign* in the place of [her] birth and citizenship." The questioning, masquerading as simple curiosity, actually creates and perpetuates foreignness, otherness. Peñaloza continues: "There is an invisible power structure embedded in that question; having the audacity and privilege to ask, *'Where are you from?'* means having the power to assert, *'Obviously, you don't belong here but I do.'"*[46]

Nguyen's story, described in *Slander* (1999), has a slightly different inflection. *Slander* is a quarter-sized zine that Nguyen created as a replacement for her earlier zine, *Slant*. She explains that, in her experience, the "where are you from?" question typically functions as a come on, "nothing short of 'hey baby' in disguise."[47] Rather than offering a conversational template as Peñaloza does, Nguyen re-creates a specific encounter with a stranger at a restaurant. When she tells him that she's from Vietnam (deciding, she explains, "to forego the smart-ass answer (Minnesota)"), he asks her to recommend Vietnamese writers, and then French ones. When Nguyen declines and turns away, she explains:

> He gets resentful. I can tell he is fuming. It's common enough, men expect you to be available, flattered by their attention, they want you to jump when they speak, open wide, they imagine you to be public property just because you are out in public. We are supposed to make nice, be grateful, be submissive. I'm used to this. . . . I expect to be accused of unfriendliness, another complaint about women I always hear. I don't care. I hardly want to be the accommodating Asian woman just to assuage a stranger's wounded male ego.[48]

This stranger responds, however, by saying, "You know, a lot of men died fighting for your country." Nguyen describes her visceral, shocked reaction, and then her retort: "So what, you want me to be grateful? *Does that mean I'm supposed to fuck everyone who survived?*"[49] Like Peñaloza, she recognizes this personal encounter as politically powerful, but she takes a different approach to unmasking the politics propelling this repeated conversation. She politicizes in part by historicizing.

Unlike Peñaloza, Nguyen doesn't explain to her reader what's disturbing about this interaction but allows this story's placement in her zine to make the indictment. Much of *Slander* #7 addresses the commodification of Vietnam as a tourist destination for white American vacationers, and she offers the "where are you from?" story immediately after a critique of a Lonely Planet video called "The Vietnam Experience." The juxtaposition is meaningful. Both stories are word-processed neatly on visually simple pages so that the emphasis is on the content, and both reveal the historical legacy and contemporary workings of U.S. imperialism. Through reading the zine (and it's likely that a reader of *Slander* might have encountered one of Nguyen's other zines and so have a broader context for understanding her), the reader knows that Nguyen is an immigrant from Vietnam. Nguyen's presence in this country is connected to a particular history of imperialism, and the responses she gets from white Americans are shaped by that history as well. Through her writings in *Slander* about representations of Vietnam on television, in public memorials, in conversations, and in her own family's life, she exposes the ways in which Vietnam has been incorporated into the apolitical discourse of the marketplace. Part of this incorporation—the marketplace work of contemporary imperialism—involves the perpetuation of particular stereotypes of the Asian American woman, and this is one common way that Nguyen encounters this imperialism. She's routinely identified as a sweet, exotic Asian woman, and when she refuses that narrative framing, she often faces anger and hostility.

It's evident from this story that she does often refuse that framing, and refuse it emphatically. Her response—*"Does that mean I'm supposed to fuck everyone who survived?"*—makes visible one of the agendas underlying the stranger's questioning of her and definitively takes Nguyen out of the discourse of the accommodating Asian woman. The stranger incorporates her into an imperialist narrative, one that implies that her body is his property because of the particular racist, sexist, and nationalist discourses that the mythogenic image of the Asian woman upholds. The oppression Nguyen is experiencing is operating on multiple levels simultaneously; it is, in other words, intersectional, and her own recuperation of a complex identity demands that her response be equally intersectional, both refusing the narrative the stranger imposes and offering her own, grounded in history.

Both Nguyen and Peñaloza unmask the "innocence" of their question-ers, revealing what is presumed to be an individualized encounter as a common cultural script that serves a number of racist, imperialist func-tions. The question marks them as hypervisibly "foreign," ethnic others whose actual belonging—U.S. birthplace, U.S. citizenship—therefore be-comes invisible. Both stories also reveal that, although this othering may not be overtly hateful—indeed, some of the questioners may believe they are being complimentary by expressing interest—it is still a form of de-humanization, commodification, what bell hooks refers to as "eating the Other."[50] The stories show the workings of racism and sexism in a "col-orblind" late-capitalist culture. It's noteworthy that both Peñaloza and Nguyen frame these conversations as not always happening with white questioners: the man in the restaurant in *Slander* is African American, and Peñaloza observes that the people who interrogate her are "not just white people."[51]

Nguyen and Peñaloza aren't reducing the problems of negotiating within a "postracial" culture to whites versus everyone else; instead, they note that a colorblind perspective can affect anyone. When someone believes that racism is a problem that has been solved—or that only affects certain populations (i.e., African Americans rather than Asian Americans)—then they don't recognize the loaded politics propelling their questioning of Peñaloza and Nguyen. The zines make those underlying political motiva-tions visible.

The invisibility/hypervisibility paradox doesn't involve only race or ethnicity. Martin's zine *Quantify* is a quarter-sized, neatly word-processed zine that often features card stock, screen-printed covers, and lengthy essays. She uses her zine to articulate her experience of being in the world in a body that's multiply "anomalous, androgynous, at times even amorphous"—in terms of gender, ethnicity, and sexuality.[52] In *Quan-tify* #4, she describes the reactions this ambiguity triggers in the world: "'What the fuck *is* that thing?' people sneer as I pass them by. Sometimes I am invisible; that is, sometimes people look right through me. Mostly people stare and I am right at center-stage, in the spotlight, vulnerable & up for inspection, pressed to please explain myself."[53] Because her body isn't legible according to standard stereotypes, strangers attempt to place her in familiar narrative frames, to label her, and she lists some of these labels that are called out to and at her as she walks through New York

City: " 'Sexy Chinita!' 'Psst . . . hey sweetie,' 'Fuckin' faggot,' 'Hey Chinese girl,' 'Mira mira, ¿como se llama?' 'Is that a guy?'"[54]

The question implied in Martin's public encounters—"What are you?"— is another version of the "Where are you from?" query that Peñaloza and Nguyen expose. Both questions reveal the effort to pin people down to flat, simplistic, easily categorizable identities. Martin refuses the flattening, even as she acknowledges the dangers of doing so. Her visibility in an ambiguous body makes her vulnerable; indeed, she and other zinesters note that the ambiguous body becomes a public spectacle because making a body a spectacle is a process by which bodies are disciplined and contained in appropriate (if invisible) hierarchical structures. Most of the reactions Martin lists place her in social locations that are dangerous because of being an ethnically exoticized sexual object ("Sexy Chinita!") or possessing a sexual identity that is seen as deviant ("Fuckin' faggot"). Similarly, in a later zine she notes, "All the Laurens get harassed."[55] Martin's experiences give the lie to the notion of the colorblind society. If we were truly postracial and postgendered, then people wouldn't care "what" Martin was—there wouldn't be the drive to pin her down to clear and unambiguous racial and gendered categories, but those categories retain their appeal because they continue to designate status and power.

Simplistic racial and gender categories correlate to a set of cultural narratives into which individuals can be placed. Martin's experiences, like Nguyen's, point to the power of the realm of the symbolic—the power of certain stereotypes to shape what's available to see and to feel, and to shape the notion of "normal" and "natural." As they negotiate within public spaces, these zinesters are constantly bumping up against these stereotypes and having to negotiate with them. What their zines reveal are the ways in which these stereotypes operate. They also reveal the ways in which zine creators can use the densely mythogenic material of their culture to resist and to create tactical subjectivities and intersectional identities.

## *Who Are You? Stereotypes and Self-Representations*

The stereotypic images of the dominant culture are omnipresent in these zines, in subtle and overt ways, and the zinesters expose them, resist them, and leverage their own self-representations against them. Indeed, these zines reveal the creative and sophisticated ways that girls and women can engage with this cultural material, from stereotypes evoked in advertising imagery to more ephemeral stereotypic notions like that of the silent Asian woman, and use that material as part of their own identity construction. Stereotypes and self-representations are almost always intertwined in these zines, because the stereotypic images and ideas are some of the raw material zinesters have to work with, and they are components of the visual construction of race and ethnicity.

One example of creative engagement with stereotypic imagery is a full page in *Slant* on which Nguyen reprints and critiques a newspaper article on "Who Were the Heroes of Vietnam?" The article takes up the left half of the page, and the right side features Nguyen's handwritten commentary, distinctive visually and in terms of its content. Four smiling white faces are featured in the newspaper article, with each interviewee identifying American soldiers and citizens as the "heroes of Vietnam." In fact, the one interviewee who says, "You had heroes on both sides," clarifies that what he means is that the American soldiers who fought *and* the draft resistors were both heroes. There is no sense at all in any of the answers that the Vietnamese themselves were even human beings in this war. When one commentator notes that the heroes were "the guys and gals who were over there in the jungles and swamps," she clearly implies that those "guys and gals" were American citizens, not the people for whom "the jungles and swamps" might have been home. Their responses to the question both reiterate standard notions of heroism and naturalize a certain definition of "we." The presumed readership—and, by extension, the presumed American who would be interested in this question—is white, nonimmigrant. The interviewees seem cheerful, sincere. Like the people who ask Peñaloza and Nguyen "Where are you from?" these interviewees seem to believe that they are offering completely individualized opinions without a larger political context. They demonstrate no awareness that their statements might be in any way exclusive, and the only controversy they seem aware of is that between the soldiers and the war protestors.

In response, Nguyen articulates the unspoken assumptions about Vietnamese people that underlie the interviewees' answers. She writes, "in books and movies we are: gooks, VC commies, slant-eyed slopes, monkeys in trees, speaking in 'alien' tongues. (making it easier to mis-translate or ignore our existence in the world, in the present.)." She goes on to say, "sometimes in movies we are lucky enough to live long enough to fuck rambo/chuck norris before we die for the love of an 'american.'"[56] Nguyen clearly identifies and indicts the stereotypes of the Vietnamese that make it possible for the newspapers' interviewees to ignore this population entirely in considering the question of the "heroes of Vietnam." Nguyen and her family—refugees—are not only not legible within a script of heroism, which is reserved for white Americans, they are invisible—"disappeared," she writes in thick felt-tip marker print. Mainstream media imagery, according to Nguyen, makes it "easier to mis-translate or ignore our existence in the world," and the newspaper article confirms this. Furthermore, the stereotypic images of the sexually available (and also disposable) Asian woman who "live[s] long enough to fuck rambo/chuck Norris" undergirds the sexual predation women like Nguyen experience, the kind of predation she describes in the "Where are you from" encounter in *Slander*. Her handwriting—with mistakes crossed out but left visible, and with selected words emphasized with felt-tip marker or hand-drawn arrows and boxes—offers a visual earnestness that undercuts the apparent sincerity of the newspaper interviewees. They come across as slick, ignorant, and unfeeling, while Nguyen's anger and pain are much more visually evident. Nguyen reveals the ways in which

Page from *Slant*,
courtesy of Mimi Nguyen.

corporate media artifacts can perpetuate the intersectional oppression she faces, and she responds by making that oppression visible and bringing her own critical perspective into the conversation.

Other grrrl zines also demonstrate complex negotiations with racist and sexist cultural iconography, even when this iconography is communicated through ephemera like advertising. *With Heart in Mouth* #3 demonstrates one zinester's grappling with expressing her own identity in a cultural context of stereotyped imagery. Incorporating original woodcut prints, handwriting, line drawings, iconic pop culture imagery, and typed text cut into strips and rearranged on the page, *With Heart in Mouth* communicates not simply through words but through a range of visual tropes. The zine is in digest format, made of plain white paper. Its creator, Anna Whitehead, identifies as a biracial black woman, and her zine explores the

Last summer I became involved in a fledgling people-of-color (poc) collective in DC, tentatively called the anti-capitalist people of color. *see earlier for more discussion of this (the wacky concept.* collective's short term goals were something along the lines of organizing a conference to coincide with the well-known (and well known to be underrepresented by racial minorities) NCOR—National Conference for Organized Resistance. I'm not really sure what acpoc's long term goals were... ...I guess something like world peace and racial unity. There were a plethora of problems with acpoc by the end of July, I was growing more and more dissatisfied particularly with some of the males in the group who I felt were either domineering or unrealistic. However, one of the main problems with acpoc was its naïve assumption— (held by most of us when we entered that situation, including me) that we were all one oppressed people. This manifested itself in our action-plans for outreach. Week after week we congregated in our meeting space in the dc imc building and discussed how we would reach "our," people" for the conference. "Our people" all apparently lived in South East DC. (For those who don't know the political geography of our nation's capital, this area is extremely black and latino.) "Our people" would transform into "those people" as we would sit and discuss how to make South East residents realize the detrimental effects capitalism was having on their lives as poor people of color. See, because we understood this — we were all one oppressed people, remember? We all had the unlucky fate of being born with minority status, so therefore we all had the same oppression **lawzee!** —it was just that *some of* mekkin' pancakes is us had taken the path to punk-rock thing ah does, than redemption, and were now in a better position to which dere aint no better, effen ah does explain to "those people" how their lives were say so! Jes mah flour being AUNT JEMIMA corrupted by our common and water on de griddle PANCAKE FLOUR enemy (THE MAN). and——whuf! dey's done honey. *Grab em!*

What we were doing in our little secluded imc meeting space was using body as an identifier. We were assuming that the social significance that has been placed on each of our bodies was not only the same, but strong enough to bind us to anyone in the same socio-political situation dictated by their body. That is, economics, geography, family background, culture, etc, became irrelevant. As

Page from *With Heart in Mouth*, courtesy of Anna Whitehead.

complexities of being a radical person of color involved in feminist and other kinds of political activism.

The words and the visual elements of this zine tell competing stories, offering a point and counterpoint perspective. One essay in the zine illustrates this dynamic particularly well. Whitehead discusses her experiences in a "people of color collective" and her recognition that identity is much more complicated than the group had been treating it. As her words (word processed and then cut into strips) describe the conflicts in the organization, the imagery tells a concomitant story: she has arranged the strips of text on top of a set of indeterminately old advertising images for Aunt Jemima Pancake Flour. The images feature a stereotyped "Aunt Jemima," who is in every way enacting the mammy icon. In addition to a picture of this dark black woman with wide white eyes and smile, holding a stack of pancakes that is at least three times taller than she is (surrounded by a swarm of white children holding plates), the ad includes dialect text: " 'Lawzee!' mekkin' pancakes is th' mos' impawtines thing ah does, than which dere aint no better, effen ah does say so! Jes mah flour and water, on de griddle and—whuf! dey's done honey. *Grab em!*"[57]

Whitehead's words are so fully integrated into the Aunt Jemima imagery that in some places it is difficult to follow the text. Whitehead's sentences are divided into small, two- and three-word chunks so that they don't obscure relevant parts of the imagery; therefore, the reader is forced to concentrate, to reread; it is unclear what path the words follow. In addition, it's not always possible to distinguish between Whitehead's words and the words of the Aunt Jemima advertisement; this deliberate obscuring blurs the distinctions between Whitehead and Aunt Jemima. On the one hand, this formatting forces the reader's engagement with the text; because of the concentration required to follow the narrative, the reader becomes a more active participant in the essay. At the same time, on the other hand, this formatting dramatizes a counternarrative. While Whitehead's words are fragmented and mobile, and give the illusion of being able to be blown off the page, the words of the advertisement are in one coherent block near the middle of the page; they assert a presence that the rest of the text seems to orbit around, or to be fragmented by. Whitehead's language is shattered and scattered by the smiling image of Aunt Jemima; the stereotyped dialect usurps her voice. Yet clearly, Whitehead is in charge of this text. Her writing destabilizes the notion of the body as identifier, offering an intelligent postmodern deconstruction of bodily binaries. And even as she does this, the image of Aunt Jemima speaks a more complicated story; even as Whitehead's narrative asserts her own middle-class background and her "two married parents with PhDs," the imagery tells the story of a culture that will group her as a black female with Aunt Jemima, that will read her according to bodily stereotypes that may bear no relation to her actual body but that will come to be imposed on her physicality.

There are no pictures of Whitehead in the zine, but Aunt Jemima appears three times in different places. Aunt Jemima is an overwhelming icon against which African American women continually have to defend themselves and from which they must differentiate themselves. Like the compliant and eroticized Asian woman that Nguyen describes, Aunt Jemima is a densely mythogenic image that implies that African American women are asexual, unattractive, and fulfilled by domestic service to whites.[58] Whitehead never addresses the icon directly, never analyzes or explains the imagery, but it stands as a representation of voiceless, stereotyped African American womanhood. The familiarity of this image even today gives the lie to the notion that our culture has transcended race. Whitehead uses this image in order to complicate her discussion of identity and to undercut simplistic apolitical public discourse around race.

Unlike Whitehead, other grrrl zinesters do offer visual representations of themselves in their zines, photographs and drawings that directly or indirectly engage with and counter the stereotypic images that pervade dominant culture. These images are strategic: self-representation may seem to be offering a clear and unambiguous sense of who these zinesters are, but it's important to remember that these artifacts of self-representation are as carefully crafted as anything else in the zines. Indeed, one thing that happens in a number of zines is that by including images of themselves, the zinesters paradoxically hide as much as they reveal. Under pretense of self-disclosure, they obscure and disrupt the spectacle of their own public visibility.

For instance, Nguyen offers a variety of images of herself in her zines. The full-page cover of *Slant* #5 features a drawing of two Asian American women carrying weapons—a gun and a baseball bat. One has a shaved head, the other scraggly ear/chin-length hair, and this second image looks not unlike the drawing of Nguyen (labeled as such) inside the zine. Both women are fierce, staring directly at the reader, smiling knowingly. These figures directly challenge the notion of the docile, compliant Asian woman who might "fuck rambo/chuck norris," debunking both raced and gendered stereotypes.

They resonate with historical images she also includes in her zines: in both *Slant* and *Slander* she features drawings from a book about the Trung sisters, "Vietnamese women warriors . . . who led the first of many uprising[s] against the Chinese Han in 40 AD and kicked total ass."[59] These pictures show women expertly wielding swords and toppling male warriors, and they make up the front and back covers of *Slander* #7. They demonstrate a historically specific, intersectional reworking of stereotypes of gender and ethnicity, with a family resemblance to some that we've seen already, and they provide a different context for Nguyen's self-representations than the standard media imagery she routinely debunks.

*Slander* also features visual images of Nguyen. *Slander* is slightly different from Nguyen's previous zines, such as *Slant* and *Evolution of a Race Riot*. The zine is smaller, ostensibly more confessional, a more seamless

Cover of *Slant,*
courtesy of
Mimi Nguyen.

Cover of *Slander*, courtesy of Mimi Nguyen.

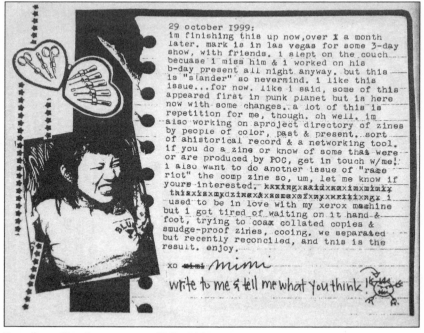

29 october 1999:
im finishing this up now, over ½ a month
later. mark is in las vegas for some 3-day
show, with friends. i slept on the couch
becuase i miss him & i worked on his
b-day present all night anyway. but this
is "slander" so nevermind. i like this
issue...for now. like i said, some of this
appeared first in punk planet but is here
now with some changes. a lot of this is
repetition for me, though. oh well. im
also working on a project directory of zines
by people of color, past & present. sort
of a historical record & a networking tool.
if you do a zine or know of some that were
or are produced by POC, get in touch w/me!
i also want to do another issue of "race
riot" the comp zine so, um, let me know if
yours interested. ~~xxxxxxxxxxxxxxxxxxxxx~~
~~thixxisxmxdxinexxxsomexxfxmyxwritinxx~~ i
used to be in love with my xerox machine
but i got tired of waiting on it hand &
foot, trying to coax collated copies &
smudge-proof zines, cooing. we separated
but recently reconciled, and this is the
result. enjoy.

xo ~~mimi~~ mimi

write to me & tell me what you think!

Page from *Slander*, courtesy of Mimi Nguyen.

merging of personal and political reflections, and the photographs she includes seem to participate in this project. She doesn't figure herself as an icon of female resistance and aggression, as with the cover of *Slant*; instead, she seems to be rehabilitating a kind of familiar femininity, as we saw with zines such as *Grit & Glitter*. Throughout the zine, she pastes small photos of herself making a number of different facial expressions—surprised, aloof, or laughing with her boyfriend. They're often hard to interpret; indeed, one particularly ambiguous photograph that she pastes near the conclusion of the introduction to the zine shows her with her hands out to her sides as if pushing something away, grimacing with closed eyes and teeth bared. She could be enacting anger, physical exertion, or something else entirely.

Many of the photos give the feeling of having been taken in a photo booth—they offer a sense of playful spontaneity. At the same time, they seem almost like film stills, significant staged moments frozen without their explanatory context. As such, they offer a portrayal of Nguyen that is intriguing and glamorous: her long, dark hair, lipsticked lips, and necklace suggest pictures of classic film stars.

Indeed, near the end of the zine she muses about such a representation: "I want to be all surface and celluloid, a walking film still vaguely recalling b&w flicks in which the girl—sick and tired of having to look over her shoulder, wary and watchful—strolls away from the burning building a just-lit cigarette in hand." This is at the end of a lengthy zine—eighty pages—that has been concerned with complex representations, with using visual, rhetorical, historical, and other tools to counter racism and sexism. At the end of all this complexity, she muses on the possibility of being flat, "all surface," an image that might offer escape from the constant effort of having to struggle for her humanity to be recognized. And yet she longs for a particular kind of flatness, one that is opaque and dangerous: she wants to be the unreadable woman whose feeling of being "sick and tired" leads her, perhaps, to burn down a building or at least to light her cigarette from its flames. She is drawing on the reclaiming of the "bad girl" that emerges in zines like *Bust*; however, she's also longing for the opacity of "the girl"— not necessarily demarcated as good or bad—in a black and white movie.

This image rejects the hypervisibility that she and other zinesters have described, and the presumptions of people in the public world that she is easily interpreted according to stereotypic narratives. It's a flatness that is a tactical mask, covering over depths that she chooses not to share—or, as the small photos throughout the zine suggest, that she chooses to share only in fragments and glimpses. Her use of visual imagery thus illustrates her multivalent attempts at self-representation in ways that prose alone can't. The images show Nguyen attempting to work out the ways in which her body is visually available to others, and what this visual availability might mean.

A series of photographic self-representations in *Quantify* also challenge visual stereotypes and the notion of a transparently readable female body. *Quantify* #5 features a filmstrip of four head shots of Lauren Jade Martin. Each picture offers only subtly different facial expressions, but Martin has used a pen to draw on the second, third, and fourth head shots—eyeliner and lipstick on the one, glasses on the next, and a mustache on the final frame. This photo montage, which accompanies her essay about being like a Transformer or Clark Kent/Superman ("more than meets the eye"), emphasizes the multiple ambiguities of her public identity: she can be female, male, or genderqueer, white or Asian, "a big ol' dyke" or "a flaming fag," depending on her performance and her accessories.[60] Indeed, this photo illustrates the notion of identity as performative rather than inherent or essential. Like Nguyen, Martin is offering bodily opacity rather than an appearance that fits a simplistic cultural script. Her body becomes a starting point, a component of an expressive repertoire, rather than something that communicates who or what she is.

Martin's playful reconfiguring of these head shots supports her assertion that her identity is "hella pomo"—not unified, essential, or fixed—and also figures her ambiguous identity as a location of potential power, something she can manipulate and have some control over. Indeed, Martin shows herself as a sort of trickster figure, making use of and undercutting expectations about identity even as these expectations shape how she is received in the world.[61] She describes the challenges of an ambiguous public presentation but also celebrates it, refusing an identity that is more easily defined. The trickster is a mobile presentation of the self that leverages cultural expectations against each other.

Image from *Quantify,* courtesy of Lauren Jade Martin.

In a two-page essay in *Quantify* #4, Martin describes her own silent responses as a trickster tactic of resistance, allowing her to shift her perceived identity. In this essay she repeats the phrase, "If I keep my mouth shut, I can pass" five times, with each repetition of the phrase prefacing an example of the kinds of passing she can do: passing as a boy, for instance, or as a Chinese immigrant. She notes, "If I try to answer back, my trickster façade faces away."[62] Withholding of her voice, then, becomes a strategy that allows her to maintain a fluidity of public identity, to "pass." Although she's always bumping up against other people's expectations, stereotypes, and assumptions, by being a sort of trickster, she is not fully constrained by these external factors. This is a key tactic to emphasize about many of these grrrl zinesters: they are forced to operate within constrained circumstances, to be sure, but those constraints do not define them or the selves they construct within their zines. In fact, the constraints often become some of the raw material that they use for their self-constructions.

There are many other examples of girls and women leveraging cultural constraints and stereotypes as part of their self-representations in their zines. For instance, in discussing her trickster role, Martin engages with the notion of silence as a tool of resistance. Silence is a component of gendered expectations for performances of appropriate womanhood: the good girl keeps her mouth shut. This expectation has particular resonance for women of color, as Asian American women often have to negotiate the stereotype of the silent Asian woman. While a common tactic within grrrl zines by white women and women of color is to emphasize voice, speaking out, several Asian American women zine creators offer a different perspective on silence, reclaiming it as a resistant response.

Nguyen, for instance, discusses silence as a means of resisting both colonizing forces and also the colorblind discourse of white feminism. Rather than simply denying the image of the silent Asian woman, Nguyen argues that silence can be an effective form of resistance, particularly when speaking can make her visible and vulnerable: "But speech (as the imagined opposite of silence) does not always = truth, okay? I think this is fucking offensive: silence is one way I've *always* resisted and I'm so fucking sick of whitegirls negating—and I mean *actively* refusing to recognize—the ways in which I resist their/*your* fucking intrusions."[63] Choosing not to share, especially in contexts where she feels she's been made into a consumable other or a hypervisible spectacle, is therefore a powerful act that both ties her to traditions of Asian womanhood and challenges the way those practices have been understood in mainstream white American culture. As discussed throughout this book, this is an example of a zinester taking a given subject position and using it as a space of resistance.[64]

Sabrina Margarite Alcantara-Tan, in contrast, offers a manifesto on loudness in her zine *Bamboo Girl*, refusing to accommodate herself to the silent stereotype. *Bamboo Girl* is a full-sized zine that has been in regular production since 1995 and that often features Alcantara-Tan's "annoyance, anger, and rage."[65] In an essay titled "On the Backlash of Asians Being Vocal," she explains: "I think that saying 'it's wrong to be so loud' totally smacks Asian feminism in the face. Sure, not everyone needs to be or has to be vocal, but for those of us who are, is it wrong to be loud? Wrong to be vocal about anger?"[66]

What we see here, as elsewhere in the world of grrrl zines, are contradictory representations without a need for consistency or closure. Nguyen advocates the tactical use of silence but also celebrates the ferocity of historical Vietnamese women warriors; Martin generates multiple incarnations of herself without settling on one "real Lauren"; Whitehead allows her words to become jumbled with Aunt Jemima advertising text. They respond to the flattening, essentializing discourses of the marketplace and the street by using that material as a means of creating intersectional identities. This is part of the "radical generativity" that Radway identifies with grrrl zines: zinesters' ability to leverage cultural expectations and discourses in sometimes surprising ways. What this work within densely mythogenic images shows, however, is that these grrrl zines are not simply constructing identities. The girls and women are shaped and constrained by their social locations, and the materials that make up these social locations become part of the zinester's toolkit or creative cultural repertoire.

In chapter 3, I conclude with a discussion of the political significance of "first-person singular feminism," the emphasis on self-description and construction that we see in grrrl zines and that has become a defining characteristic of third wave feminism. Many feminist scholars have been critical of this turn to introspection, identifying it as a regression, a denial of politics and theory. As part of her analysis of "the new colorblind racism," Collins, too, voices concern about third wave feminist rhetoric that foregrounds the personal at the expense of the political. She concludes a discussion of third wave texts such as *When Chickenheads Come Home to Roost* and *Colonize This!* with a moment of celebration and critique:

How wondrous and fearful it must be to step out into that space of possibility where you define yourself on your own terms, to craft a new
multiethnic, gender-bending, biracial, sexually dynamic, fluid personal
identity that is seen and respected by all sorts of people who seem so
different from oneself. The responsibility and potential freedom that this
promises are boundless. Yet it is obvious that these new personal identities can never occur without fundamental structural change that makes
such identities possible for everyone.[67]

Collins notes the elation that can occur when girls and women are
free to construct complex, ambiguous identities, but she warns that these
identities depend on "fundamental structural change"—change that she
implies is not necessarily part of a third wave agenda. What zines in this
chapter demonstrate is that construction of intersectional identities isn't
incompatible with theoretical analysis and attention to structural inequities. In fact, I argue that zines like *Slant, Slander, With Heart in Mouth,*
*Evolution of a Race Riot, Matapang,* and *Quantify* use intersectional analyses as a way of combating marketplace discourses of diversity that flatten
identity and perpetuate white and male privilege.

A certain presumption of innocence is pervasive in the worlds these
zinesters describe, from the white girls who want an easy sisterhood to
the interviewees who describe the heroes of Vietnam; from people asking
"Where are you from?" to those catcalling Martin on the streets. Through
visual, rhetorical, and pop cultural approaches, the zinesters in this chapter unmask the innocents and reveal the hierarchies of status and power
that the innocent façade protects and perpetuates. By articulating their
own intersectional identities, these zinesters make hidden power structures visible so that they can be addressed and altered.

In generating complex subjectivities and challenging their social locations, these zine creators, by necessity, are engaging in sophisticated, resistant ways with the symbolic terrain of their culture, a symbolic terrain
that buttresses structural hierarchies. What's more, the zines also function
in a material way to counter problematic marketplace discourses, as their
existence outside a mass-marketed capitalist system allows them to offer a
counternarrative through their creation and distribution. Since the zinesters featured in this chapter don't have to be concerned with advertisers
or focus groups, they can put forth ideas and identities that are complex,
challenging, and theoretically rich. Their work to step into what Collins
calls "that space of possibility" is linked to an agenda of social change. In

this way, their work can be seen as engaging in new forms of activism. As discussed in chapter 5, zines by girls and women deploy activist tactics that may be unfamiliar to those who are used to the activist efforts of the 1960s and 1970s social change movements, but these are activist modalities particularly attuned to the constraints and possibilities of this cultural moment.

# 5

# Doing Third Wave Feminism
## Zines as a Public Pedagogy of Hope

This magazine is about theorizing and fostering a transformation
of pop culture.

—Lisa Jervis, *Bitch* #1 (1996)

But you can do everything.
That's what I think.
Our lives are long and full and if we love and work and want, we
can do it all.
everything
everything.
  even more than we are able to imagine.

—Cindy Crabb, *Doris* #24 (2007)

In an essay called "Ohio" in *Doris* #24, Cindy Crabb muses on
a number of things—determining a turtle's age from the rings on its shell,
change in her life over the years, how she has come to reconsider her own
fears and assumptions, and the tools for social justice work that she's as-
sembled from groups she's been involved with and from her own reading.
It's not an essay with a linear trajectory; instead, it's a kind of rhizomatic
collage of thoughts, with links that work in multiple directions. The essay consists of typewritten and handwritten text surrounded by and interspersed with small illustrations, comic strips, and hand-drawn graphics
like hearts, stars, arrows, and text boxes. It is a representative grrrl zine
piece—seemingly chaotic but ultimately thoughtful, rich, and multivalent.
At the end of the essay, Crabb cites a friend of a friend who warns, "you
can't do everything you dream of. At some point you need to narrow it

down, prioritize." Crabb responds by breaking from prose into a poetic structure and offering a hopeful assertion, cited in the epigraph to this chapter, about her own and the readers' ability to, in fact, do everything, "even more than we are able to imagine."[1] This typewritten statement, framed with two small hand-drawn hearts, may not immediately seem to be making a political intervention. However, this emphatic declaration of possibility represents one kind of political work grrrl zines can do. When she suggests that "we can do it all," Crabb offers a pedagogy of hope.

Crabb's hopefulness is linked to a history of feminism and political resistance—it's part of the feminist legacy discussed in chapter 1. Crabb's optimism is a direct descendent of the radical hope expressed in many feminist publications. Although feminism can be understood as an ideology grounded in dissent and critique, the feminist impulse is ultimately a hopeful one. One of the strongest statements of radical hope comes from the anthology *This Bridge Called My Back*, in which coeditor Cherríe Moraga explains:

> But what I really want to write about is faith. That without faith, I'd dare not expose myself to the potential betrayal, rejection, and failure that lives throughout the first and last gesture of connection. . . . I am talking about believing that we have the power to actually transform our experience, change our lives, save our lives. Otherwise, why this book? It is the faith of activists I am talking about.[2]

This is a somewhat surprising assertion in *This Bridge*, a book that identifies serious problems in feminism and in the larger culture. When I read it for the first time, I wasn't expecting Moraga to begin talking about faith, a concept I associated with spiritualized passivity, not with fierce activism. And yet Moraga explains faith as a necessary component of activist work. Why would anyone do this work—engage in protest, write a book, create a zine—if they didn't believe that the world could be different than it is? If they didn't believe that we could foster real human connection, "change our lives, save our lives"?

This "faith of activists"—the belief that we can "actually transform our experience"—is at the heart of Crabb's statement, her assertion that, despite all the reasonable voices arguing otherwise, we can change "more than we are able to imagine." Crabb is clearly part of a feminist legacy. She herself identifies as such, and in this essay she explicitly discusses the importance of knowing the history of social change movements, contending that young activists need to have a sense of how social change has been accomplished in the past if they are to imagine a changed future.

But Crabb's hopeful assertion isn't simply a historical homage. She's speaking directly from—and to—the early-twenty-first century moment in which she's writing. Her statement is aligned with the utopian love letter sentiments of many grrrl zines, from the "Splendiferous Oath of Riot Grrrlz Outer Space" to the fierce disappointment and refusal to give up in *Evolution of a Race Riot*; from *Bust*'s "SEX" scrawled on a pregnant stomach to *With Heart in Mouth*'s assertion that "the world is still crazy and terrifying and filled with hope."[3] These zines make free-wheeling claims that are elating and empowering. Although Crabb and other grrrl zinesters address cultural constraints head-on and in great detail, statements like the one Crabb makes seem to dismiss such constraints easily, and in so doing, they provide a glimpse of a new paradigm, a new set of possibilities. In offering her readers this glimpse, Crabb is intervening in the symbolic realm. She is altering her readers' sense of who they are and what is possible, and this is a political intervention that can have far-reaching effects in the material world.[4] By bringing her readers along through an essay that feels like a rambling journey, Crabb is inviting them to let down their defenses, their cynicism, and to be free to imagine a better world. She offers them the feeling of possibility, and her zine becomes a primer on how to hope.

In this chapter, I consider the cultural and political work that zines like *Doris* do, the kinds of interventions they make into the world around them. These interventions are hopeful; indeed, they function as pedagogies of hope, showing the zines' readers ways to resist the culture of domination.[5] Because grrrl zines don't offer one monolithic kind of intervention but, instead, use a range of strategies, here I provide three case studies, each of which illustrates a different pedagogical model. The first is a set of narratives in the zine *Greenzine*, narratives that address violence against women. *Greenzine* offers personal stories with a political emphasis. These narratives emphasize self-revelation and publicize a healing process as both a political and personal act; they model what I am calling a "pedagogy of process." The second case study is *Bitch*, a publication that was created explicitly to bring about social change. *Bitch* demonstrates a familiar model of activism, with a third wave twist. It invites its readers to become active critics of popular culture and shows them the intellectual tools with which to do it, thus offering a "pedagogy of active criticism." The final case study is *Doris*, a zine that exhibits a new kind of activism emphasizing self-reflection and becoming fully human—changing the subject-position of the reader and thereby offering a model of intervention uniquely suited for this cultural moment. *Doris* models a hopeful, resistant subjectivity—what I term a "pedagogy of imagination"—and invites its readers to try it on. These pedagogies are doing political work. By teaching strategies for change, reflecting on their own process of creation, and providing space for seeing and feeling differently, these zines allow their readers to hope—and they show that hope can be a political intervention.

Up to now, I have considered the form and content of grrrl zines. Here I ask what these zines *do*—what sorts of cultural interventions, if any, they can make. All three sets of zines examined operate not simply through their subject matter but by offering models of how to change your thinking, your perspective on the world. They function as hybrid public/private sites of self-expression and social change aimed at a broader cultural norm rather than a specific political or electoral outcome. For these hopeful pedagogies to be effective, they mobilize embodied communities. In this chapter, I consider the zines' interventions—their tools and tactics. What I'm arguing is that the cultural work that grrrl zines do is a new kind of political work, and taking this work seriously *as* political work provides a new context for understanding not just zines but also third wave politics. In the next section, I lay out the theoretical scaffolding for this chapter, and the following sections demonstrate this theory at work in grrrl zines.

## Theoretical Context

The political work that grrrl zines do may not be immediately obvious because this work doesn't fit with models of traditional political engagement. It doesn't fit for several reasons: because grrrl zines are generally acting at the level of the symbolic order rather than at the level of institutional change, because they operate out of personal modes of expression, and because they mobilize small-scale embodied communities rather than large-scale voting blocs. Zinesters have developed these modes of engagement in part because they see that zines are intervening in a deeply cynical culture. The past twenty years have been a difficult time for activists and those concerned with social change.

Girls' studies scholar Anita Harris describes the late-twentieth century—a period starting with the Reagan era and stretching through 9/11 and beyond—in terms of "the forces of fragmentation and decollectivization that characterize social and political life in late modernity."[6] Feminist scholar bell hooks describes this moment using the term "dominator culture," meaning a culture in which the politics of hierarchy and power over others are prevalent. She argues: "A profound cynicism is at the core of dominator culture wherever it prevails in the world."[7] Indeed, this widespread cynicism—which scholars have called "the single most pressing challenge facing American democracy today"—has emerged at this particular historical juncture because of the convergence of a backlash against the social justice movements of the 1960s and 1970s and a late-capitalist, neoliberal, consumption-oriented cultural climate.[8] This climate, explains hooks, assures us that things can't ever be substantially better than they are right now, that private sector industries will solve all our problems, and that if we buy the right product, we'll feel much better. She calls this phenomenon "the pedagogy of domination."[9] This pedagogy teaches that since the world of consumer capitalism will solve our problems, we have no action to take. We can either view ourselves as being in the best possible position or, as zine creator Sarah McCarry puts it in a 2004 issue of her zine *Glossolalia*, we can see ourselves as being "completely, totally fucked and things are not going to get better."[10] Either viewpoint engenders apathy and resignation, leading to withdrawal from efforts at change.

Failure of imagination seems integral to this phenomenon: hope and a vision of a better future can come to seem almost pathetically naive.[11] In this way, cynicism forecloses social justice activism; it functions to make all forms of challenge to the status quo seem hopeless in the sense that many of us are unable either to imagine something better or to imagine that better thing actually coming into being. This translates into a cultural moment in which resistance seems limited or impossible. Feminist theory and efforts at social change, then, can appear completely outdated, irrelevant, or inadequate at the very time when they are most necessary. This is the world in which grrrl zines and third wave feminism emerged, and it's the world in which they're intervening. Because of this, grrrl zines like *Doris* are uniquely situated to awaken outrage and—perhaps more crucially—imagination, and in so doing enact what hooks and others have called for: public pedagogies of hope. hooks uses the term "pedagogy of hope" to describe the creation of hope and possibility within the realm of the classroom, but this is a concept with viability far beyond literal pedagogical spaces; indeed, I am adopting her term and broadening it to encompass the political work of grrrl zines. Pedagogies of hope—manifested in a variety of ways in grrrl zines—function as small-scale acts of resistance. By modeling process, active criticism, and imagination, grrrl zines make political interventions targeted to this late-capitalist cynical culture.

Scholars' expectations of what political work and activism look like, however, might blind us to the work that zines do. If we want a form of expression and activism that will cause large-scale social change, something equivalent to the social justice movements of the 1960s and 1970s, then we'll be disappointed in zines. Indeed, there is often a tension around this question within the zine community. Many zinesters have expressed anxiety about their zines actually making a difference in the world—an anxiety that I see as centering on the zinesters' sense that their zines aren't participating in traditional political engagement. In the zine *Slant*, Mimi Nguyen talks about feeling useless: "I feel stupid because I wonder, stepping back, what the outcome of all my written rage will be, and I can't help but imagine that it'll be practically nil."[12] In an interview, Lauren Jade Martin shared a similar skepticism, explaining that in the world of zine creation, "I feel like the personal is an excuse for the political and anything that's personal, it's like, 'Well, it's personal, so therefore its political. I'm doing a zine, therefore I'm doing something.'" She continued, "I feel some people use [zine making] as an excuse for not doing more activist work, like, 'This is my activist work, I'm doing a zine.' People say that all the time."[13]

Scholars like Stephen Duncombe also express this anxiety, questioning whether zines actually accomplish any significant cultural work. Duncombe asserts that, in the context of dire global crises, "creating an alternative underground world—no matter how novel and supportive it is—and putting out a 'radical' zine—no matter how irreverent, expressive, and fun—seem incomplete, and woefully inadequate, responses in the face of all this disaster. There has to be something more."[14] Near the end of his book exploring the larger zine phenomenon, Duncombe wonders whether zines really make any difference, or whether they're "woefully inadequate" attempts. Elsewhere in his study, Duncombe characterizes zines as "pre-political."[15] This characterization implies a condemnation: zines are somewhat childlike, offering a perspective on the world that has potential but isn't yet mature enough to recognize the need for political actions.

I think Duncombe and the anxious zinesters are applying a model of political intervention that may not work for zines, that may, in fact, be somewhat anachronistic. Lisa Jervis, cofounder of *Bitch*, sees it this way: "It's like, we see what's happening and we just don't think that those modes of protest or activism are useful right now, and you know what, they're not, because they're not working. Our electoral system is so badly broken, that's not where we want to put our energy."[16] As I discuss later in this chapter, Jervis was interested in a form of activism that didn't involve election reform, picket lines, or the traditional kinds of protest, so she and Andi Zeisler started the zine *Bitch: Feminist Response to Pop Culture*. To judge *Bitch* using the paradigm of traditional politics would mean to miss the political work that the zine is actually doing—work that is viable, thoughtful, and keyed to this cultural context.

This question of what counts as political—or what is appropriately political—is particularly salient for grrrl zines, because the work of young women is also often not recognized as political. In the same conversation, Jervis explained, "I am so sick of being told that young women aren't active enough or aren't active in the right ways or active around the right issues. You know, if you want us to be engaged in feminism, let us be engaged in feminism in ways that engage us, and appreciate that, and I mean 'appreciate it' not in the sense of 'be grateful' but almost in the medical sense of feel it, see that it exists."[17] What Jervis recognizes is that the political work that she and other young women do is often not even visible to the people who are condemning young women for their apathy. She requests that their work simply be identified—"see that it exists."

Harris has studied this misapprehension, this lack of seeing, and identifies it as being a particular late-modern historical phenomenon: "Whereas once young people's resistance politics, and young women's feminist activism in particular, could be easily identified, today these seem obscure, transitory and disorganized. . . . Young women have new ways of taking on politics and culture that may not be recognizable under more traditional paradigms but deserve to be identified as socially engaged and potentially transformative nonetheless."[18] Indeed, where Duncombe suggests that zinesters might be too childlike to recognize the need for political interventions, and where other scholars see young women as apathetic, Harris's research suggests just the opposite: that young women in particular (like Jervis) *get* the current cultural and political scene, and their disengagement from politics traditionally configured is thus not ignorance but "active disengagement" from traditional modes of doing politics, which she suggests might best be understood as "a healthy disregard for formal politics and its agendas."[19] What replaces traditional political engagement, in the world of grrrl zines, are pedagogies of hope. These hopeful interventions are not identical to traditional modes of doing politics, but they are political nonetheless, because they are drawing attention to what's wrong with the world, awakening their readers' outrage, and providing tools for challenging existing power structures.

What's required, then, is an altered understanding of what counts as political so that we can break away from the traditional paradigms that obscure our view of what's happening now. We have to attend to the personal and the cultural, the local, the quirky, as real and meaningful sites of political intervention. Scholars of girls' culture and third wave feminism have called for a recognition of these new kinds of politics. Harris argues that the "individualization . . . that characterizes late modernity has made the level of the personal rather than the structural a more compelling site of change and traditional social movement activism more difficult to sustain."[20] In her study of third wave feminism, Astrid Henry notes, "in its current manifestation, third-wave feminism is more about textual and cultural production, local forms of activism, and a particular form of feminist consciousness than it is a large-scale social justice movement."[21] Shelley Budgeon terms this phenomenon "micropolitics," a political approach that emphasizes individual actions and choices made within a feminist interpretive framework.[22] I am broadening this term beyond Budgeon's original usage to describe what I see happening in grrrl zines.

Grrrl zine creators, too, have argued for an altered understanding of politics that will account for the work of grrrl zines. Tobi Vail identifies zines as "a form of cultural activism . . . as girls start to articulate reality as they experience it inside their heads and through their bodies and what they see in terms of making culture that makes sense to them they start to intervene in reality. . . . This is all about making the transformation from being an object that is acted upon to becoming a subject that is an active participant in the world."[23] Similarly, China Martens notes that "women's unofficial writing to each other has always created social change, and we don't see these undercurrents, and I think that's what women's zines can change—how we talk to each other, we need personal, informal spaces but it comes out into influencing society."[24]

All these commentators argue that, due to the political and cultural climate since the late 1980s, large-scale activism is no longer prevalent (or perhaps even viable). They note that, particularly for girls and women and those involved in third wave feminism, we should be looking to the personal, the local, and the microlevel for political action. And they contend that these are legitimate sites and strategies. My understanding of grrrl zines' cultural work has been informed by all these thinkers; indeed, grrrl zines are ideal sites at which to see this personally attuned, micropolitical work taking place.

In addition to these feminist scholars, I've found a useful theoretical framework for assessing this new paradigm of activism in the work of communication scholar Clemencia Rodriguez. Rodriguez offers a formulation of the work done by what she calls "citizens' media" that identifies this work as explicitly political, and which fits with Jervis's and Crabb's assertions and with grrrl zines in general. Although she focuses on electronic media, particularly television and radio, zines do fit under the rubric of citizens' media, a term she uses because it "implies first that a collectivity is *enacting* its citizenship by actively intervening and transforming the established mediascape; second, that these media are contesting social codes, legitimized identities, and institutionalized social relations; and third, that these communication practices are empowering the community involved, to the point where these transformations and changes are possible."[25] As this description implies, she sees citizens' media as doing significant political work because "democratic struggles have to be understood as processes of change that also include practices of dissent in the realm of the symbolic."[26] She notes that some of the unique features of citizens' media are "blurred boundaries between sender and receiver, closeness to the audience's cultural codes, political idiosyncrasies, and noncommercial goals"[27]—all characteristics of zines.

While a cynical culture—and one attuned to old-paradigm politics—would suggest that zines are doing "practically nil," in the words of Mimi Nguyen, Rodriguez presents an alternative model for assessment, one that emphasizes political intentions rather than political effects: "While traditional scholarship weighed alternative media by their capacity to alter the empire of media megaliths, I suggest redirecting our focus to understanding how citizens' media activate subtle processes of fracture in the social, cultural, and power spheres of everyday life."[28] Indeed, she argues for a new way of understanding the work of these media—not expecting them to eradicate corporate culture, for instance, but, instead, recognizing the local, small-scale, ephemeral ways that they foster and propagate democracy. Rodriguez suggests viewing democracy not as an end-point but as a process, something organic and in motion. She doesn't figure transience and limited reach as automatic weaknesses but, instead, as components of a new activist paradigm.[29] Citizens' media does political work—work that I would characterize as micropolitical—because it alters power structures by strengthening individual subjectivities.

This is the work that grrrl zines are doing. They break away from linear models through a fluid pedagogy of process. They offer tools for awakening outrage and engaging in protest through pedagogies of active critique. And they invite readers to step into their own citizenship through pedagogies of imagination. Because of the sorts of linear expectations scholars have had of alternative media and activist work more broadly, the resistance and political interventions of grrrl zines (and third wave feminists) have been hard for many scholars to recognize, but by recognizing the dominator culture and reframing what it means to be political, these interventions become visible.

Although I discuss each pedagogy as if it were a distinct and insular approach, in fact, these pedagogies are overlapping and intertwining in grrrl zines. For instance, a zine that invites an imaginative investment may also provide the tools for active criticism, and a zine that maps a healing process may do so in such a way as to provoke an imaginative response. Further, the three pedagogies I identify here don't represent a complete list. Grrrl zines mobilize numerous hopeful pedagogies—the pedagogies of process, active criticism, and imagination are prevalent and revealing, but additional pedagogies also emerge from grrrl zines and are worth attention. The embodied zine community creates the environment for these pedagogies of hope, as does the gift economy in which zines operate. All these pedagogies represent a new model of political engagement, one that counters the stifling effects of cynicism. Through their pedagogical work, grrrl zines engender hope, a process that is necessarily political.

## Greenzine *and Pedagogies of Process*

Violence against women is one of the most common subjects in grrrl zines. In part, this is because zines provide a space for girls and women to discuss issues that otherwise are socially taboo and therefore hidden. We have seen this throughout the book, from Tobi Vail's defiant explanation that "If I didn't write these things no one else would either" to Lauren Jade Martin's demand for recognition: "Hello, I exist." Violence against women has been a particularly secretive issue, one that second wave feminists began addressing in speak-outs, participatory media, and books—modes we now generally recognize as political—and that third wave feminists have often publicized through zines. As mentioned in chapter 1, many of the early Riot Grrrl zines discussed the creators' experiences of rape and incest, and their frank, angry discussions were so surprising that the media fixated on these elements. But this use of the zine medium to discuss violence isn't limited to Riot Grrrl zines; many grrrl zines address this issue, and in a wide variety of ways—from cathartic personal stories to more explicitly didactic guides on how to respond. They then become a kind of micropolitical merger of public and private; rather than simply being revelations of victimization, they become calls to solidarity.

The word I would use to describe these zines' mode of political intervention is "process," a word that has two distinct but related meanings in the context of these zines. In one sense, process points to the fact that grrrl zines emphasize the means rather than the ends—the means of creating a zine itself, along with creating a network of sympathetic readers. In addition, these zines offer their creators a space to publicly process the violence done to them and to make their healing a public act. By making visible the emotional, mechanical, and theoretical processes involved in creating their zines, and by articulating their own healing processes, these zinesters counter consumer capitalism and make use of an embodied community for personal and social transformation.

By detailing the abuse suffered by the zinesters and its aftermath, these zines often function as a component of a healing process. Neely Bat Chestnut, who has written a number of zines about her experiences of incest, explained to me that "making a zine is one of the best therapeutic things anyone can ever do." She identified it as therapeutic on three levels: "There's one where you are writing, and then there's two where you are putting it together with images you like in this really soothing, comforting way, and then there's the act of giving it out to people and seeing their response."[30] This healing process is evidence in many grrrl zines about violence—and it's worth noting that it's a process that Chestnut describes as corporeal and community-building, not merely psychological.

The "process" part of the healing process is important—both in terms of what Chestnut describes (the multiple parts of the process of creating a zine) and in terms of viewing the zine as something that's not finished. Zine creator Cristy Road discusses her process of identifying and healing from rape in *Greenzine* #13 and #14. *Greenzine*, a digest-sized zine that Road has been producing since she was fourteen, is filled with drawings and narratives by Road and sometimes her friends. It describes many aspects of Road's life, but one of the more prominent in issues 13 and 14 is her experience of rape, her efforts to heal, and her attempts to garner support for herself and other survivors. She recounts the event itself and the immediate aftermath in issue 13 and a later encounter with the rapist in issue 14. In both, she is skeptical of her own reactions, in part because she wasn't initially comfortable describing the unwanted sex as rape. In a neatly typed narrative called "Consensual Sex Is So Hot" in issue 13, a narrative in which she expounds on the value of consensual sex by describing the trauma of rape, she explains, "I didn't know how to avoid him for the coming months. I made a comment about it the morning after in an almost sarcastic tone—as he responded in an equally sarcastic gesture. I felt like I was wrong for feeling discomfort and was accusing him of something that was socially acceptable." She describes her confusion, "feeling insane—nothing made sense," as well as her self-judgment: "Associating myself with a group of powerful feminists seemed like a token of hypocrisy" to her since she wasn't responding the way she thought a feminist would.[31] And yet she validates these "imperfect" responses, describing how she came to have compassion for herself, thanks to the support of female friends.

She offers a particularly multivalent story in *Greenzine* #14. In this issue, she describes encountering the rapist in the midst of an anti-globalization protest that has drawn violent police response. As her friends are being beaten, shot with rubber bullets, and tear-gassed, the rapist greets her. On solid black pages with white typed text, she describes a painful collision of the personal and the political, as her fear of assault from the police is worsened by interacting with the man who actually assaulted her. While he acts as though they are friends and seems surprised at her aloof response, she is thrown into emotional turmoil, crying while police in riot gear force her cohort off the street and into a restaurant. Again she questions her own reactions, writing, "At this moment, I punished myself for refraining from attacking in return on that one night in July when he saw my unconscious body as an advantage to his sickening fantasies," but she quickly moves to a place of self-acceptance: "I felt held back by trepidation and tears—but this is who I am. This is the point I am at, and Im not going to scold myself for how far I haven't come."[32]

The work Road does in *Greenzine* is an example of micropolitics. Although Road herself does a great deal of political work around violence against women (participating in an activist group in Philadelphia, contributing to other antiviolence zines like *Support*), the focus within her own zine seems to be on finding her way out of the debilitating pain caused by being a victim. This personal processing certainly makes the zine a space that is psychologically useful, but Budgeon's concept of micropolitics suggests that we view this function beyond the individual level and consider this, too, to be political work. Because the process of self-

Images from *Greenzine*,
courtesy of Cristy Road.

construction involves negotiating within cultural discourses, and because "these discourses—including gender, race, and sexuality—also organize social relations into hierarchical arrangements," Budgeon explains, "they are inherently political."[33]

Road would agree. She frames her psychological process in *Greenzine* #14 as political. The two are intimately intertwined, as she makes clear in the conclusion of her essay:

> Today I had my home town embedded with tear gas and hundreds of my allies imprisoned. Today I had twenty of my closest friends holding me and understanding the validity of my reaction. Today I collected myself. And to myself, I said that the next time there wouldnt be police threats and high tension consuming what was left of my self-confidence. Next time, I see verbal attacks toward the man who made me question my judgement on assault and my sexual boundaries for a year. . . . Today it was perfectly fine to cry.[34]

The emotional healing and self-acceptance she experiences are as important as the protest she's involved in, the more traditional model of political engagement. In *Greenzine*, then, the politics are in the process—indeed, *are* the process.

Road's emphasis on process is also political because it can be a means of resisting consumer capitalism. Something that's a process isn't a product, a commodity to be consumed. A cynical culture or a dominator culture functions in part by encouraging people to be passive except for the consumption of consumer goods; indeed, at its most cynical, our culture can offer consumption as a form of politics, as in President George W. Bush's post-9/11 exhortation to Americans to "go shopping" as a means of defeating terrorism. By emphasizing process, zines like *Greenzine* are resisting this cynical cultural model and offering an inviting space for readers of the zine to consider creating zines of their own.

Duncombe has usefully theorized this function of zines, coining the term "emulation" to describe the process of "turning your readers into writers" that is a crucial effect of zinemaking.[35] He explains that the non-professional, do-it-yourself approach that characterizes zines contributes to emulation because it demystifies the medium:

> The seamlessness of commercial culture and the technical virtuosity of high art encourage spectators/consumers to stand back and utter

in awe, "Wow. That's amazing. How did they do that?" Zines—with all their seams showing—encourage the opposite response, encourage you to come close, and say, "I see how they did that. That's not too hard. Anybody can do that."[36]

By being sloppy and rough rather than glossy and professional, *Greenzine* invites its readers to feel like potential creators. *Greenzine* features typical zine characteristics such as cut and pasted text, a mixture of handwriting and typed narrative, and varying background images (although Road's zines are somewhat distinctive because they feature her professional-quality drawings).[37]

As explained in chapter 2, because the constructedness of zines is generally so visible and simple—from the plain white paper or household objects from which they're made to the staples or rubber bands that bind them together—they are an extremely accessible medium. The visibility of *Greenzine*'s construction makes it inviting, and this inviting quality has political effects, encouraging readers to participate in their culture as creators rather than merely consumers. Rodriguez notes that demystification of the media is a common feature of citizens' media, and this demystification has political effects.[38] As Duncombe explains, "Having readers become writers and writers become readers circumvents a fundamental tenet of the logic of consumer culture: the division between producers and consumers."[39]

This is particularly significant for girls and women, who are often figured in mainstream and scholarly discourses as cultural consumers rather than producers. Girls' studies scholars note that many of the empowerment strategies for girls figure girls as shoppers, who can empower themselves by purchasing girl-power products. This emphasis on consumption has also affected scholarship on girls, which then overemphasizes girls' consumption rather than their acts of creativity and production. As Mary Celeste Kearney explains, "Feminist scholars have repeatedly placed their attention on girls' interactions with the commodities mass-produced by the mainstream culture industries" rather than examining girls' own creations.[40] *Greenzine*'s emphasis on personal healing, intimate revelations, and visible construction, then, are best understood as strategies for intervention in a cynical consumer culture. The zine is doing the work that Rodriguez identifies with citizens' media, functioning as a "small force" that demonstrates that "democratic communication [is] a live creature."[41]

To expand on Duncombe's point, the invitation zine readers feel to become part of the zine community, the emulation effect, takes place not only because of the visibility of the construction of zines but also because of the emotional complexity and even confusion zines like *Greenzine* exhibit. By refusing to offer a neatly resolved story of assault that matches some idealized version of "what a feminist would do," Road shows a version of her emotional life "with all the seams showing." When I asked Cindy Crabb what inspired her to create her zine *Doris*, she described the imperfections in the content of *Snarla*, one of her favorite zines: "[The authors of *Snarla*] didn't have it down, they were crazy, and they were writing about it. It was amazing, it was like, this makes the theory make more sense to me. It's not making actual total sense, but it's making the theories seem like something that I can bring into my life, too, and I don't have to have it perfect to be able to start to integrate it or something. So that was the big inspiration to me."[42] Because *Snarla* was not adhering to a seamless consumer culture industry standard, because the authors used the zine as a site to work through ideas rather than as a site to showcase fully formed concepts, the zine was inviting to Crabb. It was one of the things that inspired her to create *Doris*. The process of zine creation, then, is mechanical, emotional, and even theoretical, and by making all aspects of the process visible, grrrl zines such as those describing violence against women are engaging in a political intervention and inviting their readers to engage in these processes themselves.

Within the relatively safe, embodied grrrl zine community, these authors are sharing painful personal stories, both for their own healing and to change the public discourse. Indeed, zinesters like Crabb identify sharing people's intimate selves as inherently an act that changes the broader world. When I asked Crabb what zines *do*, what effect they have, she said:

> Do you know the quote that's like, "What would happen if one woman told the whole truth about her life? The world would explode"? Well, that was sort of the basis [for creating *Doris*]. I was like, maybe it wouldn't explode, but there are so many secrets, and it just seemed like it really did make a huge difference. It seemed like it made a huge difference in the women's movement of my mom's time, when sexual abuse was first starting to be talked about. . . . I really felt like if everybody talked about it, the world would have to change and it would have to not happen anymore. That silence was such a huge factor in perpetuating abuse.[43]

In other words, sharing true events from her own life and her deep reflections on them were acts that she saw as deeply political and important, not only because it would be part of her own healing but also because "the world would have to change." This is a kind of updated and expanded version of the second wave consciousness-raising group, where the personal can be made political.

By emphasizing and making visible the idea of process and processing, zines like *Greenzine* challenge consumer capitalism and the silencing of women's voices, and they make space for a multivalent micropolitics. Although the subject matter Road addresses is painful, her zines—and others like them—are performing a positive intervention, enacting a pedagogy of hope. I don't mean to suggest that their cultural work is somehow complete, that these zines will singlehandedly eradicate violence against women—indeed, as I argue in this chapter, this is the wrong rubric under which to evaluate zines. Instead, they provide a space, a means, and a process for the voices of girls and women to enter the public world.

## Bitch *and Pedagogies of Active Criticism*

*Bitch* is a publication that performs a different kind of public intervention than *Greenzine*. Although there are elements of personal disclosure in the zine, Lisa Jervis and Andi Zeisler started *Bitch* in 1996 to challenge pop culture's representations of women—in other words, rather than being about personal expression, this is a publication explicitly about intervening in the symbolic order. In the first editor's letter, Jervis contextualizes the significance of the symbolic order for girls:

> When I was twelve years old I was looking for something to reflect who I thought I was. I wanted to confirm that I was not a freak, that my feelings and desires were normal. Unfortunately, in the mass media I found affirmation only for my I-desperately-need-to-be-skinny and I-need-to-have-a-"boyfriend" longings. And those weren't even mine, they were just the charred remnants of I-really-want-to-like-myself and what-are-these-urges-and-what-can-I-do-to-satisfy-them?[44]

This editor's letter describes the kinds of pressures girls face as a result of mainstream cultural norms, pressures that are enacted and exacerbated by corporate culture industries.[45] As discussed in chapter 3, grrrl zines routinely disrupt the mainstream models of appropriate gender performance by offering alternatives—from the sexy, fun adult feminism of *Bust* to the radical appropriation of femininity in *Grit & Glitter*. Like these other zines, *Bitch* is identifying and challenging cultural norms surrounding gender. Jervis notes that her natural girlhood anxieties—human anxieties about sexual feelings and self-esteem—were interpreted and framed by the mass media she consumed simply in terms of achieving a skinny body in order to get a boyfriend. Her identity was flattened, and her legitimate questions were distorted. Like many grrrl zines, *Bitch* takes a critical stance on the distortions and amputations of girlhood and womanhood performed by the mainstream culture industries.

What I focus on in this section, however, are not the alternative models of womanhood that *Bitch* offers but the zine's methodology, its use of what I call a "pedagogy of active criticism." After discussing her twelve-year-old anxieties in her first editor's letter, Jervis goes on to say, "*This magazine is about theorizing and fostering a transformation of pop culture.*"[46] When we spoke, some ten years after that first letter was written, Zeisler explained that *Bitch* was started with activist intentions: "It was kind of this idea of wanting to do something, wanting to write about pop culture and things that were still at that point considered kind of fluffy in the mainstream media. Now, of course, pop culture journalism is huge, but at the time it really wasn't. So knowing that we had no clout, we had no pull, and we had no way of getting published in mainstream magazines, we just figured we'd do it ourselves."[47] This impulse—the recognition that something needs to be done, and since no one else is doing it, we might as well—is at the heart of the zine endeavor. Clearly this do-it-yourself approach represents an activist impulse, and *Bitch* enacts a familiar version of activism, one with obvious ties to previous generations of feminist publications.

*Bitch* offers this familiar version of activism with a twist: it draws on the rhetoric, iconography, and aesthetics of grrrl zine culture, and it addresses a subject matter—pop cultural representations—that is characteristic of the third wave. As the editors of *Third Wave Agenda* explain, "third wave activists are well aware of the power of representations to promote or contest domination. Since we understand the 'real' as an effect of representation and understand that representational effects play out in material spaces and in material ways, we take critical engagement with popular culture as a key to political struggle." They note that popular culture is an activist site often seen as problematic by second wave feminists, but they contend, "we take popular culture as just one pedagogical site that materializes our struggles with some of the ways power works."[48]

What *Bitch* does, then, is manifest this sort of passionate engagement with popular culture, an engagement that is both critical and embracing.

They critique the media and also consume it hungrily, but in both modes they take it seriously, recognizing that the symbolic realm is an important site for democratic struggle. In so doing, Jervis and Zeisler offer a model of resistant consciousness to their readers. *Bitch* aims to function as a how-to guide for its readers to become actively engaged in their cultural moment rather than assuming that the readers are the kind of passive consumers who fulfill the ideals of the dominator culture. It offers its readers training in pop cultural criticism and intervention and thus provides a pedagogy of active criticism.

*Bitch* began in 1996, a cultural moment in which grrrl zines were an established phenomenon—at least in Oakland, where Zeisler and Jervis lived—and in which the pop cultural terrain for girls and women was fraught. The Riot Grrrl movement had diminished, fallen back below the radar of mainstream media, and prominent voices were proclaiming feminism dead, even as the first books began to be published announcing and defining feminism's third wave. In its first several issues (Jervis and Zeisler published four issues between 1996 and 1997), *Bitch* took on daytime talk shows, films, and women's and girls' magazines. In particular, they savaged *Sassy* magazine, which Zeisler said had become "Bizarro-*Sassy*" by the time they started *Bitch*. The second headline on the cover of the first issue is "Special Section: *Sassy* Sucks." This was one of the things that inspired them: *Sassy*'s demise from a feisty, feminist publication to simply another mindless corporate magazine aimed at selling beauty products to girls felt like a betrayal to young women like Zeisler and Jervis.[49] They spent a great deal of time on more mainstream women's magazines, as well, as in their second issue when they offered six pages of detailed reviews of *Glamour, Cosmopolitan, Marie Claire, Allure, Mademoiselle,* and *Self,* including for each a "percentage of the magazine you might actually want to read" (none higher than 27 percent). However, *Sassy* earned special vitriol because it had been so encouraging and empowering for them.

Even in its early days in 1996, *Bitch* straddled zine and magazine status. This straddling was related to the publishers' vision of the work they wanted *Bitch* to do: to teach the skills to actively critique pop culture to a world beyond the self-identified zine community. *Bitch* started out with a fairly professional philosophy and aesthetic. The first issues were word-processed and offset printed, so they had a clean, professional look rather than the deliberate scruffiness of many zines.[50] *Bitch* continued to professionalize quickly. Although they were aware of zines and positioned themselves within the zine community—in fact, the idea for *Bitch* became crystallized when Jervis and Zeisler were on a train on the way back from a panel on the politics of zines, when both women were in their early twenties—they were always thinking of becoming a magazine. They identified themselves as "a zine with magazine aspirations," and their design and distribution reflect that goal.[51] Because they were in the San Francisco Bay Area, Jervis and Zeisler had access to already-existing zine distribution channels, including many independent book and music stores. Ironically, these healthy zine networks facilitated the movement of *Bitch* into "magazine" terrain.

The first issue sold for $1.00 (subsequent issues were $2.50), and sales were so robust that by their second issue they had a distributor, and by their seventh issue they had a glossy color cover and had begun verging into an identity as a magazine rather than a zine. Both Zeisler and Jervis noted that the sense of audience can differentiate a zine and a magazine— a zine, in their view, is more concerned with the personal expression of the author, while a magazine wants to offer certain information for an audience.[52] Zeisler and Jervis were intent on social change, not personal expression, and they were always planning to grow. Zeisler also noted that a concern for timetables—a sense of urgency—characterized *Bitch* from the beginning, and that's more common for magazines than for zines. They were attuned to bookstore distribution schedules.

Today *Bitch* has a print run of forty-seven thousand and is distributed through more than fifteen hundred bookstores and newsstands nationwide, including such major outlets as Borders, Barnes and Noble, and even grocery stores like Whole Foods. They accept advertising (although with fairly strict guidelines for advertisers).[53] Zeisler and Jervis, however, still identify it with zine status. As Zeisler said, "a zine is always something that is done for love and not money, and by that definition [in unison with Jervis] we're still a zine."[54] Indeed, in 2008, *Bitch* was still reasonably priced, with a newsstand cost of $5.95 an issue and an annual subscription rate of $15.00. Although they now have a staff of six and the ability to pay their contributors, they are a nonprofit organization and regularly seek donations from readers and others in order to stay in print. Their nonprofit status is, at one level, a sign of the difficulties the publication faces, helping it stay afloat in an increasingly competitive media marketplace; as recently as September 2008, the publishers were asking for donations from readers to be able to print the next issue.[55] Being a nonprofit also aligns *Bitch* with the gift culture impulse of zines. Although the publication isn't free, as a publication produced "for love and not money," it operates more as a gift than as a commodity. And because readers donate money to keep *Bitch* in print, they are obviously recognizing it as something more than a product to be purchased.

Both Jervis and Zeisler see the debate over zine/not-zine as unproductive, tied to tired progressive conversations around "selling out," which they suggest might also be connected to a fear of success within progressive communities, as if success—in terms of either finances or distribution—is automatically corrupting. They explain that their goal was always to reach a broader community and get their ideas out beyond the insular zine community of the Bay Area. They wanted to succeed, but they don't see this as being indicative of their losing their ideological commitments. Jervis notes, "To me, selling out involves changing your content in order to get money or distribution or whatever, and if you can reach a wider audience without changing your content, then how in the fucking world is that bad?"[56] Indeed, the publication has maintained its emphasis on a multiissue, nonmonolithic feminism, and even the look in 2008 was similar to that in 1996: despite its glossy color covers, *Bitch* is still a black and white, cleanly word-processed publication with hand-drawn illustrations accompanying the articles.

*Bitch* exhibits many of the characteristics of grrrl zines and of the third wave more broadly. Each issue offers a playful combination of outrage and delight at pop culture—what third wave scholar Merri Lisa Johnson terms the third wave's embrace of "the conflict. And the glee."[57] The name of the zine is clear evidence of this phenomenon: Zeisler and Jervis deliberately chose a name that they saw as provocative and that would allow them to reclaim sexist terminology. In their first editor's letter, Jervis explained, "This magazine is about thinking critically about every message the mass media sends; it's about loudly articulating what's wrong and what's right with what we see. This magazine is about speaking up. Will that make us bitchy? Yeah. *You wanna make somethin' of it?*"[58] Later, the explanation would become, "When it's being used as an insult, 'bitch' is an epithet hurled at women who speak their minds, who have opinions and don't shy away from expressing them, and who don't sit by and smile uncomfortably if they're bothered or offended. If being an outspoken woman means being a bitch, we'll take that as a compliment, thanks."[59]

From the first issue, Jervis and Zeisler strove for a tone that was chatty and relatable, while still being fierce when necessary; the writers were as comfortable using the term "fuck" as saying that actor John Travolta

walks "like his hip joints are primed with Astroglide."[60] Throughout the
zine, they offer playful iconography combined with serious content, such
as their "Mad as a Wet Hen" and "Whee!" sections—short takes on media—which by their second year became "Love It"/"Shove It" (and which
are still part of the publication today). For the first several issues, the back
covers offered clever bricolages of feminine icons and feminist messages
that are, again, characteristic of grrrl zines and the third wave, like the
image on the back of the second issue, which featured a woman with her
hair in curlers, sitting under a big plastic hairdryer at a beauty parlor,
calmly loading a shotgun. The caption stamped across the image reads,
"riot don't diet," a slogan that challenges the beauty culture and suggests
that women can be dangerous rather than simply objects to view.

Early issues of *Bitch* also featured playful covers, such as the third issue's drawing of two girls lamenting of their Barbies, "No matter how
many times you pop her head off, they're always gonna just make more."
In recent years, the covers have become more professionalized, but they
are often still playful.

But *Bitch* is also characterized by its long, intellectually driven analyses of pop culture terrain's treatment of women. Rather than offering up

Image from *Bitch* (left), courtesy of Andi Zeisler and Rhonda Winter.
Cover of *Bitch* (right), courtesy of Andi Zeisler.

Covers of *Bitch*, courtesy of Andi Zeisler.

simplistic observations about female sexual objectification, for instance, *Bitch* puts forth sophisticated critiques.[61] Observing the media very closely, Jervis, Zeisler, and their contributing authors are sensitively attuned to the nuances of these representations and, more important, their consequences. For instance, the second issue features an article by Jervis called "Talk Shows: TV's Culture of Categorization." Jervis's main contention is that popular 1990s talk shows such as *Geraldo* and *Jenny Jones* distort and pathologize female sexual desire. She frames the article carefully, to counteract the argument that this issue is unimportant: "The problem is not simply that individual girls get insulted and ignored by these particular episodes of these particular shows, but that huge chunks of our entire culture are built on the repression of female sexuality, and these shows are a symptom and a demonstration of that sad fact—and a mode of perpetuating it."[62] Jervis identifies talk shows as a space where harmful, sexist ideas are circulated and magnified, and she explains that the popularization of these ideas has consequences not only for individual girls and women but also for how we're able to talk and think about female sexuality.

She goes through the shows in detail, noting each time that the girl panelists' own explanations for their sexual behavior are ignored or denied by hosts and "experts," and pointing out that, counter to our mainstream cultural narratives that pathologize female sexuality, these girls are very clear about saying that they are having sex because they enjoy it. "Behind the fear of sexuality," she argues, "is a fear of female agency and power. No one can stand the thought of girls and women doing what they want to do with their own bodies." The article achieves a tone that comes to characterize *Bitch*: smart and snarky, regularly using slang, as well as phrases like "'reputation' is a misogynist social construction" and "the hegemony of the conventional."[63] The publication not only takes on the media but strives to offer a version of smart, young feminism with bite—and in so doing, models this mode of critical cultural engagement to its readers.

Although *Bitch* does have a specific focus on feminist responses to pop culture, Jervis and Zeisler intentionally conceive of the terms in that description—particularly "feminist" and "pop culture"—as being broad and open to multiple perspectives. As they were beginning to solidify the identity of the publication, the stances that it was going to take, Jervis explained, "one of those stances is kind of a non-stance of, like, we're not going to define what feminism is, or police what's an appropriate *Bitch* opinion. Writers are going to say stuff that we might personally disagree with, and that's going to happen, and it's important for that to be okay."[64] Indeed, this comfort with multiple opinions is printed on the masthead of every issue of *Bitch* in ever-changing statements such as "Opinions expressed are those of their respective authors, not necessarily those of *Bitch*. We have many—and sometimes conflicting—opinions."[65]

Both founders explain that they never want the publication to become "frozen" or entrenched; a notion of fluidity was and is important to them. According to Zeisler, "you want to always have the ability and the freedom to evolve your thinking."[66] Part of the activist work *Bitch* does, then, is to challenge the notion of a monolithic feminism and to embrace political approaches that are diverse, changing, and even contradictory. This, I contend, makes *Bitch* a publication that is enacting third wave feminism. Since the third wave has positioned itself as multiissue, fragmented, and nonmonolithic, *Bitch* is offering tools for cultural intervention without dictating how those tools should be used. This is the activist incarnation of the diverse, fragmented third wave subjectivities that grrrl zines construct.

And yet this multi-issue approach can be challenging, as well. Jervis explains,

> I get really burned out sometimes because there are so many huge problems and issues, and where do you put your activist energy? I mean,

everything is so important, and it can become very paralyzing. Especially when you're getting judged by other people on, like, the issue that you're working on is not important enough, there are more important issues out there, you're not doing activism the right way. And I think that inhibits coalition building. But the flip side of this is that there is so much activism and there is so much coalition building and alliance building, it's really exciting. It's this weird dualistic thing.[67]

*Bitch*, along with other third wave feminist endeavors, has been criticized for not taking on important enough issues, or for being on the "wrong" side of issues. As I discuss in the introduction, *Bust* has been lambasted for embracing sexual pleasure as a valid feminist terrain, and *Bitch*, too, has been seen as addressing trivial matters—*Sassy* magazine, MTV, even the reclaiming of the word "bitch"—rather than the "real" stuff of sexism.[68] Jervis's statement not only speaks to these critiques but also captures the stultifying and enabling aspects of this cultural moment. The paralysis that Jervis mentions can be misidentified as apathy; as Courtney Martin argued in a recent opinion piece about twenty-somethings, "We are not apathetic. What we are . . . is totally and completely overwhelmed."[69] Indeed, she coins the term "generation overwhelmed" to describe her cohort. In the absence of a means of responding or resisting, the paralysis and the experience of being overwhelmed can become cynicism.

Jervis and Zeisler both seem to be able to take that paralysis and do something with it. Jervis recognizes the potential in it—the fact that there are so many issues that people are working on can be exciting and freeing, opening up possibilities for connecting with other activists. And Zeisler, taking a somewhat different approach, embraces the productive power of pessimism: "Personally, I'm incredibly pessimistic, and I feel like there's a lot to be said for pessimism. I mean, I often think that social movements, as much as they come out of idealism, they also come out of pessimism in the sense that if everything sucks, there's really no harm in trying to change stuff. You really have nothing to lose."[70] What Zeisler is calling pessimism, I would identify as a version of hope, or a necessary prerequisite for hope: her sense that "there's really no harm in trying to change stuff" frees her from the paralysis of being overwhelmed and allows her to make some sort of intervention, even if it's small. This is partly what defines the activism of zines—that they are evidence of resisting that paralysis. By their very existence they testify to the importance of doing something.

*Bitch* is a publication that in many ways characterizes the third wave. Although it differs from the violence against women zines—deviating from their cut-and-paste aesthetic and their highly self-disclosing content—like them, it's a publication that is engaging in micropolitical interventions. Rather than offering a pedagogy of process, *Bitch* trains its readers in thoughtful, critical engagement with the popular culture in which they're immersed by demonstrating the use of feminist analytical tools. *Bitch* doesn't model a strictly condemning take on mainstream media productions. Instead, the editors and contributors show the pleasure of active criticism: they exhibit a love/hate relationship with pop culture and demonstrate enthusiasm even when critiquing the latest incarnations of sexism, racism, and homophobia. And by offering their readers not only the intellectual tools of active criticism but also the concrete mechanisms for enacting it—addresses and websites to write letters and learn more— *Bitch* attempts to propagate the protest.

Letters from readers, steady circulation, and readers' willingness to donate money to support *Bitch* document the importance of the publication in the lives of its readers. Readers often share with the editors of *Bitch* how much they value the community that the publication allows them to feel part of. In addition to this feeling of belonging, they describe their responses to the pedagogy of active critique. As early as volume 2, issue no. 1, a self-identified seventeen-year-old reader wrote in to say that "not only did [*Bitch*] reaffirm everything that I have been thinking all along, but it also opened [my friend's] eyes to a lot of the crap that is fed to women by these so-called 'teen magazines.'"[71] In other words, the magazine's modeling of active critique validated the reader's own criticisms and made the sexism of teen magazines visible to the reader's friend.

Other readers don't just explain that they've been inspired to become cultural critics; instead, they demonstrate it, as is the case with a letter from Ann W., who takes issue with an article criticizing the sexism of girls' toys. She writes, "I understand your dismay when wandering the aisles of Toys 'R' Us, and yeah, it's pretty clear that toy manufacturers are forcing some fucked-up ideals on young girls, but I have to ask you: Didn't you gals ever put Barbie on top of Ken? Didn't you dress up in make-up and feathers and pretend you were international spies? Come on!" She goes on to explain that girls often play with their toys in resistant ways, thwarting the intentions of the manufacturers, and she signs her letter "Ann W, who read the entire *Sweet Valley High* series and still turned into a radical feminist."[72] This sort of letter became common and is still the type most often printed in the "Dear Bitch" section. Readers like Ann W. show their own engagement in active critique by engaging in thoughtful, sophisticated, and not always compliant ways with the arguments raised in *Bitch*. Ann W. is an active critic, bringing her own intellectual judgments and life experiences to bear on an argument about girls and popular culture (and in the process making an argument about girls' agency that girls' studies scholars make, as well).

Of course, not all of the responses to *Bitch* are positive. The magazine has drawn criticism not only from some older feminists but also from younger girls and women. For instance, in response to the magazine's September 2008 budget struggles, one feminist blogger wrote, "Maybe the reason why *Bitch* isn't succeeding is because, although it's trudged along for twelve years, it just *isn't successful*. Has anyone stopped to think that it's the content, and not the mean, evil corporate world that's costing them money? A lot of women don't really subscribe to the stilted rhetoric of first-year women's studies. And it would seem that a lot of women don't really subscribe to *Bitch* either."[73] The comments on this post demonstrate a range of opinions on the publication, from those who defend *Bitch*—"I actually find Bitch to be an awesome magazine, completely relevant to my issues"—to those who write of the magazine, "I have no desire to pay for someone to tell me how Jem and the Holograms are actually tools of THE MAN keeping girls down."[74] Some readers find the active criticism in *Bitch* heavy-handed, while others enjoy it, but in either case the publication is publicly circulating a model of intervention in the symbolic order, a model of resistance.

## Doris *and Pedagogies of Imagination*

*Doris* is substantially different from *Bitch*. Although, like *Bitch*, it's a long-running publication (*Bitch* has been in existence for twelve years, *Doris* for fifteen), it's all zine, in terms of philosophy, aesthetic, and distribution. Spanning the time period discussed in this book (Crabb began producing it around 1993 from her home at that time in California), *Doris* is filled with cut-and-pasted typewritten and handwritten narratives, along with small, friendly stick-figure cartoons of Crabb and her dog, Anna. The zine isn't content-driven; as with many grrrl zines, her content varies, depending on what she's thinking about. The zine addresses topics such as violence against women, environmentalism, anarchism, bike riding, and reproductive rights, almost all of them presented in terms of personal stories and musings. But all of the zine is infused with Crabb's own theorizing about activism and resistance and what they might look like in the current cultural moment.

Although the zine started small, with only a few hundred copies printed, in the last several years Crabb estimates her circulation to be around three thousand zines per issue, sold through online distros, as well as through the traditional zine channels of independent book and music stores and direct mail order from Crabb herself. *Doris* shares qualities with the violence against women zines—offering self-disclosure as a political act—but takes that a step further. *Doris* isn't just about the political and pedagogical possibilities of process, nor is it a zine that models the sort of active criticism shown in *Bitch*. Instead, the emphasis in *Doris* is on the transformative potential of imagination.[75] In some ways it reads like a fifteen-year meditation on the possibility of individuals creating social change.

Even in the very early days of the zine, Crabb was grappling with what it meant to attempt social change in a deeply cynical culture. She identified her zine as a space that would resist the cynical lure of the easy answer and would strive for complexity:

> And what I love best is the writers who embrace complexity & try to make sence of it. It makes me feel like there's so many more possibilities for fundamental social change when I'm looking at how complex everything is, and trying to fit it all together. Because simplifying seems like a huge boring trap to me & I feel surrounded by it; by people trying to make struggle understandable by making it simple, like people suck and should all die, like men suck and they should all die, like rich people suck and they should all die. It is not that easy.[76]

This seems to me to be a foundational assumption on which *Doris* operates: that making things simple isn't the answer to social change. Indeed, this effort at simplicity is cynical, in part because it is so firmly rooted in a conception of politics beginning and ending with the individual: if I can't change it, or imagine the change easily, then change is impossible. And, of course, this sense that change is impossible is at the heart of a cynical, dominator culture. Crabb strives to capture the complexities of human life, and rather than finding these complexities daunting, she finds them hopeful, productive. Crabb's philosophy relates to Rodriguez's celebration of the transient, nonlinear work of citizens' media; rather than seeing these qualities as weaknesses, Rodriguez identifies them as evidence of strength, of democratic possibility, as does Crabb.

Although Crabb certainly suggests actions to her readers, as in *Doris* #15 where she offers an extensive guide on how to deal with depression, *Doris* is not a zine—like *Bitch*—that is propelled by specific how-to tips for cultural change. Instead, Crabb creates the zine to be a space that invites her readers to think and feel deeply and carefully—and in complex ways—about the world and their place in it. She explained to me, "I think there is something about modeling a deep self-reflection, a strong desire for real emotion and real honest closeness, that helps people to do this in their lives—counterbalances the messages that tell them to stay shallow and safe."[77] She is particularly critical of the consumer culture that encourages people to go for the quick fix, the easy answer, or to think only in terms of their individual needs.

In her zine, she consistently showcases her own emotional terrain, lets her readers see inside her own efforts at processing and making sense of the world. Reading the zine over a number of years lets you see Crabb's long-term emotional journey. The zine has both documented and been part of Crabb's own healing process, in a way very much like many of the violence against women zines (indeed, Crabb writes about her own struggles as a survivor of abuse in many issues of *Doris*). More than this, though, what Crabb is doing in *Doris* is inviting her readers to have their own emotional experience. She told me that she tries to make each issue of *Doris* contain a full range of human emotions so that the zine can provide a kind of emotional journey for the reader.

I'm intrigued with her idea of "modeling a deep self-reflection," because I do see this as both resistant and interventionist, and yet not in ways that we might recognize if we're looking for old-paradigm activism. Indeed, this might not fit many people's definition of "political" work at all. For Crabb, however, this is explicitly political, a point of view she has developed more fully in recent years. In her "Ohio" essay, she writes, "I don't think our lifestyle choices are in and of themselves political. The political part is whether our lifestyle choices help us to become more human. If they help us feel a sense of personal integrity, and if that integrity gives us the power to fight further, to imagine deeper, to want more."[78]

For Crabb, then, the political is what encourages us to become more fully human. She is interested in calling her readers back to their own human integrity, a quality she believes is not nurtured in the culture at large but which is necessary for the work of changing the world. And it's important to see that she figures this work of world change not only in terms of "fight[ing] further" but in terms of imagination and desire. Indeed, social justice activists like Paulo Freire have argued that imagination and the belief in change are crucial components of any social justice efforts. Freire argues, "In order for the oppressed to be able to wage the struggle for their liberation, they must perceive the reality of oppression not as a closed world from which there is no exit, but as a limiting situation which they can transform."[79] It's as if Crabb is taking the zine concept of emulation to a different level: not only does she invite her readers to emulate the production of the zine itself by creating a material object with "all its seams showing," but also she invites them to emulate her process of self-reflection, because she shows all the seams there, as well.

You could pick up almost any *Doris* zine and find this emphasis on becoming more fully human—an emphasis that Crabb conveys with words and imagery. For instance, in *Doris* #20 (2002), Crabb discusses the death of her mother and the friend who came to ease her through her numbness. Through these personal reminiscences, she outlines her process of healing. She describes the full human connection she feels with her friend,

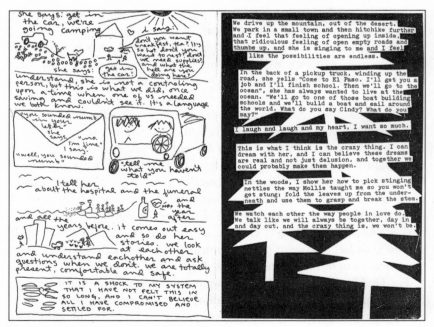

Image from *Doris*, courtesy of Cindy Crabb.

a connection that's manifested by their sharing stories with each other, beginning when the friend says, "tell me what you haven't told." At the bottom of this page, Crabb draws a box with a simplified, abstracted picture of a heart in a ribcage with the caption, "It is a shock to my system that I have not felt this in so long, and I can't believe all I have compromised and settled for."

Further on in this story she explains: "This is what I think is the crazy thing. I can dream with her, and I can believe these dreams are real and not just delusion, and together we could probably make them happen." Again, even in the context of discussing her own healing process, her emphasis is on dreaming, imagining. Crabb is enacting what Rodriguez sees as one of the powerful functions of alternative media like grrrl zines: "Alternative media spin transformative processes that alter people's senses of self, their subjective positionings, and therefore their access to power."[80] Philosopher Jonathan Lear, too, stresses the importance of imagination as part of ethical interactions with an uncertain future.[81] Unlike *Bitch*, which offers information, outrage, smart arguments to rebut mainstream representations—all very good things—*Doris* works in a different way: by inviting readers to imagine more, to allow their sense of self to be transformed. The zine models an imaginative process and therefore offers what I am calling a pedagogy of imagination.

It's a fascinating form of activism, one that might be described in terms of micropolitics. Certainly, this is part of what's going on in *Doris*: Crabb has developed an explicitly feminist framework, one that is broad-based and historically informed. She has studied the history of feminism along with the history of other social justice movements, and she's been involved in a number of political organizations. She incorporates these ideas into her zine through her own personal narrative. And yet, while the women Budgeon interviews enact micropolitics accidentally—this is a term Budgeon creates to describe the sorts of unconscious interventions these girls make—over the years that she's produced *Doris*, Crabb has become increasingly conscious of the emotionally sensitive interventions she's making through her zine. Her pedagogy of imagination is not an unconscious or accidental process.

Unlike some grrrl zinesters, Crabb is confident that her zine has made a difference in the world. Correspondence that Crabb receives from readers confirms for her that her zine has an effect. For instance, in one letter that Crabb characterizes as typical, a woman explains, "I think it's so important for women to see that there is an empowered network of other amazing women out there. We just have to find and support each other. Please know you have my support."[82] This illustrates the embodied community, because *Doris* helped to facilitate a real human connection between Crabb and this reader, a connection that helped the reader feel supported and inspired her to want to convey that same sense of support to Crabb in a letter. Crabb explained that this sort of response is common: "I get a lot of mail from people who I know personally it has affected. . . . I feel like it's helped some people not kill themselves. It's helped me not to kill myself, and I think it does help. I'm sure other zines are like that, too. I know *Snarla* helped me. I think it helps people to not just go where they're told to go. Zines help a lot of people to explore more options in their life, both emotionally and physically."[83]

In other words, Crabb sees *Doris* as a zine with a pedagogical effect, the effect of helping people "to explore more options in their life." This is clearly an important issue for Crabb, one that serves as a kind of framework for her zine. She states this idea as well in an early issue of *Doris*:

> I have this strong empathy for the way people struggle and the ways they get by in this fucked up world. I wonder all the time about what people would be doing if they were presented with options that they didn't normally see. How they would be living and relating to each other and looking at the world and what they wanted, if there were alternatives that were real and strong.[84]

She's fascinated with the options people "[don't] normally see," with real alternatives, and she sees her zine as space that can make those options visible and thereby teach people to hope. Zines like *Doris* can change power structures by giving individuals a sense of their own power, helping people "not just go where they're told to go."[85] This what it means to offer a pedagogy of imagination.

This relates back to the idea of zines as operating in the tiny spaces in mainstream culture, a notion which Crabb herself voices in *Doris* #24: "I needed to experience a world created in the cracks and fissures and forgotten places."[86] This level of political operation can have very tangible individual effects, such as encouraging someone not to commit suicide. And it can also have broader reaching effects that are harder to track but no less real and significant, effects such as promoting full humanity and citizenship and encouraging readers to feel that they belong in the world, that they have the right to be there, and that they can make a difference.

These effects are a necessary component of propagating democracy, which is why I argue that the pedagogy of imagination is, in fact, a new form of political engagement.

What does it mean to have cultural interventions that are made up of such things—of empathy, imagination, possibility, human connection? This is not what we're used to. This doesn't look like activism to many of us. And yet it's a kind of activism sensitively attuned to this cultural moment. In his most recent book, *Dream: Re-Imagining Progressive Politics in an Age of Fantasy*, Stephen Duncombe calls for just this sort of thing, a set of activist interventions that not only rely on the rational and well-argued but also tap into our human need for something more, which he encompasses in the umbrella term "spectacle." According to Duncombe, spectacle is "a way of making an argument. Not through appeals to reason, rationality, and self-evident truth, but instead through story and myth, fears and desire, imagination and fantasy. It realizes what reality cannot represent. It is the animation of an abstraction, a transformation from ideal to expression. *Spectacle is a dream on display.*"[87]

This, then, is what I argue that Crabb achieves in each issue of *Doris*. *Doris* is, in some senses, a dream on display. She imagines a world in which people are allowed to achieve their full humanity, and she offers glimpses of that world. She invites her reader to imagine with her, to feel what she is feeling. And because she has the zine medium to work with, with her own handwriting and the little pictures of Anna the dog, because she enters the reader's home and hands, she taps into the potential of the embodied community. The zine medium invites the reader to let her guard down, and Crabb steps into that small space, that fissure, where she can offer a pedagogy of hope.

I don't mean to suggest that *Doris* is a zine that offers mindless uplift. Over the years, Crabb has discussed horrible pain that she's suffered—and she makes that pain viscerally real. She discusses rape, abortion, sexual harassment, the death of people she couldn't bear to lose. And she discusses the larger cultural traumas of the first and second Gulf Wars, the state-sanctioned murders of indigenous people in South America, and the halted history of union organizing in the United States But rather than framing these issues by resorting to easy, familiar, cynical narratives, she frames them in terms of hope:

> Do you believe in happy endings? Because sometimes they do happen. Something inside shifts, something outside comes together, and your

fight becomes more purposeful, your rest becomes actually restful, your hurt becomes something you can bear, and your happiness becomes something that shines out with ease, not in lightning manic bursts that fill and then drain you, but something else, something steady, something you can almost trust to stay there.[88]

In fact, Crabb's zine seems to operate within the kind of activist location bell hooks describes in *Yearning: Race, Gender, and Cultural Politics*, a location of resistant marginality that allows for a new sort of subjectivity. hooks explains: "We come to this space through suffering and pain, through struggle. We know struggle to be that which pleasures, delights, and fulfills desire. We are transformed, individually, collectively, as we make radical creative space which affirms and sustains our subjectivity, which gives us a new location from which to articulate our sense of the world."[89] Crabb herself is a woman who's lived much of her adult life— the time that she's been producing *Doris*—on the margins of mainstream society. She has lived in small radical collectives in such places as Portland, Oregon, and Asheville, North Carolina. She's lived in transit and has spent time in jail. She's made money at various times through subsistence farming, public assistance, and working retail jobs. When I visited with her in July 2007 in Asheville, she was sewing funky skirts and contributing to an organic bread-baking cooperative. These lifestyle choices of intentional marginality have perhaps helped her sustain the kind of "radical creative space" that hooks describes, a space that allows her—in the pages of *Doris*—to theorize social change and invite her readers to do the same.

In chapter 2, I discuss people's motivation for creating a zine. People often say they do their zine because it's fun—"tactiley" fun, fun to express themselves and to become part of a community. Beyond this, I suggest that grrrl zines are often tapping into the pleasures of social change efforts. Changing culture is hard; as hooks says, it's struggle. I've written elsewhere about the work involved: "In this era of instant gratification, we don't hear much about committing ourselves to a difficult struggle, and yet this must be the guiding philosophy of feminist consciousness in the twenty-first century."[90] Bernice Johnson Reagon articulates the visceral challenges of social justice work particularly clearly when she writes, "I feel as if I'm gonna keel over any minute and die. That is often what it feels like if you're really doing coalition work. Most of the time you feel threatened to the core and if you don't, you're not really doing no coalescing."[91] Committing ourselves to a difficult challenge, one that's potentially painful and almost certainly going to experience more setbacks than successes, is not the prevailing ethos of this cultural moment. Reagon's words seem daunting.

And yet these zinesters are expressing the joy of the struggle, what hooks describes as "that which pleasures, delights, and fulfills desire." Crabb says again and again, throughout the fifteen years of *Doris*, that not trying to change the world would be boring. Issues of *Bitch* repeatedly couch the publication's efforts at social change in terms of enjoyment, as in a 2008 editors' letter that explained, "As always, we've got far more questions than answers in this issue, but putting it together was more about fun than frustration."[92] In *Greenzine*, Road describes her heart as "a muscle that blossomed by way of movement rather than contentment" and voices the importance of community: "The realization that kindled my impulse is the one that said I wasn't alone in this lifelong quest. That quest about hope and an agenda that went beyond a radical cliché."[93] Other zines describe the pleasures of struggle, as well, as when Lauren Jade Martin writes, "There is a rush, a certain kind of euphoria (way better than drugs, I'm sure) that comes with political work and organizing. . . . Every time I hear a domestic violence survivor assert in a workshop or a support group or on the hotline that she has a right to be safe and free from violence, I get a shiver of hope down my back."[94]

This is yet another way that grrrl zines can enact a pedagogy of hope, by demonstrating the satisfaction of involvement. Crabb told me, "When I look at my friends' lives, who don't have any hope and who are cynical, they seem to have not very happy lives. Maybe they do fun stuff a lot, but they don't seem very fulfilled, and I feel like working for social change is really fulfilling. It can be not very fulfilling, but you can find ways to make it super fulfilling, and then that gives hope, even in a hopeless situation."[95] Zine making is one of the fulfilling ways that some girls and women have found to "give hope, even in a hopeless situation." Grrrl zines provide hope not only to the maker but also to the reader. This is one component of zines' embodied community: their ability to transmit the corporeal experience of hopefulness and the pleasures of resisting the resignation of a cynical culture.

The recently published book *Unmarketable* explores corporate megaliths and their quick and effective coopting of cultural resistance and underground modes of expression. Author Anne Elizabeth Moore—herself a zine creator—argues that smart alternative cultural producers can't outthink the marketers or attempt to subvert their strategies through mocking or parody; for instance, in the new world of marketing, the grrrl zine *Hey There, Barbie Girl*, which parodically critiques the Barbie enterprise, ends up functioning as an ad for Mattel. But Moore suggests that if we can't destroy this marketing mentality, we can disrupt it, in part by recognizing it (as the pedagogy of active critique encourages readers to do), opting out of it (as happens in the pedagogy of process), and forming our own non-product-based emotional investments (as with the pedagogy of imagination).[96]

Moore's book is not particularly hopeful, but her arguments do implicitly reinforce the importance of the pedagogies of hope that grrrl zines can mobilize. Indeed, to return to Moraga's ideas from *This Bridge Called My Back*, a foundation for all social justice work must be the belief "that we have the power to actually transform our experience, change our lives, save our lives."[97] This "faith of activists" underlies, to greater or lesser extents, all grrrl zines. No matter how pessimistic or cynical the subject matter of the zine is, the fact that the zine exists—that the creator felt motivated to take action, to produce this artifact and share it with others in what can become an embodied community—gives evidence of hope. Many grrrl zines, from *Greenzine* to *Bitch* to *Doris*, have made it their business to propagate that hope and teach others to be hopeful, as well.

## Disrupt, Subvert, Change

In my initial assessments of grrrl zines, I found myself wanting to make them fit existing political models in order to prove their validity. I wanted to show that they affected zinesters' and readers' engagement in political protest, that they encouraged voting, or that they helped decrease the prevalence of eating disorders or helped spread awareness of emergency contraception. And while I still think it would be interesting to know to what extent these things are true, I've come to feel that the political work of grrrl zines is more subtle and differently resistant than my earlier line of questioning allowed me to see.

What I'm interested in now are these new modes of doing politics, these micropolitical pedagogies that operate in the fissures and forgotten places, that offer dreams on display, that provoke outrage, that invite all kinds of emulation. Viewing grrrl zines in this way not only makes their interventions more visible and valuable but also gives a framework for evaluating the larger world of third wave feminism. These zines become case studies that materialize the arguments that third wave scholars and girls' studies scholars have been making—arguments about girls' and women's agency and about what it means to resist in the current cultural moment.

Grrrl zines demonstrate the interpenetration of complicity and resistance; they are spaces to try out mechanisms for doing things differently— while still making use of the ephemera of the mainstream culture. They demonstrate the process, the missed attempts as well as the successes. They aren't the magic solution to social change efforts; instead, they are small, incomplete attempts, micropolitical. They function in a different way than mainstream media and than previous social justice efforts. Indeed, my work with these zines has helped me understand one of the central paradoxes of third wave feminism: the contradiction between the emphasis on the personal and intimate on the one hand, and the need for broader collective action on the other hand. In some ways, grrrl zines merge the two: they are clearly intimate, personal artifacts, and they create embodied communities. But these aren't communities that become large protest groups or voting blocs. They are communities that operate in the cracks and fissures, that—as Moore suggests—aren't equipped to bring down the megacorporations but to disrupt them, to offer some static, what Rodriguez describes as the bubbles in the swamp that show that democracy is still fermenting. They show that change is still possible—"even more than we are able to imagine."

# Conclusion

> I thought about stories, and when are people going to stop telling
> the ones with easy punchlines, dramatic conclusions; when are
> they gonna stop talking about chictracks and crankshafts. What
> the hell do they actually think about anyway? It can't be as shallow
> as all this. I thought about: when do we start to tell the stories that
> sound mundane, but actually make up our real lives.
>
> —Cindy Crabb, *Doris* #22 (2004)

## "I Think I Made a Zine"

Recently I gave a presentation on zines for an undergraduate American
literature class. I described zines, showed slides of zine pages, and discussed the wide variety of things people do with and in zines. At the end
of the class, a quiet student approached me.

"So, zines are, like, little booklets you make on paper, and photocopy,
and give to people?"

I told him yes.

"Could they have poetry in them?"

"Of course! Lots of them do."

"Then, I think I made a zine." He reached into his backpack and pulled
one out and gave it to me. It was digest-sized, filled with photography and
poetry. He was carrying them around to give to friends.

As I was finishing up this project, a colleague alerted me to the fact that
his college-aged daughter, Anna Eisen, was doing what she called "feminist scrapbooking," creating beautiful collages of pictures, comics, and
typed and handwritten text to document her everyday life. She showed
me some of these pages, and they struck me as akin to one-off zines and
the feminist scrapbooks of the nineteenth and early twentieth centuries. When I asked her why she made scrapbooks rather than blogging,
she said, "I prefer to work first in the scrapbook format because I love
combining textures and adding dimension to pages. I am not opposed

to digital scrapbooking if it serves the purpose of giving women an artistic outlet, but it is simply not for me. More importantly, compiling these collected pages into a volume adds a level of permanence (I'm not sure this is the word I'm looking for) that I don't feel on the internet."[1] Her response is similar to that of many zine creators: she's committed to the materiality of the medium both for its historical longevity and for its expressive potential.

At another point during my research, I redirected a letter that was inadvertently delivered to my house. A few weeks later, I received an elaborately decorated manila envelope in the mail from the high school student who had sent the original letter. She explained to me that she does mail art, and she sent me this art—an envelope covered with playing cards, cut-up bits of old photographs, cancelled stamps, and magazine pages—as a thank you gift. Inside the envelope were old camera negatives and a mix CD of some of her favorite music. This package wasn't quite a zine, but it was certainly in the family—an expressive artifact created from ephemeral, culturally prevalent materials.

These public-private modes of self-expression, community-building, and societal intervention sometimes emerge spontaneously. While some zinesters start off positioning themselves self-consciously within a zine

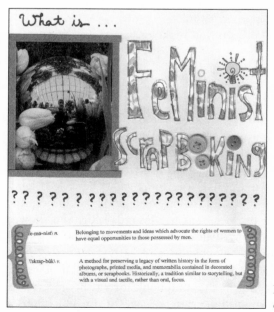

Feminist scrapbook page, courtesy of Anna Eisen.

Envelope art, courtesy of Lauren Moore.

community, invited or inspired to participate by reading zines, others stumble on zine making accidentally.

I was one of those.

As I've talked with zine creators over the past several years, many of them have asked me about my own zine story. Did I ever make a zine myself? The answer is yes. In high school, in 1990, I spearheaded the production of a compilation zine called *Naked*. I didn't know it was a zine, nor did any of my friends—I'm not sure that the rhetoric of the zine had made it to rural Tennessee by that time. But the concept certainly had. Our production, distribution, and tone all fit us within the zine medium. We combined typewritten text with hand-drawn headlines, cartoons, and other graphics, and we wrote in ways that were—to us at the time— shockingly explicit. My editor's letter, for instance, was called "Whispers (Foreplay and General Introduction)." We did our photocopying for free, at my dad's office after hours. We handed copies out to friends and left them at independent music stores and comic book shops. The yellowed copies of *Naked* I still have tucked away are immediately identifiable to me now as zines.

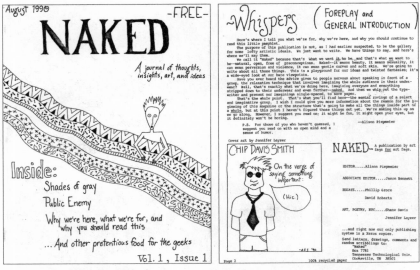

Cover and page from *Naked*.

My story isn't identical to those of many of the zine creators in *Girl Zines*. I didn't come to feminism through zines; it wasn't until the next year that I, like many proto-third wavers, would encounter Susan Faludi's *Backlash* and with it feminism. It wasn't until I was researching third wave feminism that I encountered the *Action Girl Newsletter* and *Jigsaw*.

And yet, like many girls and women who have made and continue to make zines—and like their predecessors with their mimeograph machines and scrapbooks—I had something to say that I couldn't say using traditional, professional channels. I believed the rhetoric that I'd been taught, that women could do anything, and I didn't want to fit my identity into any of the easy boxes that mainstream media presented to me as the norms of girlhood. And I thought it was great fun to sit on the floor of my bedroom, cutting and pasting together pages with my friends, creating an artifact that was meaningful to us and imagining other people holding it, reading it. That zine tells me something about my teenaged life and the culture of which I was part that no other artifact can convey. As Eisen explained of her own creations, "By scrapping my feelings of angst now, I am not only able to release those feelings from my system, but also provide a better picture of what life was like in the 2000s."[2]

These accidental zinesters' stories show, too, that the questions that have propelled this study—What is life like for girls and women on the ground? What do the creative acts of girls and women tell us about their lives, and about contemporary feminism? What do we find if we look outside the standard cultural productions that the corporate world and the academic world deem worthwhile?—apply to more things than just grrrl zines. There is a world of material imagination, ephemeral creativity, and feminist intervention out there that is happening informally, under the radar.

One of the things that has struck me about the zine world and the world of material imagination of which it is a part, is that it's fundamentally a gift culture. It's a space where girls and women are offering objects and ideas—beautiful ones like Eisen's scrapbooks; painful ones like Chestnut's reflections on her grandmother or Whitehead's entanglement with Aunt Jemima; angry ones like Nguyen's disgust with the question, "Where are you from?"; or funny ones like the Action Girl paper dolls—without an expectation of financial reward, simply for the pleasures of expression, community-building, and the possibility of making cultural changes, even tiny ones. The grrrl zine culture is grounded in a gift economy, at a small but profound remove from the capitalist marketplace and the operations of the consumer culture industries. These girls and women are putting their thoughts and material artifacts out there for others. Even when their zines are for sale, zines aren't a financially motivated undertaking; instead, they're community motivated. This is an idea I examine in chapter 2, but it informs the whole book and the whole grrrl zine undertaking. This community-minded generosity provides a space, Eisen told me, where "women can tell their stories," "stories," as Crabb explains in the epigraph, "that sound mundane, but actually make up our real lives."[3]

Furthermore, grrrl zines are sites for the articulation and illustration of third wave feminist theoretical work. Within these documents, girls and women develop conceptual apparatus to identify, make visible, and address long-standing—but shifting and innovative—social justice issues. They challenge misogyny, racism, and homophobia in individual and symbolic manifestations, from personal experiences of sexual assault to media representations of women's sexuality, from culturally prescribed body hatred to the particular kinds of hostility meted out to bodies that aren't white, straight, and gender normative. Grrrl zinesters take on these personal and cultural phenomena in playful, angry, and unruly ways, even as they reclaim and reinscribe certain aspects of the culture—using femininity strategically, for instance, or embracing sexist terminology and iconography for their own ends. Although not all grrrl zinesters identify as third wave feminists, the feminist work they are doing draws from second wave insights, the theoretical work of U.S. third world feminists, and the specificities of this late-capitalist cultural moment, synthesizing those components in ways that come to characterize the third wave. Because zines are scrappy, informal, sometimes deliberately immature and provocative, and able to be produced by almost anyone, they haven't generally been recognized either as a meaningful part of feminist history or as sites for feminist theory production, but they are both.

The theoretical mechanisms of zines operate on multiple levels—not simply at the level of their textual content but at the level of their visual and material construction and their distribution. Eisen's feminist scrapbook pages convey meaning as much by their thoughtful visual components as by their words. Furthermore, when girls and women distribute their publications to others, they activate embodied communities. I was swept into such a community when the high school student sent me her mail art, when I touched and opened the envelope, felt the textures of the ephemera taped and glued to it, and experienced a physical, sensory connection to the person who had created this artifact and sent it to me. I created my own affectionate community networks with my high school zine. These embodied communities are spaces that allow for personal and political exploration, that allow girls and women to reinscribe and shape the public reception of their bodies, as well as their own intimate corporeal experiences. Because these embodied communities are sites of vulnerability and care, they are part of what makes it possible for girls and women to articulate complex, fragmented identities in their zines and to try out different modes of intervention. They are what inspires the gifting, the generous creativity and expression that keeps zining alive. These embodied grrrl zine communities are linked to feminist communities of the past; examining these cultural productions as part of long-term feminist efforts reveals linkages between the incarnations of feminism, even as grrrl zines make visible the innovative ways girls and women in the late-twentieth century and early-twenty-first enact agency and resistance.

## How to Find Zines

Once I discovered other people's zines, I was hooked. Although zine distribution channels are more hidden than the obvious mechanisms of the corporate consumer marketplace, all it takes is getting into the zine world a bit to learn your way around. Most zines offer reviews or shout-outs to other zines, with contact information, so getting connected to the zine network is sometimes as simple as getting your hands on one zine and going from there. One zine is often enough to bring a person into the zine community: if you order the zines that the first zinester recommends, and then order the zines that those folks recommend, you're on your way. A friendly handwritten note is appreciated, and sometimes if zinesters know you care, they'll alert you when they produce a new zine. A few (like *The East Village Inky*) offer subscriptions, but this is certainly the exception, since many zine creators don't have a sense of when or whether they'll be producing another zine.

There are other ways to acquire zines, as well. Zine review guides like *Zine World* and *Xerography Debt* offer reviews of hundreds of zines, with full information for ordering them. Also zine yearbooks, such as *Best Zine Ever!*, select excerpts from what they consider the best zines of a given year, and they are great ways to be introduced to new zines. There are also several thriving online distribution sites, or distros, that make ordering zines as easy as ordering from Amazon.com. Microcosm Publishing is probably the most prominent of these distros, but others include Fall of Autumn, Sweet Candy Distro, and Parcell Press.

Independent bookstores and record stores around the country still sell zines. These include such large, well-known stores as Quimby's in Chicago and Reading Frenzy and Powell's in Portland, as well as stores like Baltimore's Atomic Books and New York's Bluestockings. Zines are also available in such possibly unexpected sites as Boxcar Books in Bloomington, Indiana; Malaprop's Bookstore in Asheville, North Carolina; and 52.5 in Charleston, South Carolina.

Libraries are increasingly cataloging zines as a way "to protect history's precious first draft."[4] A number of research libraries collect zines as archival material; prominent among these are the Sallie Bingham Center for Women's History and Culture in Duke University's Special Collections Library and the Barnard College Library, both of which emphasize girls by zines and women in their collections. The Smith College Library, the New York State Library, the Wisconsin Historical Society, and the West Coast Zine Collection at San Diego State University also have prominent zine collections. A growing number of public libraries have also recognized the value of zines, and they often allow zines to be more freely circulated, like any library book. Among these are the Baltimore County Public Library, the Salt Lake City Public Library, and the Cleveland Public Library. Community-supported libraries or infoshops, such as ABC No Rio in New York, Papercut Zine Library in Cambridge, Massachusetts, and the Zine Archive and Publishing Project in Seattle, are grassroots collection sites for zines. Again, these libraries are not just on the coasts—the Denver Zine Library is large and active, and even in places like Nashville, Tennessee, the Firebrand Community Center is assembling a zine library. *Zine World* is compiling a list of zine libraries and distros that appears to be the most comprehensive available.[5] According to their records, thirty states now have either a zine library or an infoshop.

Finally, zine festivals ("fests") happen across the country and are great places to meet zine creators and discover new zines. As the Portland Zine Fest website explains, these events exist "to create greater communication and community between diverse creators of independent media and art. This fun and free event helps people promote their work and to share skills and information related to zines and zine culture."[6] Richmond, Virginia; Portland, Oregon; Madison, Wisconsin; San Francisco, California; and a number of other cities have annual zine fests, and conferences such as the Allied Media Conference feature zine panels.[7]

Grrrl zines offer unsurpassed access to the stories, struggles, and creativity of girls and women since the late 1980s. They are rich primary sources, sites where girls and women document and construct their lives, and where they articulate and illustrate third wave feminist theory. In their negotiations with this cultural moment, their bridging of the abstract and the intensely local, their embrace of the utopian at the same time that they grapple with harsh realities, they offer a glimpse of what kinds of resistance are possible. They are, ultimately, hopeful artifacts, bringing their readers into an embodied community and encouraging them to imagine—and work for—a better world.

# Appendix
## *Where to Find Zines*

*Zine Review Guides*

XEROGRAPHY DEBT
http://www.leekinginc.com/xeroxdebt/index.htm
($3) Davida Gypsy Breier, P.O. Box 11064, Baltimore, MD 21212
ZINE WORLD:
A READER'S GUIDE TO THE UNDERGROUND PRESS
http://www.undergroundpress.org/
P.O. Box 330156, Murfreesboro, TN 37133-0156

*Zine Yearbooks*

BEST ZINE EVER!
http://www.microcosmpublishing.com/catalog/zines/1346/
P.O. Box 12409, Portland, OR 97212

*Distros*

FALL OF AUTUMN
http://www.fallofautumn.com/
alan@fallofautumn.com
Alan Lastufka, P.O. Box 254, Manhattan, IL 60442
MICROCOSM
http://www.microcosmpublishing.com/
sparky@microcosmpublishing.com
222 S Rogers St. Bloomington, IN 47404
PARCELL PRESS
http://www.parcellpress.com/

SWEET CANDY DISTRO
http://www.eyecandyzine.com/
sweetcandydistro@gmail.com
c/o Sage, P.O. Box 1833, Dallas, GA 30132

## Book/Record Stores

52.5 RECORDS
http://www.corporaterocksucks.com/
561 King Street, Charleston, SC 29403

ARISE BOOKSTORE
http://www.arisebookstore.org/
2441 Lyndale Ave., Minneapolis MN 55404

ATOMIC BOOKS
http://www.atomicbooks.com/
3620 Falls Road, Baltimore, MD 21211

BLUESTOCKINGS BOOKSTORE
http://www.bluestockings.com/
172 Allen St., New York, NY 10002

BOUND TOGETHER
1369 Haight St., San Francisco, CA 94117

BOXCAR BOOKS
http://www.boxcarbooks.org/
408 E. 6th Street, Bloomington, IN 47408

CITY LIGHTS BOOKSTORE
http://www.citylights.com/
261 Columbus Ave., San Francisco, CA 94133

COMIC RELIEF
http://www.comicrelief.net
2026 Shattuck Ave., Berkeley, CA 94704

FEED YOUR HEAD BOOKS
http://www.feedyourheadbooks.com
272 Essex St., Salem, MA 01970

LEFT BANK BOOKS
www.leftbankbooks.com
92 Pike St., Seattle, WA 98101

MALAPROP'S BOOKSTORE
http:/www.malaprops.com
55 Haywood Street, Asheville, NC 28801

NEEDLES & PENS
  http://www.needles-pens.com/
  3253 16th Street, San Francisco, CA 94103
POWELL'S BOOKS
  www.powells.com
  1005 W. Burnside, Portland, OR 97209
QUIMBY'S
  http://www.quimbys.com/
  1854 W. North Avenue, Chicago, IL 60622
READING FRENZY
  http://www.readingfrenzy.com/
  921 S.W. Oak Street, Portland, OR 97205
ST. MARK'S BOOKSHOP
  http://www.stmarksbookshop.com/NASApp/store/IndexJsp
  31 Third Avenue, New York, NY 10003

## Zine Libraries

BARNARD COLLEGE LIBRARY
  http://www.barnard.edu/library/zines/
  3009 Broadway, New York, NY 10027
NEW YORK STATE LIBRARY
  http://www.nysl.nysed.gov/
  Cultural Education Center, Empire State Plaza, Albany, NY 12230
SALLIE BINGHAM CENTER FOR WOMEN'S HISTORY
AND CULTURE IN DUKE UNIVERSITY'S SPECIAL
COLLECTIONS LIBRARY
  http://library.duke.edu/specialcollections/bingham/
  Box 90185, Duke University, Durham, North Carolina 27708-0185
SMITH COLLEGE LIBRARY
  http://www.smith.edu/libraries/libs/ssc/index.html
  7 Neilson Drive, Smith College, Northampton, MA 01063
WEST COAST ZINE COLLECTION AT
SAN DIEGO STATE UNIVERSITY
  http://infodome.sdsu.edu/about/depts/spcollections/rarebooks/zines-findingaid.shtml
  Special Collections and University Archives, Malcolm A. Love Library, San Diego State University, 5500 Campanile Drive, San Diego, CA 92182-8050

WISCONSIN HISTORICAL SOCIETY
http://www.wisconsinhistory.org/libraryarchives/
816 State Street, Madison, WI 53706-1417

## Public Libraries

BALTIMORE COUNTY PUBLIC LIBRARY
http://www.bcpl.info/
9833 Greenside Drive, Cockeysville, MD 21030-2188
CLEVELAND PUBLIC LIBRARY
http://cpl.org/
325 Superior Ave N.E., Cleveland, Ohio 44114
SALT LAKE CITY PUBLIC LIBRARY
http://www.slcpl.lib.ut.us/index.jsp
210 East 400 South, Salt Lake City, UT 84111

## Community-Supported Libraries/Infoshops

ABC NO RIO
http://www.abcnorio.org/
161 Rivington St,, New York, NY 10002
DENVER ZINE LIBRARY
http://www.denverzinelibrary.org/
1644 Platte St., Studio 107, Denver, CO 80202
FIREBRAND COMMUNITY CENTER
http://www.thefirebrand.org/
918 Ward St., Nashville, TN 37207
PAPERCUT ZINE LIBRARY
http://www.papercutzinelibrary.org/
45 Mt. Auburn St., Cambridge, MA 02138
ZINE ARCHIVE AND PUBLISHING PROJECT
http://www.hugohouseservices.org/home/ZAPP/ZAPP.aspx
noramukaihata@hugohouse.org (ZAPP currently closed)
ZINE WORLD INFOSHOPS AND
ZINE LIBRARIES COMPREHENSIVE LIST
http://www.undergroundpress.org/zine-resources/infoshops-zine-libraries/

## Zine Fests

MADISON, WISCONSIN
http://www.midwestzines.org/2.html
PORTLAND, OREGON
http://www.pdxzines.com/
RICHMOND, VIRGINIA
http://www.richmondzinefest.org/
P.O. Box 35501, Richmond, VA 23235
SAN FRANCISCO, CALIFORNIA
http://www.sfzinefest.com/

# Notes

1. Allison Wolfe was Bratmobile's lead singer, and Erin Smith was their guitarist.

2. Stephen Duncombe, *Notes from Underground* (New York: Verso, 1997), 1.

3. Duncombe cites the 50,000 figure in ibid. and estimates that 500,000 to 700,000 people were zine readers in 1997 (14). As evidence of zines' prevalence, one issue of the triannual zine review guide *Zine World: A Reader's Guide to the Underground Press* #21 (Murfreesboro, Tenn.: Self-published, May/June 2004) features reviews of 155 individual zines, while another, #24 (Murfreesboro, Tenn.: Self-published, January 2007), reviews 199 zines. Microcosm Press stocked 785 different zines as of April 2009.

4. For an explanation of participatory media and participatory culture, see Henry Jenkins, *Fans, Bloggers, and Gamers: Exploring Participatory Culture* (New York: New York University Press, 2006).

5. I use the term "grrrl zines" as girls' studies scholar Mary Celeste Kearney does, "to identify those texts that foreground an exploration of female identity and experience" (Kearney, *Girls Make Media* [New York: Routledge, 2006], 153).

6. Ibid., 136. Michelle Comstock, too, notes that zinesters are "rhetoricians engaged in the important political process of re-envisioning and revising 'feminism' and 'girlhood' in the contemporary United States" (Comstock, "Grrrl Zine Networks: Re-Composing Spaces of Authority, Gender, and Culture," *JAC* (*Journal of Advanced Composition*) 21.2 [2001]: 384).

7. Duncombe inaugurated the academic study of zines with *Notes from Underground*. Girls' studies scholars, notably Kearney (*Girls Make Media*) and Anita Harris (*Future Girl: Young Women in the Twenty-First Century* [New York: Routledge, 2004]), have examined zines. Solid sociological studies of zines by girls and women have been done by Barbara J. Guzzetti and Margaret Gamboa ("Zines for Social Justice: Adolescent Girls Writing on Their Own," *Reading Research Quarterly* 39.4 [Oct.–Dec. 2004], 408–436) and Kristen Schilt ("'I'll Resist with Every Inch and Every Breath': Girls and Zine Making as a Form of Resistance," *Youth and Society* 35.1 [Sept. 2003]: 71–97). The recent academic collection by Jo Reger, ed., *Different Wavelengths: Studies of the Contemporary Women's Movement* (New York: Routledge, 2005), features two essays on zines, Schilt's "'The Punk White Privilege Scene': Riot Grrrl, White Privilege, and Zines," 39–56, and Dawn Bates

and Maureen C. McHugh's "Zines: Voices of Third Wave Feminists," 179–194. Excellent brief analyses have been offered by Comstock ("Grrrl Zine Networks") and Janice Radway, "Girls, Zines, and the Miscellaneous Production of Subjectivity in an Age of Unceasing Circulation," lecture presented at the Center for Interdisciplinary Studies of Writing and the Literacy and Rhetorical Studies Minor, No. 18, University of Minnesota, 2001. Zines by girls and women have been studied in particular contexts, such as in terms of their representations of autobiographical strategies (Anna Poletti, "Self-Publishing in the Global and Local: Situating Life Writing in Zines," *Biography* 28.1 [2005]: 183–192); in terms of their manifestation of particular theoretical models (Adela C. Licona, "'(B)orderlands' Rhetorics and Representations: The Transformative Potential of Feminist Third-Space Scholarship and Zines," *NWSA* (*National Women's Studies Association*) *Journal* 17.2 [2005]: 104–129); or in relation to the Riot Grrrl movement (Jessica Rosenberg and Gitana Garofalo, "Riot Grrrl: Revolutions from Within," *Signs* 23 [1998]: 809–841). Deborah Siegel's *Sisterhood, Interrupted: From Radical Women to Grrls Gone Wild* also addresses zines as part of feminism's third wave, particularly in chapter 5, "Rebels with a Cause" (New York: Palgrave Macmillan, 2007).

8. Tobi Vail, *Jigsaw* #4 (Olympia, Wash.: Self-published, 1991), n.p. Vail was also guitarist for Bikini Kill, which is why the zine was available at their performances. In fact, the *Jigsaw* zine was what brought the members of Bikini Kill together.

9. According to the Experience Music Project website, "the term 'riot grrrl' came from two sources. Tobi Vail had already been writing about 'angry grrrls,' and 'riot' came from a letter written to Allison Wolfe by a DC friend, Jen Smith, who'd also played briefly in Bratmobile, discussing the recent Mt. Pleasant riots in DC following a racial shooting incident. 'We need to start a girl riot,' Smith had written, and eventually the words were flipped around to 'riot grrrl'" (Experience Music Project, "Riot Grrrl Retrospective," http://www.emplive.org/exhibits/index.asp?articleID=668).

10. Janice Radway in particular has provided a series of useful theoretical touchstones for this project, from her work on girls and zines to her earlier, groundbreaking *Reading the Romance: Women, Patriarchy, and Popular Literature* (Chapel Hill: University of North Carolina Press, 1984), which provides strategies for analyzing popular literature that does not adhere to the sorts of literary standards that scholars are taught to expect. Her recent work on zines and girl culture includes Radway, "Girls, Reading, and Narrative Gleaning: Crafting Repertoires for Self-Fashioning within Everyday Life," in *Narrative Impact: Social and Cognitive Foundations*, ed. Melanie C. Green, Jeffrey J. Strange, and Timothy C. Brock [Mahwah, N.J.: Erlbaum, 2002], 183–204), and Radway, "Girls, Zines, and Production of Subjectivity." Her work has been foundational to my own thinking about popular literature, the formation of identities in participatory media, and the role of the researcher. The growing field of girls'

studies includes many other outstanding texts, including Catherine Driscoll, *Girls: Feminine Adolescence in Popular Culture and Cultural Theory* (New York: Columbia University Press, 2002); Sherrie A. Inness, ed., *Delinquents and Debutantes: Twentieth-Century American Girls' Cultures* (New York: New York University Press, 1998); and Anita Harris, ed., *All about the Girl: Culture, Power, and Identity* (New York: Routledge, 2004).

11. Radway contends that zines "ought to be read . . . less for the way they are expressions of emerging, idiosyncratic selves or earnest, searching explorations of singular identities. Rather, I think zines should be read more for their radical generativity, for the way they combine and recombine rich repertoires of contradictory cultural fragments" (Radway, "Girls, Zines, and Production of Subjectivity," 11).

12. Lisa Jervis gave a plenary address at the 2004 National Women's Studies Association in which she argued for the abandonment of the term, and recent books such as Melody Berger, ed., *We Don't Need Another Wave: Dispatches from the Next Generation of Feminists* (Emeryville, Calif.: Seal Press, 2006) carry on this argument.

13. For more on the "I'm not a feminist, but" phenomenon, see Susan J. Douglas, *Where the Girls Are: Growing Up Female with the Mass Media* (New York: Times, 1994).

14. Rory Dicker and Alison Piepmeier, "Introduction" to *Catching a Wave: Reclaiming Feminism for the 21st Century*, ed. Dicker and Piepmeier (Boston: Northeastern University Press, 2003), 10.

15. For example, Leslie Heywood and Jennifer Drake, eds., *Third Wave Agenda: Being Feminist, Doing Feminism* (Minneapolis: University of Minnesota Press, 1997); Dicker and Piepmeier, *Catching a Wave*; Astrid Henry, *Not My Mother's Sister: Generational Conflict and Third-Wave Feminism* (Bloomington: Indiana University Press, 2004); Reger, *Different Wavelengths*; and Megan Seely, *Fight Like a Girl: How to Be a Fearless Feminist* (New York: New York University Press, 2007).

16. This differentiation is not new. In her essay "Becoming the Third Wave," a piece widely recognized as inaugurating the third wave, Rebecca Walker declares, "I am not a post-feminism feminist. I am the third wave" (Walker, "Becoming the Third Wave," *Ms.* [Jan. 1992], 39–41). A recent collection called *Interrogating Postfeminism* offers an exploration of postfeminism as a complex cultural phenomenon. The editors explain, "For us, postfeminism signals more than a simple evolutionary process whereby aspects of feminism have been incorporated into popular culture—and thereby naturalized as popular feminism. It also simultaneously involves an 'othering' of feminism . . . its construction as extreme, difficult, and unpleasurable" (Yvonne Tasker and Diane Negra, eds., *Interrogating Postfeminism: Gender and the Politics of Popular Culture* [Durham, N.C.: Duke University Press, 2007], 4). They note that a postfeminist culture is

one in which "women are assumed to have achieved equality" (13), even when there is very little evidence for such an assumption.

17. At the 2006 National Women's Studies Association Conference, five scholars (Jennifer Drake, Leslie Heywood, Astrid Henry, Ednie Kaeh Garrison, and Alison Piepmeier) were invited to take part in a Presidential Session called "New Directions in Feminist Theory." One point the scholars discussed was the fact that the third wave does not seem to have adequate theoretical foundations.

18. Carolyn Dever, *Skeptical Feminism: Activist Theory, Activist Practice* (Minneapolis: University of Minnesota Press, 2004), 4. Dever explains, as well, that "the academic canonization of theory produces a politics of exclusion both within the academy and also between 'academic' theories and those generated from contexts other than the scholarly" (4).

19. Ibid., 5.

20. Radway, "Girls, Reading, Narrative Gleaning," 199, 194.

21. For instance, as recently as March 2007, feminist scholar Rebecca Whisnant, speaking at the conference "Pornography and Pop Culture: Re-framing Theory, Re-thinking Activism," critiqued *Bust* for what she perceived as its complicity with pornography industries. She characterized *Bust* as advocating "a feminism that *acquiesces* to certain key male entitlements, while simultaneously presenting itself as bold and liberated and rebellious" and goes on to argue that "a version of feminism that supports girls' and women's desired self-conception as independent and powerful, while actually requiring very little of them as far as confronting real male power, will . . . have wide appeal. It is my contention (now jumping ahead by a decade or so) that the versions of feminism currently most popular in the academy and in United States popular culture more broadly are of exactly this kind" (Whisnant, at http://saidit.org/archives/jun06/article5.html).

22. Sarah Dyer, *Action Girl Newsletter* #10 (Staten Island, N.Y.: Self-published), n.p.

23. Often young zine commentators offer a celebratory rhetoric about zines. For instance, Francesca Lia Block and Hilary Carlip in their how-to guide for girls, announce, "By now, it's obvious: We want you to have zine mania!" (Block and Carlip, *Zine Scene* [Los Angeles: Girl Press, 1998], 117). Similarly, Elke Zobl claims that "zines reflect the unfiltered and resistant personal and political voices of youth" (Zobl, "Persephone Is Pissed! Grrrl Zine Reading, Making, and Distributing across the Globe," *Hecate* 30.2 [2004]: 156). Jennifer Bleyer asserts, "Zines basically represented pure freedom; there were no ideological police to say that women's liberation couldn't be alternately sexy, angry, emotional, feminine, combative, childish—and unapologetically contradictory" (Bleyer, "Cut-and-Paste Revolution: Notes from the Girl Zine Explosion," in *The Fire This Time: Young Activists and the New Feminism*, ed. Vivien Labaton and Dawn Lundy Martin [New York: Anchor, 2004], 50).

24. Anita Harris identifies this dichotomy in *Future Girl*, and Radway, too, is critical of these models, referring to them as the "girls at risk" discourse and

the "girls speak out" counterdiscourse (Radway, "Zines, Girls, and Production of Subjectivity").

25. Whisnant's speech at the pornography conference—which makes use of the "fuck me feminist" terminology—is an example of the kinds of feminist critiques that view the third wave as politically and ideologically aligned with patriarchal norms. In contrast, young feminists Jessica Rosenberg and Gitana Garofalo claim that Riot Grrrls are "much angrier" than second wave feminists ("Riot Grrrl," 810).

26. Martha Mahoney, "Victimization or Oppression? Women's Lives, Violence, and Agency," in *The Public Nature of Private Violence: The Discovery of Domestic Abuse,* ed. Martha Fineman and Roxanne Mykitiuk (New York: Routledge, 1994), 63.

27. These scholars offer complex poststructuralist accounts of agency and resistance. For instance, Radway explains, "Action and agency, it seems to me, are wrongly construed if they are seen as coming only from within a supposedly authentic self that is set simply in opposition to an imprisoning culture. Subjects are intertwined with culture—they are made of its very substance" (Radway, "Zines, Girls, and Production of Subjectivity," 6). Bordo challenges simplistic notions of resistance: "In assessing resistance—as I understand that activity—I am . . . looking at the concrete consequences of actions, trying to assess in what direction(s) they are moving (or reproducing) the institutions and practices of society" (Bordo, *Twilight Zones: The Hidden Life of Cultural Images from Plato to OJ* [Berkeley: University of California Press, 1997], 188).

28. Harris, *Future Girl,* 2, 4, 3.

29. Jenna Freedman, zine librarian at Barnard College and zine creator, notes, "The first question I get asked when I explain zines to someone who is new to the medium is, 'You mean like a blog?'" (Freedman, "Zines Are Not Blogs: A Not Unbiased Analysis," www.barnard.edu/library/zines/zinesnotblogs.html).

30. In 1997, Duncombe asked, "What is the future of zines? One word: computers" (Duncombe, *Notes from Underground,* 197). In a 2004 essay, Jennifer Bleyer agreed, writing of zines in the past tense and arguing that "the blank URL bar of an Internet window has proven itself in many ways to be the great cultural equalizer" (Bleyer, "Cut-and-Paste Revolution," 56–57).

31. Indeed, a 2008 book by Jeff Gomez is called, unapologetically, *Print Is Dead* (London: Macmillan, 2008), and it follows on the heels of such books as Sven Bikerts, *The Gutenberg Elegies: The Fate of Reading in an Electronic Age* (London: Faber and Faber, 2006); Jay David Bolter, *Writing Space: Computers, Hypertext, and the Remediation of Print* (New York: Erlbaum, 2001); Geoffrey Nunberg, ed., *The Future of the Book* (Berkeley: University of California Press, 1996); Roger Chartier, *Forms and Meanings: Texts, Performances, and Audiences from Codex to Computers* ( Philadelphia: University of Pennsylvania Press, 1995); Janet H. Murray, *Hamlet on the Holodeck: The Future of Narrative in Cyberspace*

(Cambridge: MIT Press, 1998); and the Media in Transition series published by MIT Press, all of which question the effect of digital media on the codex book.

32. Zinester Eleanor Whitney encounters a similar question when she discusses zines: "So, now that there are blogs, does anyone make zines anymore?" (Whitney, "In Praise of Zines: Pushing Paper in the Digital Age," *Bitch* #31 [winter 2006], 27).

33. Evidence of the continued prevalence of zines can be found in the bookstores, online distribution sites, and zine festivals that sell and distribute zines. See the appendix to this volume.

34. Jennifer Rauch published a study in 2004 that supports my interpretation of the zine/blog interaction: "Based on in-depth interviews . . . I conclude that many zine editors have resisted the Web and that those who have published online remained ambivalent about both the realities of and the prospects for this new technology. This study finds that these self-publishers perceive the Internet as a socially deficient means of distribution compared to their established practices of physically handing out, mailing, and exchanging their creations" (Rauch, "Hands-On Communication: Zine Circulation Rituals and the Interactive Limitations of Web Self-Publishing," *Popular Communication* 2.3 [2004]: 154).

35. Their study found that 35 percent of girls blog, compared with 20 percent of boys (Pew Internet and American Life Project, http://www.pewinternet.org/PPF/r/230/report_display.asp).

36. See Feministing at www.feministing.com, Blac(k)ademic at blackademic.com, Feministe at www.feministe.us/blog, Pandagon at www.pandagon.net, Angry Black Bitch at angryblackbitch.blogspot.com, and Girl with Pen at girlwpen.com.

37. At http://www.guardian.co.uk/world/2006/mar/31/gender.uk.

38. Mimi Nguyen, "Tales of an Asiatic Geek Girl: *Slant* from Paper to Pixels," in *Technicolor: Race, Technology, and Everyday Life*, ed. Alondra Nelson and Thuy Linh N. Tu with Alicia Headlam Hines (New York: New York University Press, 2001), 182–183.

39. For instance, in a study of the online newsreader Ananova, Kate O'Riordan observes that an online construction like Ananova "reproduces sexed hierarchies of difference and reintroduces one-dimensional understandings of gender, in a world where we have the need, and opportunity, to understand that gender and sex are constituted through multiple manifestations, variables, and processes" (O'Riordan, "Gender, Technology, and Visual Cyberculture: Virtually Women," in *Critical Cyberculture Studies*, ed. David Silver and Adrienne Massanari [New York: New York University Press, 2006], 251). In other words, the internet often reproduces familiar and problematic societal hierarchies of status and power rather than challenging them.

40. Jaclyn Friedman, "Wack Attack: Giving the Digital Finger to Blog Bandits," *Bitch* no. 39 (spring 2008), 48. Friedman notes many examples of the

hostile climate, including the posting of female bloggers' home addresses (the kind of attack that made technology writer Kathy Sierra withdraw from public life), the systematic harassment of women on sites such as the law school website AutoAdmit, and efforts by the group Anonymous to shut down female bloggers' sites by "interfere[ing] with [them] technically so [they] can no longer be accessed by readers" (46).

41. Ibid., 47.

42. Amanda Lenhart, "Teens, Online Stranger Contact and Cyberbullying: What the Research Is Telling Us, " Pew Internet and American Life Project, presented to the Internet Safety Task Force, April 30, 2008, http://www.pewinternet. org/PPF/r/243/presentation_display.asp.

43. Nguyen, "Tales of Asiatic Geek Girl," 186.

44. Ibid., 185.

45. Friedman, "Wack Attack," 46.

46. Indeed, Nguyen explains in a number of publications about the incredible hostility she experienced after she wrote an article in the punk zine *Maximum Rock & Roll* critiquing another columnist's eroticization of Asian women's eyelids. The columnist went on to record a song in which he discussed his desire to rape Nguyen—and these actions resulted in very little outcry from the punk community (Nguyen, "Tales of Asiatic Geek Girl," 179–180).

47. Halliday, personal interview. It's worth noting that some zine creators *do* receive "nasty comments" about their zines. For instance, Lauren Jade Martin reported, "I used to get tons of letters, you know, negative feedback, 'you're reverse-racist'" (Martin, personal interview).

48. Martin, http://theyellowperil.com/2008/05/20/the-mixed-race-queer-girl-manifesto-is-dead-long-live-the-mixed-race-queer-girl-manifesto/ (accessed June 5, 2008).

49. Halliday, personal interview.

50. Rauch found that the zine creators she interviewed made similar observations: "Although online publishing's impermanence may lend the medium flexibility, the Web also requires a lasting personal commitment to maintenance that many self-publishers would rather avoid. Just like their creations, many editors are idiosyncratic, ephemeral, irregular—and print suits the zine mentality better than the Internet. In their perspectives, the permanence or impermanence of these two media was intricately linked to physicality" (Rauch, "Hands-On Communication," 162).

51. Riot Grrrl has been the subject of numerous scholarly studies. One of the earliest was Joanne Gottlieb and Gayle Wald's "Smells Like Teen Spirit: Riot Grrrls, Revolution and Women in Independent Rock," in *Microphone Fiends: Youth Music and Youth Culture,* ed. Andrew Ross and Tricia Rose (New York: Routledge, 1994), 250–274. Kearney has published several essays on the movement, including Kearney, "'Don't Need You!': Rethinking Identity Politics and

Separation for a Grrrl Perspective," in *Youth Culture: Identity in a Postmodern World*, ed. Jonathan S. Epstein (Molder, Mass.: Beachwell, 1998), 148–188, and Kearney, "The Missing Links: Riot Grrrl–Feminism–Lesbian Culture," in *Sexing the Groove: Popular Music and Gender*, ed. Sheila Whiteley [London: Routledge, 1997], 207–229), as well as a chapter in Kearney, *Girls Make Media*. Marion Leonard has also published multiple pieces on the movement, including Leonard, "'Rebel Girl, You Are the Queen of My World': Feminism, 'Subculture,' and Grrrl Power," in *Sexing the Groove: Popular Music and Gender*, ed. Sheila Whiteley (London: Routledge, 1997), 230–255, and Leonard, "Paper Planes: Travelling the New Grrrl Geographies," in *Cool Places: Geographies of Youth Cultures*, ed. Tracey Skelton and Gill Valentine (London: Routledge, 1998), 101–118). Recent collections, Reger's *Different Wavelengths* and Tasker and Negra's *Interrogating Postfeminism*, feature essays on Riot Grrrl. While not scholarly, Nadine Monem, ed., *Riot Grrrl: Revolution Girl Style Now!* (London: Black Dog, 2007), offers a series of personal perspectives on the movement.

52. Michele Moylan and Lane Stiles, "Introduction" to *Reading Books: Essays on the Material Text and Literature in America*, ed. Moylan and Stiles (Ameherst: University of Massachusetts Press, 1996), 2.

53. Clemencia Rodriguez, *Fissures in the Mediascape: An International Study of Citizens' Media* (Cresskill, N.J.: Hampton, 2001), xiv.

54. Ayun Halliday, creator of *The East Village Inky*, sent out an email message about this research study to her subscriber database and invited readers to contact me if they were interested in being interviewed, so zine readers initiated contact with me.

55. Indeed, Duncombe explains that "examining the zines reviewed in an issue of *Factsheet Five*—the most complete listing of zines available—I found an almost two-to-one ratio in favor of small-city/suburban/rural origin over large urban areas" (Duncombe, *Notes from Underground* , 14).

CHAPTER 1

1. Dyer, personal interview.

2. Sarah Dyer, *Mad Planet* #2 (Staten Island, N.Y.: Self-published, 1993).

3. Sarah Dyer, *Mad Planet* #1 (Staten Island, N.Y.: Self-published, 1992).

4. Dyer, personal interview.

5. In her autobiography, Stanton wrote of the 1840 World Anti-Slavery Convention's exclusion of women: "It struck me as very remarkable that abolitionists, who felt so keenly the wrongs of the slave, should be so oblivious to the equal wrongs of their own mothers, wives, and sisters, when, according to the common law, both classes occupied a similar legal status" (Stanton, *Eighty Years and More: Reminiscences, 1815–1897* [Amherst, N.Y.: Humanity, 2002], 79). Similarly, Hayden and King's active involvement in the Student Nonviolent

Coordinating Committee led them to the insights they outlined in "A Kind of Memo" (1964): "Many people who are very hip to the implications of the racial caste system, even people in the movement, don't seem to be able to see the sexual caste system and if the question is raised they respond with: 'That's the way it's supposed to be'" (reprinted as Hayden and King, "Sex and Caste," in *Dear Sisters: Dispatches from the Women's Liberation Movement*, ed. Rosalyn Baxandall and Linda Gordon [New York: Basic, 2000], 22). Moraga and Anzaldúa explain in the introduction to *This Bridge Called My Back*, "We want to express to all women—especially to white middle-class women—the experiences which divide us as feminists; we want to examine incidents of intolerance, prejudice, and denial of differences within the feminist movement" (Moraga and Anzaldúa, *This Bridge Called My Back: Writings by Radical Women of Color* [New York: Kitchen Table: Women of Color Press, 1981], xxiii).

6. Trade books about zines routinely identify their origins with the Founding Fathers. For instance, Benjamin Franklin's *Poor Richard's Almanack* is cited as a zine precursor in R. Seth Friedman, *The Factsheet Five Zine Reader* (New York: Three Rivers, 1997), 10; Bill Brent, *Make a Zine!* (San Francisco: Black Books, 1997), 15; and Mark Todd and Esther Pearl Watson, *Whatcha Mean, What's a Zine?* (Boston: Graphia, 2006), 20. *The Factsheet Five Reader* also identifies Thomas Paine's *Common Sense* and Dadaist publications as zine precursors, and *Whatcha Mean?* discusses Samizdat publications. Scholarly studies replicate this genealogy, as well. Fred Wright's "The History and Characteristics of Zines" discusses Revolutionary War broadsides along with Dadaist and Samizdat publishing as part of the history of zines (*The Zine and E-Zine Resource Guide*, 1997, http://www.zinebook.com/resource/wright2.html). Stephen Duncombe, as well, identifies zines with "a tradition stretching back to Thomas Paine and other radical pamphleteers, up through the underground press of the 1960s, and on toward the internet" (Duncombe, *Notes from Underground* [New York: Verso, 1997], 15). He also links zines with Dadaist writings (34).

7. Kearney identifies second wave feminist predecessors to Riot Grrrl bands, and she contends that scholars have inaccurately implied that the fanzine precursors were male-dominated media, when, in fact, women have always been an active presence—if not the predominant population—producing fan publications (Kearney, "The Missing Links: Riot Grrrl–Feminism–Lesbian Culture," in *Sexing the Groove: Popular Music and Gender*, ed. Sheila Whiteley [London: Routledge, 1997], 207–229). Similarly, Anna Feigenbaum insists that the informal publications associated with such social movements as the Greenham Common Women's Peace Camp be understood as part of the history of zines: "I argue that Greenham's camp-based media should be considered as part of the genealogy of zine-making, rather than exclusively as 'movement ephemera' or 'social movement publications.' Placing this kind of media production alongside that of zines and their histories helps to bridge gaps in chronological histories of women's

grassroots publication and intervenes in narratives of zine-making as an individualist or 'underground' exercise" (Feigenbaum, "Tactics and Technology: Cultural Resistance at the Greenham Common Women's Peace Camp," Ph.D. diss., McGill University, 2008). Dawn Bates and Maureen C. McHugh make a brief reference to feminist predecessors to zines (Bates and McHugh, "Zines: Voices of Third Wave Feminists," in *Different Wavelengths: Studies of the Contemporary Women's Movement*, ed. Jo Reger [New York: Routledge, 2005], 181).

8. Lisa Schoenfielder and Barb Wieser, eds., *Shadow on a Tightrope: Writings by Women on Fat Oppression* (San Francisco: Aunt Lute, 1983).

9. Ellen Bass and Laura Davis, *The Courage to Heal: A Guide for Women Survivors of Child Sexual Abuse* (New York: HarperCollins, 1988).

10. Jennifer Bleyer, "Cut-and-Paste Revolution: Notes from the Girl Zine Explosion," in *The Fire This Time: Young Activists and the New Feminism*, ed. Vivien Labaton and Dawn Lundy Martin (New York: Anchor, 2004), 47.

11. Katie Roiphe, *The Morning After: Sex, Fear, and Feminism on Campus* (Boston: Little, Brown, 1993), 171.

12. Rebecca Walker, *To Be Real: Telling the Truth and Changing the Face of Feminism* (New York: Anchor, 1995), xxxiii.

13. Leslie Heywood and Jennifer Drake, eds., *Third Wave Agenda: Being Feminist, Doing Feminism* (Minneapolis: University of Minnesota Press, 1997), 3; Rory Dicker and Alison Piepmeier, eds., *Catching a Wave: Reclaiming Feminism for the 21st Century* (Boston: Northeastern University Press, 2003), 16.

14. Astrid Henry, "Feminism's Family Problem: Feminist Generations and the Mother-Daughter Trope," in *Catching a Wave: Reclaiming Feminism for the 21st Century*, ed. Rory Dicker and Alison Piepmeier (Boston: Northeastern University Press, 2003), 211, 210.

15. Feminist authors from Gloria Steinem and bell hooks to Emi Koyama have made note of this ability to alter in response to criticism as one of feminism's great strengths.

16. Suffragists and women's rights activists weren't the only women constrained by the dominant scripts; many women novelists have had to publish as men in order to have their voices heard, if their writing challenged the conventional sentimental tenets of women's writing.

17. Katherine Ott, Susan Tucker, and Patricia P. Buckler, "An Introduction to the History of Scrapbooks," in *The Scrapbook in American Life*, ed. Tucker, Ott, and Buckler (Philadelphia: Temple University Press, 2006), 3.

18. Amy L. Mecklenburg-Faenger, "Scissors, Paste and Social Change: The Rhetoric of Scrapbooks of Women's Organizations, 1875–1930," Ph.D. diss., Ohio State University, 2007, 60–61. Mecklenburg-Faenger notes that scrapbooks, like zines, have not been taken seriously by historians, art theorists, or others who might be presumed to have an interest in this medium because they are seen as unimportant (because produced nonprofessionally by women).

19. Ibid., 72.

20. Ibid., 90.

21. "It is not entirely clear who was reading Harper's books. It was fairly common for the time for women to share scrapbooks, albums, and diaries with others, so it is possible Harper would have done so. I also know for sure that at least one other (undisclosed) woman had charge of her scrapbooks while she was touring in Europe. I also know that Harper donated the volumes to the Library of Congress, which to me signals her intent that others have access to them" (Mecklenburg-Faenger, personal interview).

22. Ellen Gruber Garvey, "Scrapbook, Wish Book, Prayer Book: Trade-Card Scrapbooks and the Missionary Work of Advertising," in *The Scrapbook in American Life*, ed. Susan Tucker, Katherine Ott, and Patricia P. Buckler (Philadelphia: Temple University Press, 2006), 106–107.

23. Margaret Sanger, *Family Limitation* (New York: Self-published, 1914), 10.

24. For more information on Sanger, see Ellen Chesler, *Woman of Valor: Margaret Sanger and the Birth Control Movement in America* (New York: Simon and Schuster, 1992).

25. Constance Chen, *Mary Ware Dennett's Pioneering Battle for Birth Control and Sex Education* (New York: New Press, 1996), x.

26. For more information on Dennett, see ibid. See also Lisa Jean Moore, *Sperm Counts: Overcome by Man's Most Precious Fluid* (New York: New York University Press, 2007).

27. "Expo 96 for Women's Empowerment," http://www.now.org/nnt/01–96/expo.html (accessed August 11, 2007).

28. Susan Brownmiller, *In Our Time: Memoir of a Revolution* (New York: Delta, 1999), 44.

29. Quoted in ibid., 67.

30. Many of these documents are collected in Rosalyn Baxandall and Linda Gordon's excellent *Dear Sisters: Dispatches from the Women's Liberation Movement* (New York: Basic Books, 2000).

31. Ibid., 15.

32. Ibid.

33. Ibid., 15–16.

34. Quoted in Brownmiller, *In Our Time*, 69.

35. Baxandall and Gordon, *Dear Sisters*, 15.

36. She refers here to second wave feminists Jo Freeman, Shulamith Firestone, and Anne Koedt (Lizzard Amazon, *The Bitch Manifesto* [San Jose, Calif.: Self-published], 2).

37. Valerie Solanas, *SCUM Manifesto* (London: Olympia Press, 1971); Dawn Williams, *Function #5* (Canoga Park, Calif.: Self-published, 1993?), 33–34.

38. It's hard to know where these manifestos originated. According to Chelsea Starr, *Fantastic Fanzine* and *Bikini Kill* both printed "because" lists in 1992

(Starr, "Because: Riot Grrrl, Social Movements, Art Worlds, and Style," Ph.D. diss., University of California, Irvine, 1999). According to the film *Don't Need You*, the first Riot Grrrl manifesto was written by Allison Wolfe and Molly Neuman and printed in the zine *Gunk* in Washington, D.C., in 1991 (director Kerri Koch, Urban Cowgirl, 2006). *Riot Grrrl: Revolution Girl Style Now!* simply attributes the first "because" list to Riot Grrrl Manifesto, 1991.

39. I am referring to a Riot Grrrl manifesto printed in *When She Was Good* #1 (Sand Springs, Okla.: Self-published, n.d.).

40. Rosalyn Baxandall and Linda Gordon, eds., *Dear Sisters: Dispatches from the Women's Liberation Movement* (New York: Basic Books, 2000).

41. Chela Sandoval, *Methodology of the Oppressed* (Minneapolis: University of Minnesota Press, 2000), 62, 63.

42. Audre Lorde, "The Master's Tools Will Never Dismantle the Master's House," in *This Bridge Called My Back: Writings by Radical Women of Color*, ed. Cherríe Moraga and Gloria Anzaldúa (New York: Kitchen Table: Women of Color Press, 1983), 99.

43. Cherríe Moraga and Gloria Anzaldúa, eds., "Introduction" to *This Bridge Called My Back* (New York: Kitchen Table: Women of Color Press, 1983), 23.

44. "Revolution, Girl Style," *Newsweek* 120.21 (November 23, 1992), 85; Kim France, "Grrrls at War," *Rolling Stone* 660–661 (July 8–22, 1993), 23, 24.

45. Susan Faludi, *Backlash: The Undeclared War against American Women* (New York: Crown, 1991); Emily White, "Revolution Girl-Style Now!" *Reader* 21.51 (September 25, 1992), 18.

46. Rebecca Walker, "Becoming the Third Wave," *Ms.* (January/February 1992), 41.

47. Deborah Siegel, *Sisterhood, Interrupted: From Radical Women to Grrls Gone Wild* (New York: Palgrave Macmillan, 2007), 155.

48. Jessica Rosenberg and Gitana Garofalo, "Riot Grrrl: Revolutions from Within," *Signs* 23 (1998), 810.

49. Starr, "Because," 77.

50. Lamm, interview as part of the Experience Music Project's "Riot Grrrl Retrospective" (http://www.empsfm.org/exhibitions/index.asp?articleID=666).

51. This lack of recognition of a historical trajectory is compounded by older feminists' lack of awareness of young feminist culture in general, and zines in particular. Many of the major retrospectives being written today about twentieth-century feminism say nothing about zines. Although many more histories of twentieth-century feminism are being written right now, by and large they ignore zines. For instance, Ruth Rosen's *The World Split Open* (2001), Sara Evans' *Tidal Waves* (2003), and Estelle Freedman's *No Turning Back: The History of Feminism and the Future of Women* (2003) do not mention zines (or Riot Grrrls) at all. In fact, Kearney is one of the few scholars who has recognized the connection, arguing repeatedly for the cultural and political connection between Riot Grrrls and 1970s feminists.

52. Julia Downes, *Riot Grrrl: Revolution Girl Style Now!* (London: Black Dog, 2008), 29.

53. Tobi Vail, quoted in Red Chidgey, "Riot Grrrl Writing," in *Riot Grrrl: Revolution Girl Style Now!*, ed. Nadine Monem (London: Black Dog, 2007), 101–102.

54. Recording the history of Riot Grrrl is a project that a number of different entities and individuals have begun in recent years. For example: the EMP online project (www.empsfm.org/exhibitions/index.asp?categoryID=129&ccID=135); the documentary *Don't Need You: The Herstory of Riot Grrrl* (Urban Cowgirl Productions, 2006); and Monem, *Riot Grrrl*. See also Kristen Schilt's several articles: Schilt, "'Riot Grrrl Is . . .': The Contestation over Meaning," in *Music Scenes: Local, Translocal, and Virtual*, ed. Andy Bennett and Richard A. Peterson (Nashville: Vanderbilt University Press), 115–130; Schilts, "'A Little Too Ironic': The Appropriation and Packaging of Riot Grrrl Politics by Mainstream Female Musicians," *Popular Music and Society* 26 (2003), 5–16. See also Mary Celeste Kearney, *Girls Make Media* (New York: Routledge, 2006), as well as Kearney, "Missing Links"; Alison Jacques, "You Can Run but You Can't Hide: The Incorporation of Riot Grrrl into Mainstream Culture," *Canadian Women's Studies* 20.4 (Winter/Spring 2001): 46–51; Joanne Gottlieb and Gayle Wald, "Smells Like Teen Spirit: Riot Grrrls, Revolution and Women in Independent Rock," in *Microphone Fiends: Youth Music and Youth Culture*, ed. Andrew Ross and Tricia Rose (New York: Routledge, 1994), 250–274; Starr, "Because"; and Gillian Garr, *She's a Rebel: The History of Women in Rock and Roll* (New York: Seal Press, 1992).

55. Lora Romero makes this argument about domesticity in her book *Home Fronts: Domesticity and Its Critics in the Antebellum United States* (Durham, N.C.: Duke University Press, 1997), 109.

56. Originally included in *Mad Planet* #2 and #3, reprinted in *Action Girl Guide* 1 (Staten Island, N.Y.: Self-published, 1994).

57. Yumi Lee, *Consider Yourself Kissed* #3 (Lenexa, Kans.: Self-published, Feb. 19, 2000), n.p.

58. Sarah Dyer, *Action Girl Newsletter* (Staten Island, N.Y.: Self-published, 1993), n.p.

59. Lily Burana, "Grrrls, Grrrls, Grrrls," *Entertainment Weekly* 429 (May 1, 1998), 76

60. Lamm, personal interview.

61. Gottlieb and Wald, "Smells Like Teen Spirit," 268. Dyer explains the common misinterpretations of Riot Grrrls' gender play: "People had real issues with the fact that the Riot Grrrls were supposedly feminist and they were wearing little hair clips, you know, there's always that creepy thing where some guy says 'they're wearing baby hair clips, that's like, promoting pedophilia.' You're just like, yet you're the one who's thinking that. Don't project your creepy, creepy stuff onto everybody else" (Dyer interview).

62. *When She Was Good* #1 (Sand Springs, Okla.: Self-published, n.d.).

63. *Start a Fucking Riot* (Arlington, Va.: Self-published, 1992), n.p.

64. Second wave authors often used profanity, as did authors in the Black Power and Black Arts movement, but it wasn't as gleeful and excessive as it is in many grrrl zines.

65. Lizzard Amazon, *Slut Utopia* #1 (San Jose, Calif.: Self-published, March 1993), n.p.

66. Julia Downes asserts, "Fanzines soon became regular dreaming spaces and love letters exchanged between girls and women who yearned for an underground punk revolution they could call their own," and Red Chidgey says, "Riot grrrl was about taking risks with feminism, running away with it. Dreaming up actions and gangs" (Downes, "Riot Grrrl: The Legacy and Contemporary Landscape of DIY Feminist Cultural Activism," 18, and Chidgey, "Riot Grrrl Writing," 101, both in *Riot Grrrl: Revolution Girl Style Now!*, ed. Nadine Monem (London: Black Dog, 2007).

CHAPTER 2

1. Karen Green and Tristan Taormino, eds., *A Girl's Guide to Taking Over the World* (New York: St. Martin's Griffin, 1997); Ayun Halliday, *The East Village Inky* (New York: Self-published, n.d.); Anna LoBianco, Jody Bleyle, and Staci Colter, *Free to Fight: The Self-Defense Project* (Portland: Candy Ass Records, 1995).

2. Gregory Sholette uses the term "the culture industry" in his essay "Dark Matter: Activist Art and the Counter-Public Sphere," http://www.gregorysholette.com/essays/docs/05_darkmattertwo.pdf.

3. Many scholars have discussed the construction of a zine community. Stephen Duncombe (*Notes from Underground* [New York: Verso, 1997]) sees zines as constitutive of intimate communities; Kate Eichhorn argues that zines create "textual communities" (Kate Eichhorn, "Sites Unseen: Ethnographic Research in a Textual Community," *Qualitative Studies in Education* 14 [2001], 566); while Jennifer Sinor sees zines as a "community of life writers" ("Another Form of Crying: Girl Zines as Life Writing," *Prose Studies* 26 [2003]: 245).

4. Iris Marion Young, *Justice and the Politics of Difference* (Princeton, N.J.: Princeton University Press, 1990), 227, 238–240.

5. Nomy Lamm, "It's a Big Fat Revolution," in *Listen Up*, ed. Barbara Findlen (Seattle: Seal Press, 1996).

6. Nomy Lamm, *I'm So Fucking Beautiful* 2 ½ (Olympia, Wash.: Self-published, 1991), n.p.

7. Ibid.

8. Michele Moylan and Lane Stiles, "Introduction" to *Reading Books: Essays on the Material Text and Literature in America*, ed. Moylan and Stiles (Amherst: University of Massachusetts Press, 1996), 2.

9. Ibid., 12.

10. Gregory Sholette, "Dark Matter: Activist Art and the Counter-Public Sphere," n.p. (www.gregorysholette.com/essays/docs/05darkmattertwo.pdf). Sholette speaks of dark matter primarily in terms of its relationship to the art world, but this concept is equally applicable to the ways in which academic humanities scholarship overlooks certain kinds of texts and artifacts. A number of trade books have addressed the zine phenomenon, including Chip Rowe, *The Book of Zines* (New York: Holt, 1997), Francesca Lia Block and Hilary Carlip, *Zine Scene: The Do It Yourself Guide to Zines* (Los Angeles: Girl Press, 1998), and Mark Todd and Esther Pearl Watson, *Whatcha Mean, What's a Zine? The Art of Making Zines and Mini-Comics* (Boston: Graphia, 2006).

11. Lamm estimated that she has sold "potentially five thousand" copies of just the first issue of *I'm So Fucking Beautiful* (Lamm, personal interview).

12. Tristan Taormino and Karen Green, *A Girl's Guide to Taking Over the World: Writings from the Girl Zine Revolution* (New York: St. Martin's Griffin, 1997) anthologized excerpts from a number of zines by girls and women and has become a primary resource for scholars studying grrrl zines. In her excellent book, Anita Harris, *Future Girl: Young Women in the Twenty-First Century* (New York: Routledge, 2004), relies on *A Girls' Guide to Taking Over the World* for many of the zines she analyzes. Sholette's discussion of zines in "Dark Matter" relies on Duncombe's *Notes from Underground.*

13. Anna Feigenbaum notes a similar dismissal of formal elements in studies of the documents created as part of the Greenham Common Women's Peace Camp: the anthologies of these documents "only reproduce textual content, decontextualizing writing and drawings from its original sources. Formal aspects are lost in this preservation as typeface and layout become standardized. Likewise, drawings, borders and other aesthetic features are mostly excluded. . . . The form, production methods and distribution of these camp-based publications are not considered as sites of study in themselves" (Feigenbaum, "Tactics and Technology: Cultural Resistance at the Greenham Common Women's Peace Camp," Ph.D. diss., McGill University, 2008).

14. Victoria Law, *Fragments of Friendship: The Survival Stories* (New York: Self-published, 2004), n.p.

15. Law, personal interview.

16. "What's a Zine?" *Zine World: A Reader's Guide to the Underground Press* #21 (Murfreesboro, Tenn.: Self-published, May/June 2004), 2.

17. Martin, personal interview.

18. Quoted in Amy Spencer, *DIY: The Rise of Lo-Fi Culture* (London: Marion Boyars, 2005), 57.

19. Quoted in Todd and Watson, *Whatcha Mean?*, 18.

20. Dyer, personal interview.

21. For examples of blogs that exhibit creative design, see www.makingitlovely.com, decor8blog.com, or recordtheday.blogspot.com.

22. Dyer, personal interview.

23. Megan (no last name given), personal interview.

24. Indeed, the editors at Seal Press were explicit about not being able to accommodate the kinds of work she does in her zine: "I sent [an editor] a big stack of *The East Village Inky* and I guess they got passed around Seal Press, and they came back and they were like, 'Well, we can't really do an anthology of your zine because we wouldn't know what to do with all these illustrations and stuff, like we're not that into graphics; we wouldn't know how to promote it. But why don't you write a book for us?'" (Halliday, personal interview). Seal Press published *The Big Rumpus* in 2002.

25. Ayun Halliday, *The East Village Inky* #25 (Brooklyn, N.Y.: Self-published, Nov. 2004), n.p.

26. Elizabeth Hayes Alvarez, personal interview.

27. Judyth Stavens, personal interview.

28. Amy Jalics, personal interview.

29. Halliday, personal interview.

30. Anna Whitehead, *With Heart in Mouth* #3 (College Park, Md.: Self-published, n.d.).

31. Freedman, personal interview. See also Jenna Freedman, *Lower East Side Librarian Winter Solstice Shout-Out* (New York: Self-published, 2004).

32. Quoted in Rev. Phil and Joe Biel, directors, *A Hundred Dollars and a T-Shirt: A Documentary about Zines in the Northwest US* (Portland, Ore.: Microcosm Publishing, 2005).

33. Duncombe, *Notes from Underground*, 99.

34. Duncombe explains: "Zinesters value the bonds between the zine writer/artist, what he or she is drawing, and the person reading the zine. . . . Instead of emulating the slickness of the commercial mass media . . . the illustrations in zines are more reminiscent of the doodles and sketches in the margins of a personal letter: a style of intimate connection" (ibid., 98).

35. Duncombe refers to the phenomenon of zines encouraging readers to make their own zines as "emulation" (ibid., 123).

36. Jami Thompson, *No Better Voice* #25 (Ferndale, Mich.: Self-published, 2004).

37. Ibid. There is an interesting mixture of time frames here; this is clearly a second edition of the zine, and the reader of this edition encounters the review before she or he reaches the actual content of the zine.

38. Sholette argues that dark matter is invisible because at present "the very notion of artistic value . . . is defined by bourgeois ideology" ("Dark Matter," 4).

39. Crabb, personal interview.

40. For instance, Microcosm, one of the largest zine distros, has this to say about the zines they distribute: "We like zines containing information you'd be hard pressed to find elsewhere. We like to learn about things we didn't know we

were interested in. We like the occasional literary work. Screen printed or otherwise fancy covers are a huge plus. Creative layout never hurts either" (http://www.microcosmpublishing.com/faq/). They acknowledge the irony of applying standards to a medium as nonhierarchical as the zine: "We strongly ask you not to think of being distributed by Microcosm as a 'goal' or mark of success with your zine. Zines are one of the few non-hierarchical forms of media remaining in the world and it would be a shame to ruin that by creating echelons of success based on things as arbitrary as our tastes and the fact that we really can't distribute nearly as much as we get offered to us!" (ibid.). See the appendix to this volume for a listing of online zine distribution sites, as well as sites listing bookstores where zines are available.

41. Duncombe noted in 1997 that "swapping zines through a barter system is common and part of the ethic of participation among equals" (*Notes from Underground*, 12). The practice is on the decline, but it hasn't disappeared entirely. Although almost none of the zines reviewed in *Zine World* allow for trades as a way of getting a zine, in the years that I have been working on this book I've had a few zinesters request a trade—if not a zine, then something I've made.

42. Law, personal interview.

43. Another scholar has observed the embodied qualities of giving someone a zine: "The importance of *holding* and *hands* . . . recurred again and again in my interviews with these editors. . . . As discussed earlier, it is physicality that enables both the personification embodied in printed zines and the social interaction that material products encourage when being handed out in person, displayed in public venues, and mailed to kindred souls" (Jennifer Rauch, "Hands-On Communication: Zine Circulation Rituals and the Interactive Limitations of Web Self-Publishing," *Popular Communication* 2.3 [2004], 163).

44. Cindy Crabb, *Doris: An Anthology, 1991–2001* (Portland, Ore.: Microcosm Publishing, 2005), 36.

45. Ibid.

46. Law, personal interview.

47. Chestnut, personal interview.

48. Eichhorn, "Sites Unseen." Eichhorn is in the midst of a research project examining the preservation of zines in libraries. Sarah Dyer donated her extensive zine collection to the Duke University Special Collections Library, and she explained that the archiving of the zines would probably surprise most of the zine creators: "You know, most of these people . . . were just sort of sending this stuff out into the world and probably figured they'd all get thrown out within a couple months" (Dyer, personal interview).

49. Lauren Jade Martin noted that when her zines began being distributed primarily through bookstores and online distros, she started getting less feedback from readers: "There's virtually no feedback anymore where I used to get tons of letters. . . . It's like throwing [the zine] into a vacuum" (Martin, personal interview).

50. Halliday, personal interview.

51. Benedict Anderson, *Imagined Communities: Reflections on the Origin and Spread of Nationalism*, rev. ed. (London: Verso, 1991), 6.

52. Ibid., 35.

53. Halliday, personal interview; Kelly Love Johnson, personal interview.

54. Law, personal interview.

55. Kimra McPherson, "Notes from the Zine Underground," in *Breaking the Cycle: Gender, Literacy, and Learning*, ed. Lynne B. Alvine and Linda E. Cullum (Portsmouth, N.H.: Boynton/Cook, 1999), 148.

56. Taormino and Green, *Girl's Guide to Taking Over the World*, xiv.

57. Quoted in V. Vale, *Zines!* Vol. 1 (San Francisco: RE/Search, 1996), 102.

58. Lamm, personal interview.

59. Crabb, personal interview.

60. Mimi Nguyen, "Tales of an Asiatic Geek Girl: *Slant* from Paper to Pixels," in *Technicolor: Race, Technology, and Everyday Life*, ed. Alondra Nelson and Thuy Linh N. Tu with Alicia Headlam Hines (New York: New York University Press, 2001), 177, 178.

61. Megan, personal interview; Elizabeth Hayes Alvarez, personal interview.

62. Sholette, "Dark Matter," 6.

63. Indeed, many scholars of gift culture—including Theodor Adorno, Marcel Mauss, and Clive Dilnot—have observed that gifts function to create pleasure and community between the giver and receiver. Dilnot notes that "objects work dialogically, as a means of establishing concrete relations with the other" (Dilnot, "The Gift," *Design Issues* 9.2 [Spring 1993]: 55).

64. Michelle, *Design 816* (Madison, Wisc.: Self-published, n.d.).

65. Tracey West, *First Person: True Stories by Real People* (Sparkill, N.Y.: Self-published, n.d.).

66. Jen G. Box, *Gogglebox* #3 (New York: Self-published, 1994); Dooley, *Two Cents* #2 (San Jose, Calif.: Self-published, 1993).

67. Halliday, personal interview.

68. Henry Jenkins, *Fans, Bloggers, and Gamers: Exploring Participatory Culture* (New York: New York University Press, 2006), 175.

69. William H. Glass, "In Defense of the Book," *Harper's Magazine* 299 no. 1794 (1999), 47, 46.

70. Scholars of nineteenth-century womanhood, for instance, often posit published writing as something that freed women from the constraints of embodiment. As I have argued in another publication, however, this view of women's relationship to print culture obscures "the complex relationship between the female body and print. . . . Print is a space which can create syncretic, multivalent embodiment" (Alison Piepmeier, *Out in Public: Configurations of Women's Bodies in Nineteenth-Century America* [Chapel Hill: University of North Carolina Press, 2004], 175).

71. Kim Fern, *Fern* #7 (Normal, Ill.: Self-published, 1994?), n.p.

CHAPTER 3

1. Patricia Hill Collins, *Black Feminist Thought: Knowledge, Consciousness and the Politics of Empowerment* (New York: Routledge, 1990), 69.

2. Stephen Duncombe, *Notes from Underground* (New York: Verso, 1997), 37; italics in the original.

3. Ibid., 39. Mary Celeste Kearney, too, identifies Duncombe's remark as significant (*Girls Make Media* [New York: Routledge, 2006], 146).

4. Kathleen Hanna, "Jigsaw Youth," Jigsaw #4 (Olympia, Wash.: Self-published, 1991), n.p.

5. Lamm, personal interview.

6. Mimi Nguyen, *Slant* #5 (Berkeley, Calif.: Self-published, 1997), 2.

7. Janice Radway, "Girls, Zines, and the Miscellaneous Production of Subjectivity in an Age of Unceasing Circulation," lecture presented at the Center for Interdisciplinary Studies of Writing and the Literacy and Rhetorical Studies Minor, No. 18, University of Minnesota, 2001, 11.

8. Kearney, *Girls Make Media*, 148.

9. Clyde Taylor, *"The Game" in Black Male: Representations of Masculinity in Contemporary American Art* (New York: Whitney Museum of American Art, 1994), 169. Taylor discusses black men as "densely mythogenic" and is interested in how, "like other mythogenic people—Gypsies, Jews—the legend of the Black man outruns and awaits him through the course of his journey. And like other mythogenic people, Black men are, as if in self-defense, prolific generators of self-descriptive legends" (ibid.).

10. Farai Chideya and Melissa Rossi, "Revolution Girl Style," *Newsweek* (Nov. 23, 1992).

11. I have used a slide of this zine page regularly in presentations to audiences of college women, and it has never failed to capture the attention of the room. Indeed, when this slide goes up on the screen, many women who had been sitting passively reach for notebooks and begin copying it down. This anecdotal evidence suggests that Moore's reversal can have a galvanizing effect on young women.

12. Courtney Martin, *Perfect Girls, Starving Daughters: The Frightening New Normalcy of Hating Your Body* (New York: Farrar, Straus Giroux, 2007), 18.

13. Merri Lisa Johnson, "Jane Hocus, Jane Focus: An Introduction," in *Jane Sexes It Up: True Confessions of Feminist Desire*, ed. Merri Lisa Johnson (New York: Four Walls Eight Windows, 2003), 15.

14. Jennifer Sinor ("Another Form of Crying: Girl Zines as Life Writing," *Prose Studies* 26 [2003]: 240–264) identifies the fragmented identities in grrrl zines as being inherent in all life writing, and I agree. I want to expand beyond this point, though, to argue that the particular forms of fragmentation—unapologetic, emphatic, celebratory, often without even the fiction of a coherent

self—are grounded in the particularities of feminist youth in a late-capitalist moment.

15. Leslie Heywood and Jennifer Drake, eds., *Third Wave Agenda: Being Feminist, Doing Feminism* (Minneapolis: University of Minnesota Press, 1997), 2, 3.

16. Ibid., 3.

17. Johnson, "Jane Hocus, Jane Focus," 44.

18. Chela Sandoval, *Methodology of the Oppressed* (Minneapolis: University of Minnesota Press, 2000), 43.

19. Ibid., 58. Heywood and Drake, in particular, have identified third wave feminism as emerging specifically from the feminist interventions of U.S. third world feminists.

20. Johnson, "Jane Hocus, Jane Focus," 19.

21. "The Growing Zine Network," *USA Today*, August 7, 1992 (Lexis Nexis accessed July 11, 2007).

22. This quote is from Ginia Bellafante's much-maligned (and rightly so) piece, "Feminism: It's All about Me!," *Time* 151.25, June 29, 1998.

23. Linda Martín-Alcoff, "Who's Afraid of Identity Politics?" in *Reclaiming Identity: Realist Theory and the Predicament of Postmodernism*, ed. Paula M. L. Moya and Michael R. Hames-Garcia (Berkeley: University of California Press, 2000), 335–37.

24. Lamm, personal interview.

25. Both Kearney (*Girls Make Media*) and Anita Harris (*Future Girl: Young Women in the Twenty-First Century* [New York: Routledge, 2004]) observe the prevalence of discussions of body image in grrrl zines.

26. Naomi Wolf has argued persuasively that beauty and body issues so strongly affect girls and young women today because these are the mechanisms by which the backlash against second wave feminism is happening. She contends that struggling with one's body is a particularly third wave experience. Wolf, *The Beauty Myth* [New York: William Morrow, 1991]; Wolf, *Adios, Barbie* [Emeryville, Calif.: Seal Press, 1998]; and Martin, *Perfect Girls, Starving Daughters* also make this point.

27. Marilyn Wann, *Fat!So?* (San Francisco: Self-published); Krissy Durden, *Figure 8* (Portland, Ore.: Self-published); Jenny San Diego, *Not Sorry* (Portland, Ore.: Self-published); Pat Wilkinson, *Shameless* (Self-published).

28. Jenny San Diego, *Not Sorry* #3 (Portland, Ore.: Self-published, April 2005), n.p.

29. Ibid.

30. Suzie Cyanide, in *We Will Determine Our Own Bodies* (Memphis: Self-published, n.d.), 1.

31. River-A-Genda, in *We Will Determine Our Own Bodies* (Memphis: Self-published, no date), 25.

32. Audre Lorde, "The Master's Tools Will Never Dismantle the Master's House," in *This Bridge Called My Back: Writings by Radical Women of Color,*

ed. Cherríe Moraga and Gloria Anzaldúa (New York: Kitchen Table: Women of Color Press, 1983), 99.

33. Crabb, personal interview.

34. Chestnut, *Mend My Dress* #3 (Seattle: Self-published, summer 2006), n.p.

35. Ibid.

36. Ibid.

37. Chestnut, *Mend My Dress* #2 (Seattle: Self-published, spring/summer 2005), n.p.

38. Chestnut, personal interview.

39. Radway, "Girls, Zines, and Production of Subjectivity," 194.

40. Chestnut, personal interview.

41. Heywood and Drake, *Third Wave Agenda*, 7.

42. Maria Lugones, *Pilgrimages/Peregrinajes: Theorizing Coalition against Multiple Oppressions* (Lanham, Md.: Rowman and Littlefield, 2003).

43. Lily Burana, "Grrrls, Grrrls, Grrrls," *Entertainment Weekly* 429 (May 1, 1998), 76.

44. bell hooks, *Yearning: Race, Gender, and Cultural Politics* (Boston: South End Press, 1990), 15.

45. Debbie Stoller, personal interview.

46. Letter to the Editor, *Bust*, 1.2 (fall 1993), 2.

47. Editorial, *Bust* 7 (spring/summer 1996), 2.

48. Ibid.

49. Duncombe, *Notes from Underground*, 123.

50. *Bust* 1.4 (summer/fall 1994).

51. Stoller, personal interview.

52. Ibid.

53. Ibid.

54. Ibid. Circulation information from personal correspondence and *Bust* media kit, http://www.bust.com/2008mediakit.pdf. Interestingly, while Stoller always envisioned *Bust* as a magazine, Henzel, who has been the publication's creative director from the beginning, explained to me, "for the design part, I wasn't looking at real magazines as inspiration, I was really looking at zines. I was a big zine reader, so it had that feel because that's what I like. Obviously the early issues didn't look kind of the way they do now, and I wasn't looking at *Vanity Fair* and saying, 'oooh,' it was a zine in my mind" (Henzel, personal interview).

55. Stoller, personal interview.

56. Personal interviews with four zine creators who asked not to be identified.

57. Neely Bat Chestnut, *Grit & Glitter* (Seattle,: Self-published, March 2007), n.p.

58. Hazel Pine, in ibid.; Chestnut, in ibid.

59. Chestnut and Pine, in ibid.

60. Judith Halberstam, *In a Queer Time and Place: Transgender Bodies, Subcultural Lives* (New York: New York University Press, 200), 167.

61. Pine, *Grit & Glitter*, March 2007, n.p.

62. Kearney (*Girls Make Media*), in particular, labels grrrl zines in terms of cultural feminism.

63. Rory Dicker and Alison Piepmeier, "Introduction" to *Catching a Wave: Reclaiming Feminism for the 21st Century*, ed. Dicker and Piepmeier (Boston: Northeastern University Press, 2003), 17.

64. Merri Lisa Johnson, "Introduction: Ladies Love Your Box—The Rhetoric of Pleasure and Danger in Feminist Television Studies," in *Third Wave Feminism and Television: Jane Puts It in a Box*, ed. Johnson (New York: I. B. Tauris, 2007), 13

65. Editorial, *Bust* 1.2 (fall 1993), 2.

66. Burana, "Grrrls, Grrrls, Grrrls," 76.

67. Martens, personal interview.

68. For instance, *The East Village Inky* and *The Future Generation*, which was just published as a book.

69. Deesha Philya, "Ain't I a Mommy?" *Bitch* 40 (summer 2008), 46–52.

70. Although grrrl zines are affiliated with actual girls, five of the twelve zine creators I interviewed were over thirty and still producing their zines.

71. Heather Hewett explains: "The name 'mama,' of course, is significant. 'Mama' is to 'mother' as 'grrl' is to 'woman' . . . : it creates an alternative vocabulary that defines itself in opposition to restrictive notions of identity. 'Mama' suggests an attempt to redefine motherhood, a political project that begins for many third wavers in the realm of language and culture" (Hewett, "Talkin' 'bout a Revolution: Building a Mothers' Movement in the Third Wave," *Journal of the Association for Research on Mothering* 8.1–2 [2006], 45).

72. Halliday, personal interview.

73. Law, personal interview.

74. Ariel Gore, "Foreword" to *The Future Generation: The Zine-Book for Subculture Parents, Kids, Friends and Others* by China Martens (Baltimore: Atomic, 2007), 5.

75. Halliday, personal interview.

76. China Martens, *The Future Generation* #9 (Fairfield, Penn.: Self-published, August 1998), 21.

77. Judyth Stavans, personal interview.

78. Amy Jalics, personal interview.

79. Ayun Halliday, *The East Village Inky* #32 (Brooklyn, N.Y.: Self-published, October 2006), n.p.

80. Martens, *The Future Generation* #9.

81. Hewett, "Talkin' 'bout a Revolution."

82. Lauren Eichelberger, "The Birth of a Radical Mama," in *Mamaphiles: A Mama Zine Collaboration* (Baltimore: Self-published, 2003), 36.

83. Jackie Regales, "It's Difficult," in ibid., 103–4.

84. Noemi Martinez, "My Son Will Never Know," in ibid., 87.

85. Susan J. Douglas and Meredith Michaels, *The Mommy Myth: The Idealization of Motherhood and How It Has Undermined All Women* (New York: Free Press, 1994).

86. Victoria Law and Siu Loong Law Englander, *Nefarious Doings in Revisionist Tourist Attractions* (New York: Self-published, 2007).

87. Editorial, *Bust* 1.2 (fall 1993), 2.

88. Linda Hirshman, *Get to Work: A Manifesto for the Women of the World* (New York: Viking, 2006), 1–2.

89. Astrid Henry, *Not My Mother's Sister: Generational Conflict and Third-Wave Feminism* (Bloomington: Indiana University Press, 2004), 37.

90. Ibid., 73.

91. Henry, personal interview.

92. Hewett, "Talkin' 'bout a Revolution," 34. Hewett argues that "the writerly exploration of the complex mixture of personal desire, pleasure, and love that constitutes mothering and parenting has an essential role to play in affecting cultural constructions of motherhood. Moreover, literary and cultural productions provide access to the many realities of mothers' lives that can help to inform public rhetoric (and perhaps even provide some insights into grassroots organizing)" (48).

93. Patrice DiQuinzio, *The Impossibility of Motherhood: Feminism, Individualism, and the Problem of Mothering* (New York: Routledge, 1999), 248.

94. Hewett, "Talkin' 'bout a Revolution," 43.

CHAPTER 4

1. Sarah Banet-Weiser, "What's Your Flava? Race and Postfeminism in Media Culture," in *Interrogating Postfeminism: Gender and the Politics of Popular Culture*, ed. Yvonne Tasker and Diane Negra (Durham, N.C.: Duke University Press, 2007), 215, 216.

2. Sabrina Margarita Alcantara-Tan has an essay in *Bamboo Girl* in which she critiques the "coolness" of tattoos from Asian cultures (Alcantara-Tan, "The Acculturation of Asiatic Tattoos by Non-Asians," *Bamboo Girl* #8 [New York: Mutya, 1999], 18.)

3. The same discourse of "transcending race" dogged Barack Obama's presidential candidacy from the beginning, as if his presence as a viable candidate means that race no longer has significance in American culture. This rhetoric, of course, existed side by side with continually racially loaded commentary.

4. Mimi Nguyen, *Slant* #5 (Berkeley, Calif.: Self-published, 1997), 36.

5. Patricia Hill Collins, *From Black Power to Hip Hop: Racism, Nationalism, and Feminism* (Philadelphia: Temple University Press, 2006), 3. See also Banet-

Weiser, What's Your Flava? 201–226, and Kimberly Springer, "Divas, Evil Black Bitches, and Bitter Black Women: African American Women in Postfeminist and Post-Civil-Rights Popular Culture," in *Interrogating Postfeminism: Gender and the Politics of Popular Culture*, ed. Yvonne Tasker and Diane Negra. (Durham, N.C.: Duke University Press, 2007), 249–276.

6. Banet-Weiser, "What's Your Flava?" 216.

7. bell hooks, too, discusses this phenomenon: "Masses of young people dissatisfied by United States imperialism, unemployment, lack of economic opportunity, afflicted by the postmodern malaise of alienation, no sense of grounding, no redemptive identity, can be manipulated by cultural strategies that offer Otherness as appeasement, particularly through commodification" (bell hooks, *Black Looks: Race and Representation* [Cambridge, Mass.: South End Press, 1992], 25).

8. Radway, "Girls, Zines, and the Miscellaneous Production of Subjectivity in an Age of Unceasing Circulation," lecture presented at the Center for Interdisciplinary Studies of Writing and the Literacy and Rhetorical Studies Minor, No. 18, University of Minnesota, 2001. Indeed, these multiple possibilities are related to the "radical generativity" that Janice Radway identifies with grrrl zines, as well as the "tactical subjectivity" that Chela Sandoval links to U.S. third world feminism (Sandoval, *Methodology of the Oppressed* [Minneapolis: University of Minnesota Press, 2000]).

9. These tactics are similar to what Sandoval calls "a mobility of identity" as "a model for oppositional political activity and consciousness in the postmodern world" (Sandoval, *Methodology of the Oppressed*, 43).

10. Sandoval warns, "differential United States third world feminist criticism (which is a set of theoretical and methodological strategies) is often misrecognized and underanalyzed by readers when it is translated as a demographic constituency (women of color), and not as a theoretical and methodological approach in its own right" (ibid., 171). In this chapter, I am not simply analyzing a particular demographic group who produce zines but, instead, publicizing the theoretical and methodological approaches that these grrrl zines enact. I am arguing that these zines are producing a third wave theory.

11. For instance, NOW, the Feminist Majority, NARAL Pro-Choice America, and the Center for the Advancement of Women all have mission statements featuring intersectional goals. NOW's mission statement explains that "NOW works to . . . eradicate racism, sexism and homophobia," while the Feminist Majority's mission statement notes that it "promotes non-discrimination on the basis of sex, race, sexual orientation, socio-economic status, religion, ethnicity, age, marital status, nation of origin, size or disability."

12. Kimberle Crenshaw, "Demarginalizing the Intersection of Race and Sex: A Black Feminist Critique of Antidiscrimination Doctrine, Feminist Theory, and Antiracist Politics," *University of Chicago Legal Forum* (1989): 139–169. For instance, Sojourner Truth's famous "Ar'n't I a Woman?" speech is a powerful

statement of identity in which race and gender are mutually constituted, so that the racism she experiences as a black woman is qualitatively different from that experienced by a black man, and the sexism she experiences is qualitatively different from that experienced by a white woman. See also the work of Maria Stewart, Ida B. Wells, and Anna Julia Cooper.

13. Combahee River Collective," A Black Feminist Statement," quoted in Cherríe Moraga and Gloria Anzaldúa, eds., *This Bridge Called My Back: Writings by Radical Women of Color* (New York: Kitchen Table: Women of Color Press, 1983), 216.

14. Kimberlé Williams Crenshaw, "Mapping the Margins: Intersectionality, Identity Politics, and Violence against Women of Color," in *The Public Nature of Private Violence: Women and the Discovery of Abuse*, ed. Martha Fineman and Roxanne Mykitiuk (New York: Routledge, 1994), 94.

15. Rebecca Walker, "Becoming the Third Wave," *Ms.* (January/February 1992). For instance, the third wave anthologies *To Be Real, Listen Up, Third Wave Agenda, Catching a Wave* (and others) each feature from 20 to 30 percent women of color authors. Rebecca Walker, *To Be Real: Telling the Truth and Changing the Face of Feminism* (New York: Anchor, 1995); Barbara Findlen, ed., *Listen Up* (Seattle: Seal Press, 1996); Leslie Heywood and Jennifer Drake, *Third Wave Agenda: Being Feminist, Doing Feminism* (Minneapolis: University of Minnesota Press, 1997); Rory Dicker and Alison Piepmeier, eds., *Catching a Wave:Reclaiming Feminism for the 21st Century* (Boston: Northeastern University Press, 2003).

16. Patricia Hill Collins, *Black Feminist Thought: Knowledge, Consciousness and the Politics of Empowerment* (New York: Routledge, 1990), 13.

17. In a later book, Collins does in fact offer this critique of third wave feminist writings, as when she says of *Colonize This!*, "not only does their politics grow from their personal lives; it does not seem to go much further than this" (Collins, *From Black Power to Hip Hop*, 188).

18. Daisy Hernandez and Bushra Rehman, eds., *Colonize This! Young Women of Color on Today's Feminism* (Berkeley, Calif.: Seal Press, 2002).

19. Clyde Taylor, "The Game," in *Black Male: Representations of Masculinity in Contemporary American Art* (New York: Whitney Museum of American Art, 1994), 169.

20. Iris Marion Young, *Justice and the Politics of Difference* (Princeton, N.J.: Princeton University Press, 1990) 232.

21. Mimi Nguyen, "We Are Not Family; or break out the blackface, here comes the white girl!" *Slant* #5 (Berkeley, Calif.: Self-published, 1997), 18.

22. Martin, personal interview.

23. Collins explains: "Since the 1980s, the American nation-state has increasingly defined ideas about what it means to be American through ideas of Whiteness, Christianity, wealth, masculinity, and heterosexuality. As a result, social inequality of race, class, gender, ethnicity, and religion, among others, appear

to be natural and normal and certainly not socially constructed by public policies and everyday customs" (Collins, *From Black Power to Hip Hop*, 7).

24. Here Martin refers to her identity as "pomo," a shortening of "postmodern."

25. Anna Whitehead, *With Heart in Mouth* #3 (Baltimore, Md.: Self-published, n.d.), n.p.

26. Mimi Nguyen, ed., *Evolution of a Race Riot* (Berkeley, Calif.: Self-published, 1994). For instance, in *Shotgun Seamstress* #2, the author credits Mimi Nguyen, writing, "Race Riot got this shit started!" (Portland, Ore.: Self-published, 2007, n.p.)

27. Mimi Nguyen, in *Evolution of a Race Riot*, 82.

28. Chandra Ray, in *Evolution of a Race Riot*, 7.

29. In response to the hypothetical question, "Why can't you appreciate that white women are at least trying to acknowledge their white privilege?," Nguyen writes, "What do you want, a parade? The key to the city?" and goes on to explain, "It gets to be such an insular, self-referential cycle of re-staging your whiteness. I mean, even in confessing your privilege." Nguyen, *Slant* #11 (Berkeley, Calif.: Self-published, n.d.), n.p.

30. Mimi Nguyen, http://www.worsethanqueer.com/slander/pp40.html.

31. Gloria Anzaldúa and Cherríe Moraga, eds., *This Bridge Called My Back: Writings by Radical Women of Color* (New York: Kitchen Table: Women of Color Press, 1983).

32. Liz McAdams, in *Evolution of a Race Riot*, 23.

33. Ibid.

34. Ibid., 22.

35. bell hooks, for instance, regularly validates constructive conflict: "Rather than fearing conflict we have to find ways to use it as a catalyst for new thinking, for growth" (hooks, *Teaching to Transgress: Education as the Practice of Freedom* [New York: Routledge, 1994], 113).

36. Lauren Jade Martin, *Quantify* #4 (New York: Self-published, 2002), 4.

37. Martin, personal interview.

38. Martin, *Quantify* #4, 5, 4.

39. Nguyen, *Slant* #5, 12.

40. Ibid., 28.

41. Ibid., 36.

42. "'Hermana, Resist': Healing Communities by Writing," an interview with Noemi Martinez, by Haydee Jimenez and Elke Zobl, February 2008, http://grrrlzines.net/interviews/hermanaresist.htm (accessed May 2008).

43. Martin, personal interview.

44. Michelle Peñaloza, *Matapang* (Nashville, Tenn.: Self-published, 2003); Nguyen, *Slant* #5, 2.

45. Collins, *From Black Power to Hip Hop*, 3.

46. According to the conversational template she offers, Peñaloza doesn't verbally respond to her questioners in a way that exposes the politics of the conversation; the italics signify that the awareness remains silent, voiced only in the pages of her zine.

47. Mimi Nguyen, *Slander* #7 (Berkeley, Calif.: Self-published, 1999), n.p.

48. Ibid.

49. Ibid.

50. bell hooks, "Eating the Other," in *Black Looks: Race and Representation* (Boston: South End Press, 1992), 21.

51. Peñaloza, *Matapang*, n.p.

52. Martin, *Quantify* #4, 1.

53. Ibid.

54. Ibid., 2.

55. Martin, *Quantify* #5, 6.

56. Nguyen, *Slant* #5, 3.

57. Whitehead, *With Heart in Mouth* #3, n.p.

58. Collins explains that the mammy is an important "controlling image" of black womanhood that reflects (and perpetuates) "the dominant group's interest in maintaining Black women's subordination" (Collins, *Black Feminist Thought*, 71).

59. Nguyen, *Slander* #7, n.p.

60. Martin, *Quantify* #5, 4.

61. The trickster, according to Sandoval, is one "who practices subjectivity as masquerade, the oppositional agent who accesses differing identity, ideological, aesthetic, and political positions" in order to destabilize hierarchies of identity and work toward "egalitarian social relations." (Sandoval, *Methodology of the Oppressed*, 62.)

62. Martin, *Quantify* #4, 15–16.

63. Nguyen, *Slant* #5, 12.

64. See also Sandoval, *Methodology of the Oppressed*, 55.

65. Sabrina Margarite Alcantara-Tan, "The Herstory of *Bamboo Girl* Zine," *Frontiers: Journal of Women Studies* 21½ (2000): 159.

66. Sabrina Margarite Alcantara-Tan, *Bamboo Girl* #9 (New York: Self-published, 2000), 9.

67. Collins, *From Black Power to Hip Hop*, 196.

CHAPTER 5

1. Cindy Crabb, "Ohio," *Doris* #24 (Asheville, N.C.: Self-published, 2007), 17.

2. Cherríe Moraga and Gloria Anzaldúa, eds., *This Bridge Called My Back: Writings by Radical Women of Color* (New York: Kitchen Table: Women of Color Press, 1983), xviii.

3. Anna Whitehead, *With Heart in Mouth* #3 (College Park, Md.: Self-published, n.d.), n.p.

4. Communication scholar Clemencia Rodriguez argues that what she calls citizens' media alters "people's senses of self, their subjective positionings, and therefore their access to power" (Rodriguez, *Fissures in the Mediascape: An International Study of Citizens' Media* [Cresskill, N.J.: Hampton, 2001], 18).

5. Education theorist Paulo Freire introduced the idea of radical pedagogies, including pedagogies of hope, in his seminal *Pedagogy of the Oppressed* (New York: Continuum, 1970).

6. Anita Harris, ed., *Next Wave Cultures: Feminism, Subcultures, Activism* (New York: Routledge, 2007), 1.

7. bell hooks, *Teaching Community: A Pedagogy of Hope* (New York: Routledge, 2003), 11.

8. Jeffrey Goldfarb, *The Cynical Society: The Culture of Politics and the Politics of Culture in American Life* (Chicago: University of Chicago Press, 1999), 1. A number of scholarly and popular books from a range of disciplinary perspectives have examined the widespread cynicism that characterizes late-twentieth-century American culture; in 1999, one author noted, "Suddenly, it seems, American society is awash in cynicism. That diagnosis, unlikely just a few years ago, seems so obvious that it borders on the banal" (William Chaloupka, *Everybody Knows: Cynicism in America* [Minneapolis: University of Minnesota Press, 1999], 5). Recent related books include Russell Jacoby, *The End of Utopia: Politics and Culture in an Age of Apathy* (New York: Basic Books, 1999); Henry A. Giroux, *Public Spaces, Private Lives: Beyond the Culture of Cynicism* (Lanham, Mass.: Rowman and Littlefield, 2001); and Michael Lerner, *The Politics of Meaning: Restoring Hope and Possibility in an Age of Cynicism* (Reading, Mass.: Addison-Wesley, 1996).

9. hooks, *Teaching Community*, 11.

10. Sarah McCarry, *Glossolalia*, in *The Zine Yearbook* 8 (Toledo, Ohio: Clamor Magazine, 2004), 30.

11. As Naomi Klein explains, globalization and advertising inundation are "making it ever more difficult and more seemingly pointless to muster even an ounce of outrage" (Klein, *No Logo: Taking Aim at the Brand Bullies* [New York: Macmillan, 2002], 12.) The huge popularity of the Barack Obama presidential campaign can be explained, in part, by the fact that he tapped into this need for hope and a vision of change. He recognized the cynical culture and crafted a campaign around challenging that cynicism and promoting what his book title describes as *The Audacity of Hope*—something that was clearly much needed.

12. Mimi Nguyen, *Slant* #5 (Berkeley, Calif.: Self-published, 1997), 36.

13. Martin, personal interview.

14. Stephen Duncombe, *Notes from Underground* (New York: Verso, 1997), 174.

15. Ibid., 176. Duncombe notes that he's taken this terminology from historian Eric Hobsbawm, who argues that pre-political organizations "are made up

of 'people who have not yet found, or only begun to find, a specific language in which to express their aspirations about the world'—but they are groups which have revolutionary potential."

16. Jervis, personal interview.

17. Ibid.

18. Harris, *Next Wave Cultures*, 1.

19. Ibid., 235.

20. Ibid., 7.

21. Astrid Henry, *Not My Mother's Sister: Generational Conflict and Third-Wave Feminism* (Bloomington: Indiana University Press, 2004), 35–36.

22. Shelley Budgeon, "Emergent Feminist(?) Identities: Young Women and the Practice of Micropolitics," *European Journal of Women's Studies* 8.1 (2001), 20.

23. Tobi Vail, *Jigsaw* #4 (Olympia, Wash.: Self-published, 1991), n.p.

24. Martens, personal interview.

25. Rodriguez, *Fissures in the Mediascape*, 20.

26. Ibid.

27. Ibid., 47.

28. Ibid., xiv.

29. Ibid., 22.

30. Chestnut, personal interview.

31. Cristy Road, "Consensual Sex Is So Hot," *Greenzine* #13 (Philadelphia: Self-published, n.d.), n.p.

32. Cristy Road, *Greenzine* #14 (Portland, Ore.: Microcosm Publishing, 2004), n.p.

33. Budgeon, "Emergent Feminist(?) Identities," 18.

34. Road, *Greenzine* #14, n.p.

35. Duncombe, *Notes from Underground*, 123.

36. Ibid., 129.

37. Road's drawings are in such demand that she sells posters of them and has been commissioned to do the covers of professional books such as *We Don't Need Another Wave*.

38. Rodriguez notes that demystification of the media is a common feature of citizens' media. By "opening spaces for dialogue and participation, breaking individuals' isolation, encouraging creativity and imagination, [and] redefining shared social languages and symbols," the zine medium challenges consumer capitalism (Rodriguez, *Fissures in the Mediascape*, 63). Although Rodriguez does not study zines, her observations about citizens' media are applicable to the cultural work that zines do, the resistance within the symbolic realm. She contends that all citizens' media have "one thing in common: they express the will and agency of a human community confronting historical marginalizing and isolating forces, whatever these may be. Moving into any fissure encountered in the mediascape, colonizing their own sites of media production, citizens from all corners

of the world are using the linguistic or cultural marginalization, the alienating
effects of modern capitalism, the homogenization of cultural identities, gender
inequity, globalization, disinformation and misinformation, isolation, and economic and political repression" (ibid.).

39. Duncombe, *Notes from Underground*, 124.

40. Mary Celeste Kearney, "Producing Girls: Rethinking the Study of Female
Youth Culture," *Girls Make Media* (New York: Routledge, 2006), 289.

41. Rodriguez, *Fissures in the Mediascape*, 22.

42. Crabb, personal interview.

43. Ibid. Crabb is referring to a poem by Muriel Rukeyser which actually
reads, "What would happen if one woman told the truth about her life?/ The
world would split open" (Muriel Rukeyser, "Käthe Kollwitz," in *The Collected Poems of Muriel Rukeyser*, ed. Janet E. Kaufman and Anne F. Herzog, with Jan Hel-
ler Levi [Pittsburgh: University of Pittsburgh Press, 2005], 463).

44. Lisa Jervis, "Editor's Letter," *Bitch* #1.1 (Oakland: Amazon Girl Publishing, 1996), n.p.

45. A number of scholars have commented on the corporatization of culture,
starting with Theodor Adorno and Max Horkheimer in the mid-twentieth century, but it is a concept that became increasingly relevant at the end of the century
and the beginning of the twenty-first. David Harvey, for instance, discusses the
"commodification of . . . things that were never actually produced as commodities" as a component of a neoliberal cultural moment (Harvey, *A Brief History of
Neoliberalism* [New York: Oxford University Press, 2005], 166). Scholars from dis-
ciplines as diverse as popular culture studies and religious studies have examined
this phenomenon. For example, Stanley Hauerwas and Samuel Wells, *The Blackwell Companion to Christian Ethics* (London: Blackwell, 2006), and Toby Miller
and Robert Stam, eds., *A Companion to Film Theory* (London: Blackwell, 2007).

46. Jervis, *Bitch* 1.1, n.p.; italics in original.

47. Zeisler, personal interview.

48. Jennifer Drake and Leslie Heywood, "We Learn America Like a Script,"
in *Third Wave Agenda: Being Feminist, Doing Feminism*, ed. Heywood and Drake
(Minneapolis: University of Minnesota Press, 1997), 51, 52.

49. Zeisler, personal interview. *Sassy* played an interesting role in the world
of grrrl zines. Many Riot Grrrl zines had a love/hate relationship with the magazine, which—in its heyday—profiled grrrl zines and gave a great deal of attention
to Riot Grrrls, in ways that were both productive and somewhat damaging. As
discussed in chapter 3, Debbie Stoller found *Sassy* inspiring and, in part, created
*Bust* as a *Sassy*-type magazine for adult women. And *Sassy*'s decline then became
the partial inspiration for *Bitch*.

50. Jervis and Zeisler (personal interview) explained that the initial offset
printing was an accident—they'd told the printing company to photocopy the zine,
but it looked so good (and became popular so quickly) that they stuck with it.

51. Jervis and Zeisler, personal interview.

52. A number of grrrl zines would complicate this distinction, including zines like *Free to Fight: An Interactive Self-Defense Project* that offer information on women's self-defense, to the many grrrl zines that offer health care information.

53. On their website they explain to potential advertisers, "in keeping with our noncommercial publishing philosophy, our goal is to work with smaller, independent advertisers whose products and services are aligned with our mission of formulating replies to the sexist and narrow-minded media we consume while critically examining the images of things like femininity, feminism, class, race, and sexuality" (http://bitchmagazine.org/advertise).

54. Jervis and Zeisler, personal interview. Zeisler and Jervis attribute the definition of a zine as something made for love and not for money to Tom Lupoff, who was responsible for building the periodicals section of Cody's, a famous Bay Area bookstore.

55. See the publishers' plea to readers at http://bitchmagazine.org/post/bitchs-fate-is-in-your-hands.

56. Jervis, personal interview.

57. Merri Lisa Johnson, "Jane Hocus, Jane Focus: An Introduction," in *Jane Sexes It Up: True Confessions of Feminist Desire*, ed. Johnson (New York: Four Walls Eight Windows, 2003), 11.

58. Jervis, "Editor's Letter," *Bitch*, #1.1, n.p.

59. At http://www.bitchmagazine.org/about (accessed May 9, 2008).

60. Jervis and Zeisel, *Bitch*, #1.1, 37.

61. *Bitch* is also typically third wave in that its authors were informed by academic training in women's studies classes. They come to their work with an expertise that earlier generations of feminists had to invent.

62. Jervis, "Talk Shows: TV's Culture of Categorization," *Bitch* #1.2, 9.

63. Ibid., 13–15.

64. Jervis, personal interview.

65. Jervis and Zeisler, *Bitch* #38 (winter 2008), 4. However, even with this overt statement of multiple opinions, Jervis and Zeisler find that people want to pigeonhole the publication, identify "the *Bitch* position" on certain issues.

66. Zeisler, personal interview.

67. Jervis, personal interview.

68. Like *Bust, Bitch* has been criticized for its support of sexiness by, for instance, blogs such as Women's Space (http://www.womensspace.org/ph-pBB2/2008/09/23/bitch-magazine-bust-magazine-and-hustler-sponsor-tease-o-rama/) and Feminist Law Professors (http://feministlawprofs.law.sc.edu/?p=4121). Jervis and Zeisler report that they still hear a great deal of criticism about the publication's name, often from older feminists. More broadly, it's become common for older feminists to dismiss third wave feminism as not appropriately

political; at a conference in April 2008, a panelist at a plenary session derided the third wave for not being concerned with sexism and called for a fourth wave that would concern itself with sexism.

69. Courtney Martin, "Generation Overwhelmed," *American Prospect,* October 22, 2007, http://www.prospect.org/cs/articles?article=generation_overwhelmed.

70. Zeisler, personal interview.

71. Letter to the Editor, *Bitch,* #2.1 (spring 1997), 2.

72. Ann W., Letter to the Editor, ibid.

73. At http://jezebel.com/5050695/the-struggles-of-bitch-magazine-are-neither-surprising-nor-new.

74. At http://jezebel.com/5050695/the-struggles-of-bitch-magazine-are-neither-surprising-nor-new#viewcomments.

75. Even the title speaks to the fact that self-disclosure and ego aren't necessarily the driving forces of the zine. The author's name is Cindy Crabb, not Doris. Crabb explained why she named the zine *Doris*: "The thing about *Doris* is that it's sort of this idea that everybody is Doris, which stems from this weird thing from a waitress that I worked for. I was like, what could be a name that actually just means everybody for some weird reason? And Doris was the only name that we could think of that we didn't know anybody named" (Crabb, personal interview). Doris, then, stands in as a kind of universal name rather than referring to any single individual.

76. Cindy Crabb, *Doris: An Anthology, 1991–2001* (Portland, Ore.: Microcosm Publishing, 2005), 19.

77. Crabb, personal correspondence.

78. Cindy Crabb, "Ohio," *Doris* #24 (Asheville, N.C.: Self-published, 2007), 5.

79. Freire, *Pedagogy of the Oppressed,* 31. Similarly, political theorist Richard Rorty argues, "You have to describe the country in terms of what you passionately hope it will become, as well as in terms of what you know it to be now. You have to be loyal to a dream country rather than to the one to which you wake up every morning. Unless such loyalty exists, the ideal has no chance of becoming actual" (Rorty, *Achieving Our Country: Leftist Thought in Twentieth-Century America* [Cambridge: Harvard University Press, 1998], 101).

80. Rodriguez, *Fissures in the Mediascape,* 18.

81. "There is the possibility that our wishes could be integrated into an overall functioning of our imaginative capacity in such a way as to facilitate a creative and appropriate response to the world's challenges. We thus have room for the idea of *imaginative excellence* when it comes to ethical life" (Jonathan Lear, *Radical Hope: Ethics in the Face of Cultural Devastation* [Cambridge: Harvard University Press, 2008], 117).

82. Reader's personal correspondence to Cindy Crabb.

83. Crabb, personal interview. Crabb had additional thoughts about how zines like *Doris* can "change the world": "I wrote some articles about assault

and supporting survivors for a zine called *Slug and Lettuce*, and I've heard that those articles were a big reason a group called Support NY started—which was (is?) a group that is working on supporting survivors of rape and assault. Also, I had someone tell me that her close friend's mom died, and if she hadn't read my zine about what I needed when my mom died, she wouldn't have known how to help, or what to say or do to support her friend" (Crabb, personal correspondence).

84. Crabb, *Doris: An Anthology*, 105.

85. According to Rodriguez (*Fissures in the Mediascape*), this is how citizens' media functions.

86. Crabb, *Doris* #24, 8.

87. Stephen Duncombe, *Dream: Re-Imagining Progressive Politics in an Age of Fantasy* (New York: New Press, 2007), 30; italics in the original. It may be surprising that Duncombe, who seemed to feel somewhat hopeless about zines in *Notes from Underground*, would come to identify the importance of spectacle without identifying spectacle as one of the functions of zines. This may be because he was examining a different set of zines than I am studying here; it may be that grrrl zines are somewhat more in touch with the importance of "a dream on display."

88. Crabb, "Outroduction," *Doris: An Anthology*, 308.

89. bell hooks, *Yearning: Race, Gender, and Cultural Politics* (Boston: South End Press, 1990), 153.

90. Rory Dicker and Alison Piepmeier, "Introduction" to *Catching a Wave: Reclaiming Feminism for the 21st Century*, ed. Dicker and Piepmeier (Boston: Northeastern University Press, 2003), 19.

91. Bernice Johnson Reagon, "Coalition Politics: Turning the Century," in *Home Girls: A Black Feminist Anthology*, ed. Barbara Smith (New York: Kitchen Table: Women of Color Press, 1983).

92. Cindy Crabb, "Editor's Letter," *Bitch* #39 (Asheville, N.C.: Self-published, 2008), 5.

93. Road, *Greenzine* #14, n.p.

94. Lauren Jade Martin, *Quantify* #4 (New York: Self-published, 2002), 13.

95. Crabb, personal interview.

96. Anne Elizabeth Moore, *Unmarketable: Brandalism, Copyfighting, Mocketing, and the Erosion of Integrity* (New York: New Press, 2007).

97. Moraga, "Introduction," *This Bridge Called My Back*.

CONCLUSION

1. Eisen, personal interview.

2. Ibid.

3. Ibid.

4. Chris Dodge, "The New Monastic Librarians," *Utne Reader*, July–August 2005, 80.

5. At http://www.undergroundpress.org/zine-resources/infoshops-zine-libraries/.

6. At http://www.pdxzines.com/info/.

7. See the appendix for more information about zines and where to get them.

# Index

# About the Author

ALISON PIEPMEIER directs the Women's and Gender Studies Program at the College of Charleston, where she is Associate Professor of English. She is the co-editor of *Catching a Wave: Reclaiming Feminism for the 21st Century* and author of *Out in Public: Configurations of Women's Bodies in Nineteenth-Century America*. She lives in Charleston, South Carolina, with her husband and daughter.